First World War
and Army of Occupation
War Diary
France, Belgium and Germany

35 DIVISION
105 Infantry Brigade
Sherwood Foresters (Nottinghamshire and Derbyshire Regiment)
16th Battalion
28 January 1916 - 22 April 1919

WO95/2488/2

The Naval & Military Press Ltd
www.nmarchive.com
Published in association with The National Archives

Published by

The Naval & Military Press Ltd

Unit 10 Ridgewood Industrial Park,

Uckfield, East Sussex,

TN22 5QE England

Tel: +44 (0) 1825 749494

www.naval-military-press.com

www.nmarchive.com

This diary has been reprinted in facsimile from the original. Any imperfections are inevitably reproduced and the quality may fall short of modern type and cartographic standards.

© **Crown Copyright**
Images reproduced by permission of The National Archives, London, England, 2015.

Contents

Document type	Place/Title	Date From	Date To
Heading	WO/95/2488/2 15 Battalion Sherwood Foresters (Nottingham & Derbyshire Regiment)		
Heading	35th Division 105th Infy Bde 15th Bn Notts & Derby Regt Jan 1916-Apr 1919		
Heading	15 Notts & Derby Vol 1 35 Div January & February 1916		
War Diary	Jidworth	28/01/1916	01/02/1916
War Diary	Boulogne	02/02/1916	02/02/1916
War Diary	Renescure	03/02/1916	09/02/1916
War Diary	La Roome & La Lacque	10/02/1916	20/02/1916
War Diary	Paradis	20/02/1916	01/03/1916
Operation(al) Order(s)	Operation Orders No1 By Lieut. Col. R.N.S. Gordon Commdg. 15th. (S) Bn. The Sherwood Foresters.		
Operation(al) Order(s)	Operation Orders No 2 By Lieut. Col. R.N.S. Gordon Commdg. 15th. (S) Bn. Sherwood Foresters.	29/03/1916	29/03/1916
War Diary	Laventie	01/04/1916	01/04/1916
War Diary	Trenches	04/04/1916	07/04/1916
War Diary	Laventie	08/04/1916	12/04/1916
War Diary	Cul De Sac	18/04/1916	18/04/1916
War Diary	Paradis	18/04/1916	18/04/1916
War Diary	Trenches	19/04/1916	23/04/1916
War Diary	Le Touret (Right Bourwood)	23/04/1916	27/04/1916
War Diary	Trenches	27/04/1916	02/05/1916
Operation(al) Order(s)	Operation Orders No. 3 By Lieut. Col. R.N.S. Gordon, Commdg. 15th (S) Bn Sherwood Foresters	02/04/1916	02/04/1916
Operation(al) Order(s)	Operations Orders By No. 4 By Lt. Col. R.N.S. Gordon 15th. (S) Battn The Sherwood Foresters	08/04/1916	08/04/1916
Operation(al) Order(s)	Operation Orders No. 5 By Lieut. Col. R. N. S. Gordon Commdg. 15th (S) Bn. Sherwood Foresters.	11/04/1916	11/04/1916
Operation(al) Order(s)	Operation Orders No. 6 By Lieut. Col. R.N.S. Gordon Commdg. 15th. (S) Bn. Sherwood Foresters.	17/04/1916	17/04/1916
Operation(al) Order(s)	Operation Orders No. 7 By Lieut. Col. R.N.S. Gordon Commdg. 15th. (S) Bn. Sherwood Foresters.	19/04/1916	19/04/1916
Operation(al) Order(s)	Operation Orders No. 8 By Lieut. Col. R.N.S. Gordon Commdg. 15th. (S) Bn. Sherwood Foresters.	22/04/1916	22/04/1916
War Diary	Lacouture	02/05/1916	06/05/1916
War Diary	Les Lobes	07/05/1916	14/05/1916
War Diary	Cirro Borber	15/05/1916	26/05/1916
Operation(al) Order(s)	Operation Orders No. 9 By Lieut. Col. R.N.S. Gordon Commdg. 15th. (S) Bn Sherwood Foresters.		
Operation(al) Order(s)	Operation Orders No. 10 By Lieut. Col. R.N.S. Gordon Commdg. 15th. (S) Bn. Sherwood Foresters.	02/05/1916	02/05/1916
Operation(al) Order(s)	Operation Orders No. 11 By Lieut. Col. R.N.S. Gordon Commdg. 15th. (S) Bn Sherwood Foresters.	05/05/1916	05/05/1916
Operation(al) Order(s)	Operation Orders No. 12 By Lieut.-Col. R.N.S. Gordon Commdg. 15th. (S) Bn. Sherwood Foresters	05/06/1916	05/06/1916
Operation(al) Order(s)	Operation Orders By Major F. Vickers Commdg. 15th. (S) Bn. The Sherwood Foresters.	17/05/1916	17/05/1916
Operation(al) Order(s)	Operation Orders No. 15 By Major F. Vickers Commdg. 15th. (S) Bn. Sherwood Foresters	24/05/1916	24/05/1916

Type	Description	Date 1	Date 2
Operation(al) Order(s)	Operation Orders No. 15 By Lieut-Col. R.N.S. Gordon, Com & 15th. (S) Bn. Sherwood Foresters.	29/05/1916	29/05/1916
Miscellaneous	First Report On Operations On Night Of 30th. May 1916	31/05/1916	31/05/1916
War Diary	Croix Barbee	01/06/1916	16/06/1916
War Diary	Les Lobes	16/06/1916	17/06/1916
War Diary	Mt Bernenchon	17/06/1916	30/06/1916
Operation(al) Order(s)	Operation Orders No. 17 By Lieut-Col. R.N.S. Gordon. Commdg. 15th. (S) Bn. Sherwood Foresters.	08/05/1916	08/05/1916
Operation(al) Order(s)	Operation Orders No. 18 By Lieut-Col. R.N.S. Gordon Commdg. 15th. (S) Bn. The Sherwood Foresters.	15/06/1916	15/06/1916
Heading	105th Bde. 35th Division 15th Battalion Notts & Derby Regiment 1st To 31st July 1916		
War Diary	Mt. Bernenchon	01/07/1916	03/07/1916
War Diary	Sus St. Leger.	04/07/1916	07/07/1916
War Diary	Beauval.	08/07/1916	11/07/1916
War Diary	Warloy	12/07/1916	14/07/1916
War Diary	Bois De Billon.	15/07/1916	16/07/1916
War Diary	Trenches	17/07/1916	20/07/1916
War Diary	Talus Boise	21/07/1916	24/07/1916
War Diary	Silesia Trench.	25/07/1916	26/07/1916
War Diary	Talus Boise	27/07/1916	28/07/1916
War Diary	Dublin Trench.	29/07/1916	29/07/1916
War Diary	Minden Post.	30/07/1916	31/07/1916
Miscellaneous	First Report Of Operations 20-7-16	23/07/1916	23/07/1916
Miscellaneous	Report On Reconnaissance On New Trench Guillemont-Maltz Horn Farm.		
Miscellaneous	Register Of Messages Operations On Maltz Horn Farm.	20/07/1916	20/07/1916
Miscellaneous	Register Of Messages Operations On Maltz Horn Farm	20/07/1916	20/07/1916
Miscellaneous	Register Of Telephone Messages (Verbal) During Operations On Maltz Horn Farm.	20/07/1916	20/07/1916
Miscellaneous	To O.C. Coys. & Units.	24/06/1916	24/06/1916
Operation(al) Order(s)	Operation Order No 21 By Lieut Col. R.N.S. Gordon Commdg 15th (S) Bn. Sherwood Foresters.	06/07/1916	06/07/1916
Operation(al) Order(s)	Operation Order No. 23 By Lieut-Col RNS Gordon Cmdg 15th Sherwood Foresters	10/07/1916	10/07/1916
Operation(al) Order(s)	Operation Order No. 23 By Lieut-Col RNS Gordon Cmdg 15th Sherwood Foresters	12/07/1916	12/07/1916
Miscellaneous	Papers In Connection With Operations On Maltz Horn Farm.	20/07/1916	20/07/1916
Operation(al) Order(s)	Operation Orders. No 22 By Lieut-Col. R.N.S. Gordon Commdg. 15th. (S) Bn. Sherwood Foresters.	09/07/1916	09/07/1916
Operation(al) Order(s)	Operation Orders No. 19 By Lieut-Col. R.N.S. Gordon Commdg. 15th. (S) Bn. The Sherwood Foresters.	28/05/1916	28/05/1916
Operation(al) Order(s)	Operation Orders No. 20 By Lieut-Col. R.N.S. Gordon, Commdg. 15th (S) Bn. Sherwood Foresters.	02/07/1916	02/07/1916
Map			
Operation(al) Order(s)	Operation Orders No. 26 By H.P.G. Cochran, Commdg. 15th. (S) Bn. Sherwood Foresters.	28/07/1916	28/07/1916
Map			
Miscellaneous	Trench Map. Montauban.		
Miscellaneous	W. Coy		
Operation(al) Order(s)	Operation Order No. 25 By Major. H.P.G. Cochran Cmdg 15th (S) Bn. The Sherwood Foresters.	26/07/1916	26/07/1916
Miscellaneous	105th. (Infantry) Brigade Order No. 38	19/07/1916	19/07/1916

Miscellaneous	Attack Orders No. 1 By Lieut-Col. R.N.S. Gordon Commdg. 15th. (S) Bn. Sherwood Foresters	19/07/1916	19/07/1916
Miscellaneous	To O.C. Coys. & Units.	25/06/1916	25/06/1916
Miscellaneous	Programme Of Entrainment.		
Miscellaneous	Table "B"		
Miscellaneous	To O.C. Coys. & Units.	02/07/1916	02/07/1916
Heading	105th Brigade. 35th Division. 1/15th Battalion Notts & Derby Regiment August 1916		
War Diary	Bois De Tailles	01/08/1916	06/08/1916
War Diary	Molliens Vidame	07/08/1916	13/08/1916
War Diary	The Citadel	14/08/1916	20/08/1916
War Diary	Talus Boise	21/08/1916	22/08/1916
War Diary	Trenches	23/08/1916	23/08/1916
War Diary	Bivouacs	24/08/1916	26/08/1916
War Diary	Sandpit Valley	27/08/1916	28/08/1916
War Diary	Bois De Tailles	29/08/1916	31/08/1916
Operation(al) Order(s)	Operation Orders No. 27 By Lt.-Col. R.N.S. Gordon Commdg. 15th. (S) Bn. Sherwood Foresters.	01/08/1916	01/08/1916
Operation(al) Order(s)	Operation Order No. 28 By Lieut-Col. R.N.S. Gordon Commdg. 15th. (S) Bn. Sherwood Foresters.	04/08/1916	04/08/1916
Operation(al) Order(s)	Operation Orders No. 29 By Lieut-Col. R.N.S. Gordon Commdg. 15th. (S) Bn. Sherwood Foresters.	05/08/1916	05/08/1916
Operation(al) Order(s)	Operation Orders No. 30 By Lieut-Col. R. N. S. Gordon, Commdg. 15th. (S) Bn. Sherwood Foresters	08/08/1916	08/08/1916
Operation(al) Order(s)	Operation Order No. 31 By Lieut-Col. R.N.S. Gordon Commdg. 15th. (S) Bn. Sherwood Foresters.	10/08/1916	10/08/1916
Operation(al) Order(s)	Operation Order No. 32 By Lieut-Col. R.N.S. Gordon Commdg. 15th. (S) Bn. Sherwood Foresters.	19/08/1916	19/08/1916
Miscellaneous	Papers In Connection With Operations On Maltz Horn Trenches	23/08/1916	23/08/1916
Miscellaneous	105th. (Inf.) Brigade Order No. 48	20/08/1916	20/08/1916
Miscellaneous	Report Of Operations August 23rd. 1916		
Miscellaneous	Receipt.		
Miscellaneous	Despatch.		
Miscellaneous	Receipt.		
Miscellaneous	Despatch.		
Miscellaneous	Attack Orders No. 2 By Lieut-Col. R.N.S. Gordon Commdg. 15th. (S) Bn. Sherwood Foresters.	23/08/1916	23/08/1916
Operation(al) Order(s)	Operation Orders No. 33 By Lieut-Col. R.N.S. Gordon Commdg. 15th. (S) Bn. Sherwood Foresters.	25/08/1916	25/08/1916
Operation(al) Order(s)	Operation Orders No. 34 By Lieut-Col. R.N.S. Gordon Commdg. 15th (S) Bn. Sherwood Foresters.	26/08/1916	26/08/1916
Operation(al) Order(s)	Operation Orders No. 35 By Lieut-Col. R.N.S. Gordon Commdg. 15th (S) Bn. Sherwood Foresters.	28/08/1916	28/08/1916
Operation(al) Order(s)	Operation Orders No. 36 By Lieut-Col. R.N.S. Gordon Commdg. 15th (S) Bn. Sherwood Foresters.	28/08/1916	28/08/1916
Operation(al) Order(s)	Operation Orders No. 37 By Lieut-Col. R.N.S. Gordon, Commdg. 15th (S) Bn. Sherwood Foresters.	29/08/1916	29/08/1916
Miscellaneous	Battalion Orders By Lieut-Col. R.N.S. Gordon Commdg. 15th. (S) Bn. Sherwood Foresters.	30/08/1916	30/08/1916
Operation(al) Order(s)	Operation Orders No 70 By Lieut-Col. R.N.S. Gordon Comdg. 15th. (Service) Bn. The Sherwood Foresters.	03/08/1916	03/08/1916
Operation(al) Order(s)	Operation Orders By 43 Major W.A.W. Crellin, 15th. (S) Battn. The Sherwood Foresters.		
Operation(al) Order(s)	Operation Orders 38 By Lieut-Col. R. N. S. Gordon, Commdg. 15th (S) Bn. The Sherwood Foresters	31/08/1916	31/08/1916

Type	Description	Start	End
War Diary	Wanquetin	01/09/1916	13/09/1916
War Diary	Trenches	14/09/1916	30/09/1916
Operation(al) Order(s)	Operation Orders No. 39 By Lieut-Col. R.N.S. Gordon Commdg. The 15th (Service) Battn. Sherwood Foresters.	02/09/1916	02/09/1916
Operation(al) Order(s)	Operation Orders No. 41 By Lieut-Col. R.N.S. Gordon Commdg. 15th. (S) Bn. Sherwood Foresters.	14/09/1916	14/09/1916
Operation(al) Order(s)	Operation Orders No. 42 By Lieut-Col. R.N.S. Gordon Commdg. 15th. Sherwood Foresters.	15/09/1916	15/09/1916
War Diary	Arras	01/10/1916	16/10/1916
War Diary	Trenches	17/10/1916	31/10/1916
Operation(al) Order(s)	Operation Orders No. 43 By Major W.A.W. Crellin Commdg. 15th. (S) Bn. Sherwood Foresters.	05/10/1916	05/10/1916
Miscellaneous	15th. (S) Battn. The Sherwood Foresters.		
Operation(al) Order(s)	Operation Orders No 44 By Lieut-Col RNS Gordon Commdg 15th (S) Bn Sherwood Foresters	24/10/1916	24/10/1916
Heading	Hq 2nd		
Miscellaneous	To 105th. (Infantry) Brigade.	26/10/1916	26/10/1916
Miscellaneous	15th. (S) Battn. The Sherwood Foresters.	26/10/1916	26/10/1916
Miscellaneous	To G.C. 15th. (S) Bn. The Sherwood Foresters.		
Miscellaneous	Name of Prisoner Captured by the 15th Sherwoods.		
Miscellaneous	15th. (S) Battn. The Sherwood Foresters.		
Miscellaneous	Operations. Organization Of Raid In Enemy Trenches In G.a.12 Central		
War Diary	Arras	01/11/1916	30/11/1916
Operation(al) Order(s)	Operation Orders By No 46 Lieut-Col. R.N.S. Gordon Commdg., 15th. (S) Battn. The Sherwood Foresters.	01/11/1916	01/11/1916
Operation(al) Order(s)	Operation Orders By No 44 Lieut-Col R.N.S. Gordon, Commdg., The 15th. (S) Battn. The Sherwood Foresters.	02/11/1916	02/11/1916
Operation(al) Order(s)	Operation Orders No. 48 By Lieut-Col. J.F. Clyne. Commdg. 15th (Service) Battn. The Sherwood Foresters	09/11/1916	09/11/1916
Miscellaneous	To Headquarters, 105th (Infantry) Brigade.	26/11/1916	26/11/1916
Operation(al) Order(s)	Operation Orders. No. 49 By Lieut-Col. R.N.S. Gordon Commdg. 13th. (S) Bn. The Sherwood Foresters.	26/11/1916	26/11/1916
War Diary	Arras	01/12/1916	05/12/1916
War Diary	Bea-Fort	06/12/1916	28/12/1916
War Diary	Dainville	28/12/1916	31/01/1917
War Diary	Monts-en-Ternois	01/02/1917	08/02/1917
War Diary	St Vast-en-Chausse	09/02/1917	20/02/1917
War Diary	Camp Des Ballons	21/02/1917	28/02/1917
War Diary	Hilly	01/03/1917	04/03/1917
War Diary	Vrely Camp des Ballons	05/03/1917	14/03/1917
War Diary	Rosieres	14/03/1917	18/03/1917
War Diary	Chaulnes	18/03/1917	21/03/1917
War Diary	Puzeaux	22/03/1917	27/03/1917
War Diary	Morlemont	28/03/1917	31/03/1917
War Diary	Paradis Robecq.	01/03/1917	07/03/1917
War Diary	Le Touret	07/03/1917	07/03/1917
War Diary	Merville	14/03/1917	18/03/1917
War Diary	Paradis	19/03/1917	19/03/1917
War Diary	Estaires.	25/03/1917	27/03/1917
War Diary	Trenches.	28/03/1917	30/03/1917
War Diary	Laventie	31/03/1917	31/03/1917
War Diary	Morlemont	01/04/1917	02/04/1917
War Diary	Canizy	03/04/1917	12/04/1917

Type	Location/Title	From	To
War Diary	Tertry	13/04/1917	19/04/1917
War Diary	Mon de Garde	21/04/1917	30/04/1917
War Diary	Tertry	01/05/1917	07/05/1917
War Diary	Quarry	08/05/1917	08/05/1917
War Diary	Gricourt	09/05/1917	12/05/1917
War Diary	Mon de Garde	13/05/1917	15/05/1917
War Diary	Quarry	17/05/1917	19/05/1917
War Diary	Tertry	19/05/1917	23/05/1917
War Diary	Peronne	24/05/1917	25/05/1917
War Diary	Templeux La Fosse	26/05/1917	31/05/1917
Miscellaneous	105th. Inf. Bde.	10/05/1917	10/05/1917
Miscellaneous	Battalion Orders No. 55	09/05/1917	09/05/1917
Miscellaneous	Report on Operations on Les Trois Sauvages on Night of 9th/10th. May, 1917	10/05/1917	10/05/1917
Miscellaneous	Narrative Of Operations Right Of May 9th./10th.		
Miscellaneous	Narrative Of Operations On Night Of 15th./16th. May 1917		
Operation(al) Order(s)	Battalion Operation Order No. 57		
Map			
War Diary	Templeux La Fosse Villers Guislans	01/06/1917	17/06/1917
War Diary	Heudecourt	18/06/1917	25/06/1917
War Diary	Gauche Wood	26/06/1917	29/06/1917
War Diary	Villers Faucon	30/06/1917	06/07/1917
War Diary	Epehy	07/07/1917	15/07/1917
War Diary	Aizecourt-la-Bas.	16/07/1917	22/07/1917
War Diary	Lempire	23/07/1917	01/08/1917
War Diary	Aizecourt-la-Bas.	02/08/1917	16/08/1917
War Diary	St Emilie	17/08/1917	18/08/1917
War Diary	The Knoll	19/08/1917	19/08/1917
War Diary	Lempire	19/08/1917	19/08/1917
War Diary	Lempire & St Emilie.	20/08/1917	23/08/1917
War Diary	The Knoll	24/08/1917	25/08/1917
War Diary	St Emilie.	26/08/1917	27/08/1917
War Diary	Aizecourt-La-Bas	28/08/1917	01/09/1917
War Diary	Lempire.	02/09/1917	11/09/1917
War Diary	Villers Faucon.	11/09/1917	18/09/1917
War Diary	Birdcage Sector.	19/09/1917	22/09/1917
War Diary	Epehy.	26/09/1917	30/09/1917
War Diary	Aizecourt Le Bas Peronne	01/10/1917	03/10/1917
War Diary	Warlus	03/10/1917	13/10/1917
War Diary	Arneke	15/10/1917	15/10/1917
War Diary	Proven	16/10/1917	16/10/1917
War Diary	Elverdinghe	17/10/1917	31/10/1917
War Diary	Houlthurst Forest.	01/11/1917	01/11/1917
War Diary	Dynes Camp.	02/11/1917	04/11/1917
War Diary	Paddington Camp.	06/11/1917	14/11/1917
War Diary	Brake Camp.	15/11/1917	23/11/1917
War Diary	Kempton Park	24/11/1917	25/11/1917
War Diary	Poelcapville.	26/11/1917	28/11/1917
War Diary	Siege Camp.	29/11/1917	04/12/1917
War Diary	Langemarck	05/12/1917	08/12/1917
War Diary	Le Nouveau Monde	09/12/1917	10/12/1917
War Diary	Schools Camp.	11/12/1917	08/01/1918
War Diary	Whitemill Camp.	09/01/1918	16/01/1918
War Diary	Left Support.	17/01/1918	21/01/1918
War Diary	Left Front Sub Sector.	21/01/1918	24/01/1918

War Diary	Irish Farm.	24/01/1918	31/01/1918
Miscellaneous	105th Inf. Bde.		
Heading	105th Inf. Bde. 35th Div, 15th Battn. The Sherwood Foresters (Nottinghamshire And Derbyshire Regiment). March 1918		
War Diary	Langemarck.	01/03/1918	01/03/1918
War Diary	Huddlestone Camp.	02/03/1918	08/03/1918
War Diary	Chauny Farm Camp.	09/03/1918	23/03/1918
War Diary	Curlu Wood	24/03/1918	24/03/1918
War Diary	Curlu Maurepas Rd.	25/03/1918	25/03/1918
War Diary	Maricourt.		
War Diary	E Of Bray Albert Rd.	26/03/1918	26/03/1918
War Diary	Buire.	27/03/1918	31/03/1918
Operation(al) Order(s)	15th (S) Bn. The Sherwood Foresters Operation Order No. 16	01/03/1918	01/03/1918
Operation(al) Order(s)	15th. (S) Bn. The Sherwood Foresters. Operation Order No. 17	09/03/1918	09/03/1918
War Diary	Lahoussoye.	01/04/1918	03/04/1918
War Diary	La Neuville	04/04/1918	05/04/1918
War Diary	Herissart.	06/04/1918	06/04/1918
War Diary	Hedauville	07/04/1918	07/04/1918
War Diary	Bouzincourt.	08/04/1918	08/04/1918
War Diary	Front Line.	11/04/1918	15/04/1918
War Diary	Hedauville.	16/04/1918	16/04/1918
War Diary	Aveluy Wood.	17/04/1918	24/04/1918
War Diary	Hedauville	25/04/1918	25/04/1918
War Diary	Bouzincourt.	26/04/1918	02/05/1918
War Diary	Herrisart	03/05/1918	10/05/1918
War Diary	Forward Area	11/05/1918	14/05/1918
War Diary	Herrisart	15/05/1918	19/05/1918
War Diary	Reserve Position	20/05/1918	21/05/1918
War Diary	Bouzincourt	22/05/1918	23/05/1918
War Diary	Front Line	23/05/1918	27/05/1918
War Diary	Bouzincourt	29/05/1918	31/05/1918
War Diary	Right Front Line	01/06/1918	04/06/1918
War Diary	Forceville	05/06/1918	08/06/1918
War Diary	Line In Front Of Bouzincourt	09/06/1918	11/06/1918
War Diary	Forceville	12/06/1918	16/06/1918
War Diary	Puchevillers.	17/06/1918	30/06/1918
War Diary	Candas.	01/07/1918	01/07/1918
War Diary	Wizernes.	02/07/1918	02/07/1918
War Diary	Zermezeele	03/07/1918	03/07/1918
War Diary	Beauvoorde Wood.	04/07/1918	04/07/1918
War Diary	Reserve.	05/07/1918	08/07/1918
War Diary	Support.	09/07/1918	12/07/1918
War Diary	Front Line	13/07/1918	18/07/1918
War Diary	Reserve.	19/07/1918	20/07/1918
War Diary	Support.	21/07/1918	24/07/1918
War Diary	Front Line.	25/07/1918	30/07/1918
War Diary	Reserve.	31/07/1918	31/07/1918
Miscellaneous	105th Inf. Bde. 35th Div.		
War Diary	St Sylvestre Cappel	01/09/1918	02/09/1918
War Diary	Poperinghe	03/09/1918	04/09/1918
War Diary	Ypres.	04/09/1918	05/09/1918
War Diary	(Support)	05/09/1918	08/09/1918
War Diary	(Reserve)	08/09/1918	12/09/1918

War Diary	Front Line	12/09/1918	18/09/1918
War Diary	School Camp. (resting)	19/09/1918	21/09/1918
War Diary	Front Line	22/09/1918	24/09/1918
War Diary	School Camp	25/09/1918	25/09/1918
War Diary	Front Line.	26/09/1918	30/09/1918
War Diary	Reserve	01/10/1918	05/10/1918
War Diary	Front Line	06/10/1918	07/10/1918
War Diary	Doll's Ho.	08/10/1918	10/10/1918
War Diary	Holden Ho.	11/10/1918	11/10/1918
War Diary	Support	12/10/1918	04/11/1918
War Diary	Front Line.	05/11/1918	31/01/1919
War Diary	Beaumarais	01/02/1919	28/02/1919
War Diary	Beaumarais Camp	01/03/1919	01/03/1919
War Diary	Calais	24/03/1919	25/03/1919
War Diary	Monnecove Camp	26/03/1919	26/03/1919
War Diary	Monnecove	01/04/1919	18/04/1919
War Diary	St Omer	19/04/1919	19/04/1919
War Diary	Dunkirk	20/04/1919	22/04/1919

WO/165/2 468/2

15 Battalion Sherwood Foresters
(Nottingham & Derbyshire Regiment)

35TH DIVISION
105TH INFY BDE

15TH BN NOTTS & DERBY REGT
JAN ~~FEB~~ 1916-APR 1919

1.4

10/35.
1s Notts & Derby
Vol 1
35 Div

January + February
1916

Army Form C. 2118.

15.S. Sherwood Foresters.

WAR DIARY
or
INTELLIGENCE SUMMARY
(Erase heading not required.)

Army Form C. 2118.

Instructions regarding War Diaries and Intelligence Summaries are contained in F. S. Regs., Part II. and the Staff Manual respectively. Title Pages will be prepared in manuscript.

Place	Date	Hour	Summary of Events and Information	Remarks and references to Appendices
Tidworth	28/1/16		Regiment received orders to embark for Unknown on Jan. 29th & 30th.	
	29/1/16	9 am.	Transport of regiment entrained at Tidworth at 9 am. En route to HAVRE via SOUTHAMPTON. Strength 102 Rank & file, 21 vehicles, 9 bicycles. MAJOR THELWALL. LTS DOUGLAS & CRESSWELL.	
			Orders for entraining Battalion cancelled.	
	30/1/16		Orders received for Battalion to proceed overseas.	
	31/1/16	6 am.	Battalion entrained at TIDWORTH in 2 trains, proceeded via FOLKESTONE & BOULOGNE to ST MARTINS REST CAMP, BOULOGNE. All ranks arrived at 10.30 pm.	
	1/2/16	3 am.	STRENGTH 29 Officers, 892 Rank & file.	
			Officers:—	
			LT.COL. GORDON. R.M.S. cmdg.	
			MAJOR VICKERS. F.	
			CAPT. OTTONELL. T.T.	
			" BARNETT-SMITH. G.	
			" RENNICK. W.L.	
			" PRICE. W.	
			" CUTTS. T.B.	
			" MORELL. K.W.	
			LIEUT. MOORE A.	
			" BVOT. G.H.	
			" HODGSON A.D.	
			" JACKSON. E.C.	
			" GABRIEL. A.	
			2ND LT. WHARTON G.L.	
			" FORSYTH A.McK.	
			" CRIDGE N.	
			" MACINTOSH J.N.F.	
			" DEXTER. R.F.K.	
			" MACHUTCHEON J.	
			" COLLIER F.H.	
			" HARVEY M.M.	
			" NIGHTINGALE E.	
			" LESTER M.	
			" HOMAN R.	
			" BRIDGEWATER E	
			" DERBYSHIRE H.	
			LT & ADJ CRELLIN W.A.W.	
			LT. Q.M. FERGUSON. A.E. R.A.M.C. M.O.	
			LT. FERGUSON T.E. R.A.M.C. M.O.	
			DIV. A.M.L.O. Joined Battalion on 6th February.	
			CAPT. WADSWORTH. R. proceeded on 23rd JANY to HAVRE & rejoined Battalion on 6th February.	

Army Form C. 2118.

WAR DIARY
or
INTELLIGENCE SUMMARY
(Erase heading not required.)

13th SHERWOOD FORESTERS

Place	Date	Hour	Summary of Events and Information	Remarks and references to Appendices
BOULOGNE	2/2/16		Battalion proceeded by to ST. OMER by train, & then by route march to RENESCURE & joined up with Transport.	
RENESCURE	3/2/16 to 8/2/16		In billets.	
	9/2/16		Battalion moved by route march to fresh billets at LA ROUPIE and LA LACQUE.	
LA ROUPIE & LA LACQUE	10/2/16 to 18/2/16		In billets.	
	19/2/16		Battalion marched to ROBECQ & billets for the night.	
	20/2/16		Battalion marched to LOCON area & billets in PARADIS.	
PARADIS	20/2/16 to 1/3/16		In billets.	

Rutherford Lt Col
Comm'g 13 (S) Foresters

Operation Orders No 1.   Copy No. 5.
By Lieut. Col. R.N.S. Gordon,
  Commdg. 15th. (S) Bn. The Sherwood Foresters.

Map Sheet 36.

$\frac{1}{40,000.}$

1. <u>Destination</u>. The Battalion will proceed tomorrow and take on the Right Sector of LAVENTIE Trenches from the 2nd. Scottish Rifles.

2. <u>Distribution</u>. <u>Right Company</u>. "W" Coy. from ERITH STREET exclusive to M.24.4 inclusive. .... 3 Platoons.
   ELGIN POST KEEP .... 1 "

   <u>RIGHT CENTRE COMPANY</u>. "X" Coy. from M.24.5. inclusive to M.24.6. inclusive .. .. 3 Platoons.
   HOUGOUMONT POST KEEP .... 1 Platoon.

   <u>LEFT CENTRE COMPANY</u>. "Y" Company from M.24.7. inclusive to N.13.2. inclusive .... 3 Platoons.
   FAUQUISSART POST KEEP .... 1 Platoon.

   <u>LEFT COMPANY</u>. "Z" Company from N.13.3. inclusive to N.13.5 inclusive .... $3\frac{1}{2}$ Platoons.
   FELON POST KEEP .... 1 Platoon.

3. <u>Guides</u>. Guides will meet the Companies at LAVENTIE STATION level Cross-ing at 6-30 p.m.

4. <u>Headquarters</u>. Will be at M.12.b.5.6. adjoining Hougoumont Keep.

5. <u>Starting Point and Time.</u> X ROADS L.29.b.8.o. at 4-30 p.m.

6. <u>Route to Trenches.</u> LE NOUVEAU MONDE - LAVENTIE FT. d'ESQUIN.

7. <u>Intervals.</u> No troops will cross South of Estairs-Sailley Road before 6-15 p.m.   At this point Coys. will move at 10 minutes intervals. On reaching LAVENTIE they will move up by Platoons at 200 yards interval.

8. <u>Arrival in Trenches.</u> On arrival in Trenches Coys. will take over and report to Headquarters as soon as relief is completed.

9. <u>Trench Stores.</u> All Trench, Keep and Supporting Point Stores will be taken over on relief, duplicate receipts being retained.

10. <u>Defence Schemes.</u> Section and Sub-Section Defence Schemes and Trench Maps will be taken overc by all concerned.

11. <u>Regimental Stores</u>. All Regimental Stores taken up by Headquarters will be dumped at Battalion Headquarters. Coys. will indent on them after ascertaining their requirements.

12. <u>Avenues and Drains</u>. Coys. in the front line are responsible for the upkeep of Avenues and of drains running back behind their line of trenches as far as the RUE TILLELOY inclusive. "Z" Coy. will be responsible for the care of ROTTEN ROW.

13. <u>Order of March</u>. W.X.Y.Z. Headquarters, Transport proceeding to Trenches. Personnel remaining at LAVENTIE.
    Transport remaining at LAVENTIE.

14. <u>Taking over Stores</u>. 2nd. in Command of Coys. and Coy. S.Ms. will proceed to the trenches to take over Trench Stores tomorrow morning, they will parade at the Qr.Mr.'s Stores at 8-30 a.m. and will

be met at the level crossing LAVENTIE STATION at 10 a.m.

15. <u>Lewis Guns</u>. Lewis Gun Section A. & B. will be brigaded under the orders of the Brigade M.G.O. They will parade at 10-30 a.m. and will take all M.G. Stores, Men's Kits, 1 Blanket. Limbers will accompany them and remain with them.

16. <u>Snipers</u>. Coy. Snipers under Lieut. Forsyth will parade at 8-30 a.m. outside Q.M.'s Stores and will act under the orders of the BDE. Intelligence Officer.

17. <u>Dress</u>. Each man will take with him, his Greatcoat, Waterproof Sheet, and Cape, Water Bottle filled, Rations for Monday, and 2 sandbags per man.

18. <u>Packs</u>. Skin Coats and all Articles not being taken into Trenches will be placed in the Packs and be returned to Quartermaster's Stores by 10 a.m.

19. <u>Blankets</u>. All Blankets of men proceeding to Trenches will be rolled in bundles of ten and returned to Q.M.'s Stores by 7 a.m.

20. <u>Light Trench Stores</u>. All Light Trench Stores will be drawn from the Q.M.'s Stores and distributed amongst Companies.

21. <u>Anti-Frost-Bite Oil</u>. Coy. Commanders will see that every man proceeding to the Trenches has his feet rubbed with Whale oil.

22. <u>Uniformity of Dress</u>. Coy. & Unit Commanders will carefully inspect all their men before marching off, and see that all are dressed alike especially XXXXXXXXXXXX in regard to their Kit and Accoutrements. Greatcoats will be worn. Haversacks will be worn in place of the Pack with the Emergency Ration tied firmly on top. Mess Tin underneath Haversack and the waterproof sheet with cape folded neatly inside strapped on to the back of the belt underneath the Mess Tin.

23. <u>Reports</u>. Up to 7 p.m. to rear of Column.
In the Line to HOUGOUMONT POST.

Copies to O.C. Coys. & Units.

War Diary, File.　　　　　　　　　　　　R.N.S. Gordon, Lieut. Col.
　　　　　　　　　　　　　　　　Commdg. 15th. (S) Bn. Sherwood Foresters.

Operation Orders   No. 2.   Copy No. 5.
By Lieut. Col. R.N.S. Gordon,
         Commdg. 15th. (S) Bn. Sherwood Foresters.

                                                In the Trenches.
                                                29-3-16.

Relief. The Battalion will be relieved tomorrow night 30th. by the 16th. (S) Bn. Cheshire Regt. and will move to Billets as under :-

    Battn. Headquarters   M.4.d.
       "W" Coy.   M.4.d.6.6. and M.4.d.5.2½.
       "X" "   M.10.b.8.9½.
       "Y" "   West of Road in M.10.b.
       "Z" " On relief will take over the following posts from the
               16th. Cheshires.:-
               WANGERIE POST M.1.7.b. - 1 Officer, 2 Platoons.

MASSELOT POST M.1.8.a. - 1 Platoon.

ROAD BEND POST M.1.7.d.- 1 Officer, 1 Platoon.

Headquarters of "Z" House M.11.d.s.4.
During the night all Platoon Commanders of "Z" Coy. will sleep with their Platoons.
Coy. Commanders will detail one officer per Coy. and one N.C.O. per Platoon to visit their Billets and posts on the morning of the 30th. these will act as guides on being relieved.

O.C. "Z" Coy. will detail one Officer to take over Stores etc. of post to be occupied, on the afternoon of the 30th. he will take with him one N.C.O. for each post as a guard over the Stores.

Coy. Commanders will report when they are relieved by telephone, and will send an Officer to report when their Coys. are in Billets or new posts, to Headquarters, at M.4.d. The following posts will also be taken over on the afternoon of the 30th. :-

    By "W" Coy. DRUMEZ POST)   1 N.C.O. and 3 men.
) M.3.A.
            MUDDY LANE   )   1 N.C.O. and 3 men.

They will be posted by an Officer of "W" Coy. and will report at 16th. Cheshires Hdqrs. at 2;30 p.m.

By "Y" Coy. ESQUIN POST M.11.c. 1 N.C.B. & 6 men, they will accompany the party from "W" Coy. at the same time. Ration dump for "Z" Coy. will be at WANGERIE POST.

O.C. Coys. will send 4 Platoon Guides each to be at HQ. at 6-30 p.m. to guide the incoming Regt. These men must absolutely know their road & direction to which to take the incoming Platoons.

Duplicate Receipts. will always be taken when handing over or taking over any trench stores.

Coys. will hand over to incoming Battalions all Battalion Trench Stores i.e. :- Box Periscopes, sniperscopes, and Helmets.
They will mark them so as to be recognisable and take a separate receipt for them.

TO O.C. Coys. & Units.

Issued at 6 p.m.   S/d.   R.N.S. Gordon, Lieut. Col.
                 Commdg. 15th. (S) Bn. The Sherwood Foresters.

Army Form C. 2118.

WAR DIARY
or
INTELLIGENCE SUMMARY
(Erase heading not required.)

1/1 Vol 3
XXXV
1st SHERWOOD FORESTERS.

Place	Date	Hour	Summary of Events and Information	Remarks and references to Appendices
LAVENTIE	1/4/16		In billets	
Trenches	4/4/16 to 7/4/16		Battn relieved 16. CHESHIRES in the trenches in the LAVENTIE SECTOR. 1st CHESHIRES were on our left.	
LAVENTIE	8/4/16 to 10/4/16		In billets	
	11/4/16 to 14/4/16		In billets	
CUL DE SAC	15/4/16			
PARADIS	18/4/16		Battn marched to PARADIS & billeted for the night.	3.4.
	19/4/16		Battn moved to trenches & relieved the 9th WELCH REGT in the FERME DU BOIS sector. 1st CAMBRIDGESHIRES on right.	L.B.
Trenches	16 23/4/16		1st CHESHIRES on our left. 1st CAMBRIDGESHIRES on right. Very quiet. Enemy particularly inactive.	
LE TOURET (Richebourg)	23/4/16 27/4/16		In billets.	
Trenches	27/4/16 to 2/5/16		Relieved 14th GLOSTERS in the line	

K.W. Marsden Capt & Adjt for Lieut Col Comdg
1st Sherwood Foresters

Copy No.

Operation Orders No. 3.
By Lieut. Col. R.N.S. Gordon,
Commdg. 15th. (S) Bn Sherwood Foresters

Ref. Trench Map 36. S.W. 1.   2-4-16.

1. <u>Relief</u>.   The 15th. Sherwood Foresters will relieve the 16th. Cheshires in the Right Sub-Sector of the FAUQUISSART SECTION.

2. <u>Details</u>.   Coys. will take over same frontages as when in Trenches from 26th. March to 30th.

3. <u>Order of March and Time</u>.   Y, X, W, H.Q. Coys. to move by Platoons at 200 yards interval.   No party to pass ESQUIN POST before 7-30 p.m. "Z" Coy. will follow after "Y" Coy.

4. <u>Route</u>.   W & X Coys. via BEDFORD ROW and NORTH ELGIN STREET. Y & Z Coys. via MASSELOT ROAD.

5. <u>Taking over Stores</u>.   Coys. will detail an Officer to take over Trench Stores to report to O.C. 16th. Cheshires at 4 p.m.

6. <u>Dress</u>.   Field Marchong Order without Packs. 100 rounds ammunition to be carried.

7. <u>Water Bottles</u>.   Water bottles will be taken in full.

8. <u>Rations</u>.   Rations will be at Dump Heads at 10 p.m.

9. <u>Stores</u>.   All Coy. Stores for Trenches will be forwarded to Q.M. Stores by 5 p.m.

10. <u>Coy. Kits</u>.   All Kits not required for Trenches will be placed in Q.M's Stores by 4 p.m.

11. <u>Billets</u>. Coy. Commanders will furnish a certificate by 6 p.m. thatvtheir Billets have been thoroughly cleaned.

12. <u>Completion of Relief</u>.   O.C. Coys. will report to H.Q. by phone on completion of Relief.

13. <u>HOUGOUMONT POST</u>.   Hougoumont Post will be garrisoned by Left Reserve Battalion.   O.C. "X" Coy. will detail instead 2 N.C.Os. and 12 men as H.Q. Guard in place of one Platoon at HOUGOUMONT POST.

14. <u>Rations</u>.   Transport Officer will arrange for Transport for Rations :

   W & X at Midland Railway Head.
   Y & Z at G. Central Railway Head.
   H.Q. at HOUGOUMONT POST.

                                                R. N. S. Gordon, Lieut. Col.
Issued at 7 p.m.   Commdg. 15th. (S) Bn· Sherwood Foreste

   Copies to O.C. Coys. & Units.
           T.O.
           Q.M.
           Major Thelwall,
           War Diary
           File
           Signalling Officer

OPERATIONS ORDERS BY　　NO.4　　COPY NO.......

Lt. Col. R.N.S. Gordon,

15th (S) Battn. The Sherwood Foresters.

Ref. $\frac{1}{40000}$ Sheet 36 S.W.1.　　8-4-16.

RELIEF. 1. The 15th Sherwood Foresters will be relieved by the 16th Cheshires tonight.

DESTINATION. 2. After Relief Companies will move independently to Billets in LAVENTIE, as under,
- "W" Company to Posts MASSELOT, ~~22.13403,~~ WANGERIE, ROAD BEND.
- "X" " to Billets No 2.
- "Y" " to Billets No 3.
- "Z" " to Billets No 1,

ROUTE. 3. W and X Companies will move by BEDFORD ROW and LA FLINQUE ROAD, Y and Z Companies will move by MASSELOT ROAD and ESQUIN ROAD.

FORMATION. 4. Companies will move by Platoons at 200 yards interval.

DUTIES. 5. The following duties will be taken over by Companies as under,
X Company 1 N.C.O. and 3 men at LE DRUMEZ POST,
1 N.C.O. and 3 men at MUDDY LANE POST.
Y Company 1 N.C.O. and 6 men at ESQUIN POST.
these parties will report at Head Quarters 16th Cheshires at 3 p.m. today, and will be posted by an Officer to be detailed by O.C. X Company,

TAKING OVER POSTS. 6. O.C. W Company will detail 1 Officer to take over Stores in WANGERIE ROAD BEND and MASSELOT POSTS, from 16th Cheshires, and 1 N.C.O. per post to remain in charge of same, party to report at WANGERIE POST at 3 p.m.

BILLET STORES. 7. O.C's X,Y,Z, Companies will detail 1 N.C.O. per Company to take over Billet Stores in their respective Billets, to report at the Billet Head Quarters at 3 p.m.

BATTALION TRENCH STORES. 8. O.C. Companies will send all Company and Battalion Trench Stores to Head Quarters by 6 a.m., this will include Sniperscopes, Hyperscopes and Very Pistols.

STEEL HELMETS. 9. O.C. Companies will take with them the 50 Steel Helmets per Company issued whilst in LAVENTIE.

AMMUNITION. 10. O.C. Companies will see that every man is in possession of 100 rounds S. A. A. on leaving the Trenches.

MESS KIT. 11. All Company Stores, Officers Kit and Mess Kit will be sent to Head Quarters by 6 a.m.

RATIONS. 12. Rations for W Company will be dumped at WANGERIE POST.

STRETCHERS. 13. All long and Trench Stretchers will be taken to Billets under Company arrangements.

REPORTS. 14. On completion of Relief Companies will report by Phone to Head Quarters, and on arrival at Posts and Billets, will send an Officer to report to the Adjutant at Head Quarters at LAVENTIE.

Issued at 8 a.m.　　Signed,　　K. W. MORELL, Capt.

A/Adjt. 15th Sherwood Foresters.

Operation Orders No. 5.   Copy No.
By Lieut. Col. K.H.S.Gordon,
   Commdg. 15th. (S) Bn. Sherwood Foresters

Ref. 1/40,000   Sheet 36.   11-4-16.

1. **Relief & Destination.** The 15th. Sherwood Foresters will be relieved by the 12th. M.L. Infantry tomorrow, and will proceed to Billets round G.14.a.5.5. by road.

2. **Route.** LAVENTIE - EAST SIDE OF TRIANGLE H.4.b. - LE NAB MONDE - SAILLY FORK ROADS G.9.c., - CUL DE SAC.
   Coys. will move at 200 yards interval North of LAVENTIE.

3. **Order of March.** Hdqrs., "Z" Coy., "X" Coy., "Y". "W" Coy. will move independently on being relieved.

4. **Time & Starting Point.** Head of Column to pass LAVENTIE Railway Crossing at 8 p.m.

5. **Guides.** O.C. all Coys. will detail one Officer per Coy. and one N.C.O. per Platoon to report at Battalion Headquarters at 8-30 a.m. 12th. inst. O.C. "W" Coy. will detail in addition one guide per Platoon to report at Headquarters at 8 p.m. to guide incoming Company.

6. **Reports.** O.C. "W" Coy. will report immediately to Battn. by letter on completion of relief, and will march off to Billets to CUL DE SAC. without waiting further orders.

7. **Transport.** The Transport Officer will arrange for the following Transport
   "W" Coy.   1 G.S. Wagon.
   "X" "   1 G.S. Limbered Wagon.
   "Y" "   1 G.S. Limbered Wagon.
   "Z" "   1 G.S. Limbered Wagon.
   Hdqrs.   1 G.S. Wagon.

8. **Officers Kits & Coy. Stores.** All Officers Kits, Mess Kits, and any Coy. Stores (Signalling Instruments etc.) will be carried in the wagon attached to Coys.

9. **Kitchens.** Kitchens will be cleaned and prepared for march by 8 p.m.

10. **Water Carts.** Water Cart at Hdqrs. will move with Kitchens, Water Cart at WANGNNIE POST will accompany "W" Coy.

11. **Dress.** Men will march in Greatcoats, Haversacks on shoulders, waterproof Cape and Macintosh rolled on belt.

12. **Helmets and Signalling Instruments.** All Helmets, Signalling Instruments and Stores on Battalion charge will be taken with Coys.

13. **Stores.** All spare Stores in Coys. will be returned to Q.M's Stores by 9 a.m. 12th. inst.

14. **Officers Chargers.** Officers Chargers will meet their Coys. at LAVENTIE Railway Crossing. M.O. Chargers to Battalion Headquarters, Transport Officer to arrange. On arrival at Billets, chargers will return to Transport Lines.

15. **Returns.** On arrival in Billets the following returns will be rendered by O.C. Coys. & Units. :-

    Billet and Ration Return.
    Falling Out State.

16. **Lewis Gun Sections.**   will move independently to Billets at CUL DE SAC.

17. **Reports.**   To Battalion Headquarters at LAVENTIE till relief of all posts are completed, after to Battalion Headquarters at CUL DE SAC.

                                                R.N.S. Gordon, Lieut. Col.

                                    Comndg. 15th. (S) Bn. Sherwood Foresters.

Issued at 7 p.m.

    Copy No. 1 O.C. "W" Coy.
               2 O.C. "X" Coy.
               3 O.C. "Y" Coy.
               4. O.C. "Z" Coy.
               5 Lewis Gun Detch.
               6 Headquarters.
               7 File
               8 War Diary.
               9 T.O.
             10 Q.M.
             11 Major Cholwall.

Operation Orders, No. 6.   Copy
By Lieut. Col. R.N.S.Gordon,
Commdg. 15th. (S) Bn. Sherwood Foresters.

Ref. Map Sheet. 36 and 36a.   17-4-16.

1. **Destination.** The Battalion will march tomorrow to LES LOBES and billet for the night 18th./19th.

2. **Route.** Ble CROIX G.32.a.- CROSS ROADS R.5.a.- PONT RICQUEL-LES LOBES.

3. **Order of March.** Hdqrs., Z, Y, W, X Coys. Lewis Gun Section, 1st. Line Transport to follow in rear of "X" Coy. from Point G.26.c.3.3. 2nd. Line Transport and Kitchens in rear of Battalion.

4. **Time & Starting Point.** Head of Column to pass CROSS ROAD G.21.a.2½.2½. at 9-10 a.m.

5. **Transport.** The Transport Officer will arrange for the following Transport,
    Headquarters 1 G.S.Wagon.
    "W" Coy.   1 "   "
    "X" Coy.   1 "   "
    "Y" Coy.   1 "   "
    "Z" Coy.   1 "   "
    Q.M.   1 "   "
    The Wagons will be sent to Coys. on their arrival this evening.

6. **Kits & Blankets &c.** Officers Kits, Mess Kits, Blankets, Signal Equipment &c. will be carried in the wagon attached to Coys..
   Lewis Gun Section Blankets will be carried in Headquarter wagon.

7. **Packs.** Men's Packs will be stored by Coys. in the Q.M's Stores by 7 p.m. tonight and will be carried to Q.M's Stores in Depot at LACOUTOURE by Motor Lorries on the morning of the 19th. inst.

8. **Dress.** Marching Order with Overcoats, and without Packs.

9. **Officers Chargers.** The Transport Officer will arrange to send Officers Chargers and Horses for Kitchens to the various Units by 8 a.m. tomorrow. Pack Mules will join in behind their respective Coys. on the line of march.

10. **Advance Party.** One Officer per Coy. and one N.C.O. per Platoon and the Snipers will proceed direct into the Trenches on the morning of the 18th. inst. and remain there the night 18th./19th. O.C. Coys. will render names of above to the Orderly Room by 7 p.m. tonight. This party will parade separately with the Battalion tomorrow and be marched by the Senior Officer to the Trenches and report to the Adjutant of the 9th. Welsh Regiment.
    Haversack rations will be carried for the 18th. and 19th. inst.
    The Officer of above party will take over all Trench Stores in the Trenches, Keeps and Supporting Points - handing over details being obtained and receipts given.

11. **Returns.** On arrival in Billets the following Returns will be rendered by O.C. Coys. and Units. :-

              Billeting & Ration Return.
              Falling Out State.

Issued at 6 p.m.
                                    R.N.S.Gordon, Lieut. Col.
To O.C.Coys.   Commdg. 15th. (S) Bn. Sherwood Foresters.
   M.G.
   H.Q.
   File
   War Diary.
   Major Thelwall.
   T.O.
   Q.M.

Operation Orders No. 7.   Copy No. 5
By Lieut. Col. R.N.S. Gordon,   19-4-16.
    Commdg. 15th. (S) Bn. Sherwood Foresters.

Map Ref. 1/40,000   Sheet Bethune Combined.

1. **Relief of Trenches.** The 15th. Sherwood Foresters will relieve the 9th. Bn. The Welsh Regiment in the Right Sub-sector of the FERME DE BOIS Sector.

2. **Distribution of Coys.** Coys. are allotted the following lengths of Trenches and Posts respectively :-

    "X" Coy. From LA QUINGUE RUE (exclusive) S.21.1. S.21.2. to a point 140 yards North in S.21.3.

    "Y" Coy. From a point 140 yards North in S.21.3. to FERME DE BOIS S.21.3., S.16.1., S.16.2.

    "Z" Coy. HOPE KEEP POST - 15 men and two N.C.Os.
              DEAD COW POST   - 20 men and 3 N.C.Os.
              TUBE POST   - Remainder of Coy.

    "W" Coy. BOURNVILLE   - 2 Platoons & H.Q.
              OLD BREASTWORK - 2 Platoons.

    Battalion Headquarters - S.14.13.3.1. to which place all reports will be furnished.

3. **Order of March, & Entry into Trenches.** "Y" Coy., "X" Coy., "Z" Coy., "W" Coy.,
    "Z" Coy. will detail its Coy. to enter the Posts as under :-

              HOPE KEEP POST.
              TUBE POST.
              DEAD COW POST.

4. **Route.** Coys. will march by following Route :- LOCON- PONT TOURNANT -MESPLEAUX - RUE DE BOIS.

5. **Starting Point.** Coys. will pass the Starting Point LES LOBES at 10 minutes interval between Coys. leading Coy. to pass at 6 p.m. After passing Canal at PONT TOURNANT Coys. will move by Platoons at 250 yards interval.
    Guides will meet Coys. at S.10.d.1.5.

6. **Dress.** Men will parade in Greatcoats, with capes and Waterproofs rolled.

7. **Water Bottles.** Water Bottles will be taken up full.

8. **Rations.** Men will carry Thursday's Rations with them.

9. **Sniperscopes, Periscopes and Very Pistols.** Coys. will return to H.Q. by 1 p.m. all Trench Stores on Charge which will be taken up to H.Q. by Limber and issued to "X" and "Y" Coys.

10. **L.G. Section.** Lewis Gun Officer will detail Gun Teams for six Battle Emplacements and two mobile Gun Teams. Reserve Lewis Gun Details will be attached to "Z" Coy. and posted to TUBE POST.

11. **Stretchers.** Coys. will arrange to take their long and Trench Stretchers into the Line with them.

12. **First Aid Dressing Station.** First Aid Dressing Station is located at S.14.b.9.3.

13. **Ammunition.** O.C. Coys. and Units will see that each man takes 100 rounds into the Trenches with him.

14. **Reports and Returns.** The attention of all Unit Commanders is drawn to the revised time of Reports circulated to Coys.

15. **Guard.** O.C. "W" Coy. will detail a Guard of two N.C.Os. and 12 men for duty at Headquarters.

16. **Bounds.** Men are to be distinctly warned that no one is to pass along the RUE DE BOIS East of Battalion Headquarters.

17. **Ration Parties.** All Ration Parties will be furnished by the two Coys. in Support - "W" Coy. furnishing party for "Y" Coy. and "Z" " " " " "X" "

18. **Taking Over Trench Stores.** All Trench Stores will be taken over in daylight and receipt given, copy to be retained for reference.

19. **Completion of Relief.** On Completion of Relief O.C. Coys. will notify H.Q. that all men are posted to the places they are to occupy in case of alarm.

20. **Lewis Guns.** O.C. Lewis Gun Detachment will parade at a convenient time and proceed to Trenches to arrive at EPPINETTE POST (S.13.b.10.7.) at 9 a.m. Reserve Lewis Gun Men will be attached to "Z" Coy. and posted to Tube Post.

21. **Signallers and Bombers.** H.Q. Signallers and Bombers will parade under orders of Signalling and Bombing Officers, and will report at Battn. H.Q. RUE DE BOIS S.14.b.7.3. at 12 noon.

22. **Dump.** will be at GRUB STREET at end of Light Railway. (S.14.a.) except for H.Q.

Issued at 5 p.m.

R.N.S.Gordon, Lieut. Colonel,
Commdg. 15th. (S) Bn. The Sherwood Foresters.

To O.C. "W" Coy.	Copy No.	1
"X" "	" "	2
"Y" Coy.	" "	3
"Z" "	" "	4
H.Q.	" "	5
File	" "	6
War Diary	" "	7
Major Thelwall,	" "	8
Lewis Gun Off.	" "	9
Bombing "	" "	10
Signalling "	" "	11
Transport "	" "	12
Q.M.	" "	13

Operation Orders No.3.
By Lieut. Col. R.N.S. Gordon,
Commdg. 15th. (S) Bn. Sherwood Foresters.

Copy No. 6

22-4-16.

Ref. 1 Bethune,
  40,000 Combined Sheet.

1. **Relief.** The Battalion will be relieved by the 14th. Gloster Regiment tomorrow night April 23rd. 1916.

2. **Guides.** O.C. Coys. will detail a guide from each Platoon to report at H.Q. at 7 p.m. to guide incoming Platoons.

3. **Order of Relief.** The Battalion will be relieved in the following order :-
   Y, X, Z, W, Hdqrs.

4. **Billets.** On relief Coys. will move independently to their Billetting Areas as under :-
   "W" Coy. to D Area.
   "X" "   to B Area.
   "Y" "   to A Area.
   "Z" "   to C Area.
   H.Q. "   to E Area.
   L.G. Detchmt. " to F Area.

5. **Formation.** Coys. will move by Platoons at 250 yards intervals.

6. **Duties.** The following Posts will be furnished by "X" Coy. :-
   Z ORCHARD   S.14.b.5.8.   1 Sgt. 14 Other Ranks.
   ALBERT   S.8.d.5.4.   1 Sgt. 14   "   "

7. **Alarm Garrisons.** The following Posts will be occupied on the "Alarm" being given, to be furnished by "X" Coy. :-

   RUE DE L'EPINETTE N. (S.13.d.4.6.)   2 Platoons.
   CHAVATTES   be (S.13.b.4.8.)   ½ Platoon.

   The following Posts will/only occupied if ordered to do so, and will be furnished by "Y" Coy. :-

   LE TOURET N.   (X.10.b.4.3.)   1 Platoon.
   LE TOURET N.E. (X.17.a.8.4.)   2 Platoons

8. **Trench Stores.** O.C. Coys. will render to H.Q. by 4 p.m. a copy of all Trench Stores to be handed over to incoming Battalion. Triplicate copies to be made on forms sent to Coys.

9. **Battalion Trench Stores.** All the Battalion Trench Stores will be handed over to incoming Regiment. Triplicate Lists to be made out, one copy to be furnished to Headquarters by 4 p.m.

10. **Steel Helmets.** O.C. Coys. will hand over all Steel Helmets to incoming Regiment with the exception of 25 per Coy. which will be taken to Billets by them.

11. **Lewis Guns.** Machine & Lewis Guns will be relieved at 5 p.m. and will proceed direct to their Billetting Areas. Guides will report at Headquarters at 4 p.m.

12. **Relief of Posts.** O.C. "X" Coy. will arrange for relief of Z ORCHARD and ALBERT POSTS to be complete by noon.

13. **Transport.** The Transport Officer will detail two Limbers to take away Kits from Headquarters.

14. **Reports.** On completion of Relief Coys. will report by phone to H.Q. and on arrival at Billets will send an Officer to report to the Adjutant at Headquarters.

Army Form C. 2118

XX 15th Sherwood Foresters MAY
VOL 4

H.Y.
Gyrfelt

WAR DIARY
or
INTELLIGENCE SUMMARY
(Erase heading not required.)

Instructions regarding War Diaries and Intelligence Summaries are contained in F.S. Regs., Part II. and the Staff Manual respectively. Title Pages will be prepared in manuscript.

Place	Date	Hour	Summary of Events and Information	Remarks and references to Appendices
Laventie	2/5/16 to 6/5/16	—	In billets	Afternoon Operation orders
	7/5/16 to 14/5/16	—	Battalion in trenches as Divisional Reserve	
Estaires Bac St Maur	15/5/16 to 18/5/16		In trenches (took over from 23rd Manchesters.)	
	18/5/16		Relieved 14th KR Rifles in neighbourhood of NEUVE CHAPELLE sector.	
	22/5/16		Relieved by 1st Gloster our reserve battle till 23/5/16	
	26/5/16		Took over line from 14th Glosters trenches in Fall 31/5/16. Battalion made trenches on 30/5/16 but this was very unpopular owing to an action fought on that night when the enemy counter air fosietion (recount attached).	

Mansell Capt & Adjt
15th Sherwood Foresters

Operation Orders No. 9.   Copy No.
By Lieut. Col. R.N.S. Gordon,
   Commdg. 15th. (S) Bn. Sherwood Foresters.

Ref.   1   Bethune
      40,000 Combined Sheet
              Trench Map 8.

1. **Relief.** The 15th. Sherwood Foresters will relieve the 14th. Glosters in the Right Sub-Sector of the FERME DU BOIS SEctor tomorrow.

2. **Distribution of Coys.**

   "Z" Coy.   FROM LA QUINQUE RUE (exclusive) S.21. S.21.2. to a point 140 yards North of S.21.3.

   "W" Coy.   From a point 140 yards North in S.21.3. to FERME DU BOIS S.21.3. S.16.1. S.16.2.

   "X" Coy.   ROPE KEEP POST.   -   15 men and two N.C.Os.
              DEAD COW POST   -   20 men and 3 N.C.Os.
              TUBE POST   -   Remainder of Coy.

   "Y" Coy.   BOURNVILLE   -   2 Platoons and H.Q.
              OLD BREASTWORK   -   2 Platoons.

3. **Route.** W & Y Coys. will move by KING GEORGE'S ROAD, WHISKY CORNER S.8.b. and TEETOTAL CORNER. (S.13.a.)
   Z & X will move by EMERGENCY ROADS X.11.d. X.12.c. crossing 10 S.13.b. to Fork Roads at S.14.c.5.9.

4. **Starting Point & Time.** Starting Point for W. & Y Coys. Fork Road S.7.b. 8-30 p.m.
   Starting Point for Z & X Coys. Fork Road S-13.b. 0.9.
   Time 8-30 p.m.
   Coys. to follow at 10 minutes interval.

5. **Order of March.**   "X" Coy. will detail its Coy. to enter Posts in
   For Posts   following order :-
   "X" Coy.
                             ROPE KEEP POST.
                             TUBE POST.
                             DEAD COW POST.

6. **Reconnaissance.** All Coys. will thoroughly reconnoitre their Routes and will see that each Platoon has a guide who knows the road.

7. **Guides.** The following guides will be supplied by Coys. who, on completion of Relief will return to their Coys. :-

       "W" 4 Guides to "Y" Coy.
       "X" 4   "   " "Z" "
       "Y" 4   "   " "W" "
       "Z" 4   "   " "X" "

8. **Intervals.** Coys. will move by Platoons at 200 yards interval.

9. **Dress.** Men will parade in Greatcoats with Capes and Waterproofs rolled.

10. **Waterbottles.** Waterbottles will be taken full.

11. **Rations.** Rations will be taken up by men for Friday.

12. **L.G. Section.** L.G. Detachment will parade under orders of L.G. Officer and will relieve by daytime. Relief to be completed by 6 p.m.

13. <u>Stretchers</u>. Coys. will take Long and Trench Stretchers with them.

14. <u>Snipers and Bombers</u>. Snipers and Bombers under their Commanders will relieve by day, to be completed by 6 p.m.

15. <u>Ammunition</u>. 100 rounds per man will be taken into the Trenches.

16. <u>Guard</u>. O.C. "Y" Coy. will detail a Guard of 2 N.C.Os. and 12 men for duty at Headquarters.

17. <u>Ration Parties</u>. Ration Parties will be supplied by Coys. in Support.

18. <u>Taking over Trench Stores</u>. All Trench stores will be taken over in daylight and receipts given.
O.C. Coys. will detail an Officer to report at 14th. Gloster Headquarters at 4 p.m. to do this.

19. <u>Transport</u>. Transport Officer will detail Transport to go to SANDBAG HOUSE at 9 p.m. water cart and M.O's to accompany. One Limber for Officers Mess Kit will call round Coys. starting with "X" at 6-30 p.m.

20. <u>Completion of Relief</u>. O.C. Coys. will notify Headquarters on completion of Relief, and that all men are posted to the places they will occupy in case of alarm.

            K.W. Morell Captain & A/Adjt.
          15th. (S) Bn. Sherwood Foresters.

Issued at 5 p.m.

```
       "W" Coy. Copy No. 1.
       "X"  "    "   "   2.
       "Y"  "    "   "   3.
       "Z"  "    "   "   4.
    H.Q.)
        )    "    "   "   5 & 6.
    File         "    "   7
    War Diary    "    "   8.
    L.G. Officer "    "   9.
    Bombing   "  "    "   10.
    Signalling   "    "   11.
    Transport    "    "   12.
    Q.M.         "    "   13.
O.C.14th.Glosters "    "  14.
```

Operation Orders No. 10   Copy No. 12
By Lieut. Col. R.M.S.Gordon, File
Commdg. 15th. (S) Bn. Sherwood Foresters.

Ref. 1/40,000   Bethune Combined Sheet.

May 2 1916

1. **Relief.** The Battalion will be relieved by the 14th. Gloster Regt. tonight May 2nd. 1916.

2. **Order of Relief.** The Battalion will be relieved in the following order :- W, Z, X, Y.

3. **Billets.** On relief Coys. will move independently to their Billeting Areas as under :-

   W Coy.   D Area.
   X "   B   "
   Y "   A   "
   Z "   C   "
   H.Q. "   E   "
   L.G. Detmt.   F   "

4. **Route to Billets.** Coys. will return to Billets by same Routes as on Relief on 27th. "Y" Coy. will move by RUE DU BOIS by Sections at 50 yards interval.

5. **Formation.** Coys. will move by Platoons at 200 yards intervals.

6. **Duties.** The following Posts will be furnished by "Y" Coy.
   Z ORCHARD   S.14.b.5.8.   1 Sgt.   14 other Ranks.
   ALBERT   S.8.d.5.4.   1 "   14   "   "

7. **Trench Stores.** O.C. Coys. will render to H.Q. by 6 p.m. a copy of all Trench Stores to be handed over to incoming Battalion. Triplicate copies to be made out on forms sent to Coys.

8. **Lewis Guns.** Machine and Lewis Guns will be relieved at 12 noon and will proceed direct to their Billeting Areas, moving by sections. O.C. L.G. Detachment will leave a Guard of one N.C.O. and three men to look after L.G. Mountings and remove same to GRUB STREET at 8 p.m.

9. **Relief of Posts.** O.C. "Y" Coy. will arrange for relief of "Z" ORCHARD and ALBERT POSTS to be completed by 12 noon.

10. **Transport.** The Transport Officer will detail transport to be at GRUB STREET for removal of Stores at 8-30 p.m.

11. **Reports.** On completion of Relief Coys. will report by phone to H.Q. and on arrival at Billets will send an Officer to report to Adjutant at H.Q. in Area E.

Issued at 7 a.m.

                                              Captain,
                                              A/Adjutant,
                                              15th. (S) Battalion,
                                              Sherwood Foresters.

O.C. "W" Coy.   Copy No. 1.
     "X" "   "   "   2.
     "Y" "   "   "   3.
     "Z" "   "   "   4.
L.G. Detachment   "   "   5.
     H.Q.   "   "   6.
                  "   "   7.
     War Diary   "   "   8.
Transport Officer "   "   9.
     Q.M.   "   " 10.
O.C. 14th. Glosters. " " 11.
     File.   "   " 12.

Operation Orders No. 11.   Copy No.
By Lieut. Col. R.N.S. Gordon,
        Commdg. 15th. (S) Bn. Sherwood Foresters.

                                                            5-5-16.

Map Ref.   I   Bethune
           40,000 Combined Sheet.

1. **Relief.** The Battalion will move into Divisional Reserve Area on the 6th. and will be billed in LES LOBES area R 32.

2. **Guides for Relief of Posts.** O.C. "X" Coy. will detail 4 guides to meet garrisons of the H.L.I. taking over Z ORCHARD)
                                                                ALBERT   ) at X5.a.3.0.
                                                                EPINETTE)
                                                                CHAVATTES) at 10 a.m.
   on the 6th.

3. **Receipts of Post Trench Stores.** Lists of all Trench Stores in Z ORCHARD and ALBERT POSTS will be made out in triplicate and copy sent to H.Q.

4. **Route.** The Battalion will move by following Route :-
   MESPLAUX X.14.b. LOCON X.7.

5. **Starting Point and Time** Battalion Headquarters at 5-30 p.m.

6. **Order of March.** "Y" Coy. "X", "W", "Z", H.Q. L.G. Detachment, Transport.
   East of Canal Companies will move by Platoons at 200 yards interval.
   West of Canal Companies will move as Units at 10 minutes interval.
   W, X, & Z Coys. will move from their Billets to Starting Point by Emergency Road X.11.c. X.10.d.

7. **Billets.** Coys. will be billeted as under :-
   W in C Area   R. 31. a.&d.
   X in D Area   R.32.c.
   Y in B Area   Q.36.d.& X.1.a.
   Z in A Area   X.1.b.& d.
   H.Q. & L.G. Detachment in E Area X.2.a.
   Q.M. Stores & Transport R.20.a.5.2.

8. **Cookers and Watercarts.** All Cookers and Watercarts will be returned to Transport Lines by 2 p.m.

9. **Guides for Incoming Battalion.** O.C. Coys. & Units will detail 4 guides per Coy. and one Guide per Unit to meet the 18th. H.L.I. at X.5.a. 3.0. at 1.45 p.m.

10. **Reports.** On Arrival in Billets all reports will be made to Battalion H.Q. at X.2.a.5.6.

                                                    Lieut-Col.
                                        Commdg. 15th. (S) Bn. Sherwood Foresters.

Issued to O.C. W Coy. Copy No.1
              X   "   "   " 2
              Y   "   "   " 3
              Z   "   "   " 4
         L.G. Detchmt. " " " 5
              H.Q.   " " " 6
              File   " " " 7
    Major Vickers   " " " 8
    Transport Officer " " " 9
    Quartermaster   " " " 10.
    War Diary   " " " 11.
                       " " " 12.

Operation Orders, No. 12.
By Lieut-Col. R.H.S. Gordon,
Commdg. 15th. (S) Bn. Sherwood Foresters

Copy No.

5-5-16

Map. 1
40,000. Bethune Sheet.

1. **Relief.** The 15th. Sherwood Foresters will relieve the 23rd. Manchester Regiment in the Right Reserve Line of the NEUVE CHAPELLE Section.

2. **Billets.** Coys. will be billeted in the following areas as shown on accompanying maps :-

Headquarters	Area E.
"W" Coy.	" A.
"X" Coy.	" B.
"Y" Coy.	" C.
"Z" Coy.	" D.

3. **Posts.** The following Posts will be furnished by "Z" Coy. Relief to be completed by 5-30 p.m.

   ST. VAAST   Garrison   1 Officer,
   H.33.c.o.o.   50 men.

4. **Lewis Guns.** Lewis Gun Detachments will be furnished for the following Posts :-

   PORT ARTHUR   S.4.d.9½.1½.   1 Gun & Detachment.
   LANSDOWN   S.3.d.8½.8.   1 Gun & Detachment.
   ST. VAAST   H.33.c.o.o.   1 Gun & Detachment.
   POINT LOGI N. S.4.a.9½.8½.   2 Guns & Detachment.
   POINT LOGI S. S.4.a.9½.8.   1 Gun & Detachment.

   These Posts will be relieved by 7 a.m. on the 14th.

5. **Reconnaissance.** O.C. Coys. will detail one Officer per Coy. and/from each a representative Platoon to ascertain their Billeting Areas, and take over stores.

6. **Guides.** Platoon Representatives who will act as Guides will meet Platoons at R.33.d.9½.1. at 5-30 p.m.

7. **Route.** Coys. will march to their Billets by following Route :-
   LOGON ZELOBES ROAD -- VIEILLE CHAPELLE -- LACOUTURE QUEEN MARY'S ROAD.

8. **Distances.** West of the LAWE RIVER Coys. will move intact. East of the LAWE RIVER Coys. will move by Platoons at 200 yards interval.

9. **Order of March.** Z., X., Y., W., H.Q.,.

10. **Starting Point and Time.** Cross Roads R.32.d.8.7. Leading Coy. at 5-15 p.m. Intervals of 10 minutes between Companies.

11. **Transport.** One G.S. Wagon and one G.S. Limbered Wagon will accompany each Coy. to carry all Kit, Blankets etc. and these will report at Coy. H.Q. by 3 p.m.

12. **Position of H.Q. etc.** Transport will remain at R.20. Central.
    Q.M. Stores will be located at R.20. Central.
    Battalion Headquarters will be located at H.31.d.5.7.
    Brigade Headquarters   "   "   "   " R.30.c.4.9½.

13. **Stores etc.** All Billet Stores will be handed over to incoming Unit and receipts taken, copy to be furnished to H.Q. by 9 a.m. 15th. May.

All Billet Stores, Maps etc. will be taken over from relieved Unit, copy of receipts to be furnished to Headquarters by 9 a.m. 18th. May.

14. **Cleanliness.** All Billets will be thoroughly cleaned before being vacated.

Issued at 10 p.m.

                                                     Captain,
                                                   a/Adjutant,
                                        15th. (S) Bn. Sherwood Foresters

```
O.C. "W" Coy.    Copy No. 1.
     "X"  "       "    "  2.
     "Y"  "       "    "  3.
     "Z"  "       "    "  4.
L.G. Detachment         "  5.
     H.Q.         "    "  6.
Major Vickers    "    "  7.
     File        "    "  8.
     "           "    "  9.
Transport O.     "    " 10.
     Q.M.        "    " 11.
23rd. Manchesters "   " 12.
```

Operation Orders,　　　　　　　　　　　　　　　　　　Copy No.
By Major P. Vickers,
Commdg.15th. (S) Bn. The Sherwood Foresters.

17-3-16.

1. **Relief.** The 15th. Sherwood Foresters will relieve the 14th. Glosters in the NEUVE CHAPELLE Right Sub-sector on the night of the 18th.

2. **Distribution.** "W" Coy. Right Coy. S.10.4. to S.10.5. inclusive.
   "X" Coy. Centre Coy. S.10.6. S.11.1.
   "Y" " Left Coy. S.5.1. S.5.2.
   "Z" Coy. in Posts.
   HELLS REDOUBT　30 men under a Sgt.
   LANSDOWN POST　1 Officer, 50 N.C.Os. & Men.
   PORT ARTHUR　1　"　50 N.C.Os. & Men.
   HUN POST　Remainder of Coy. Coy. Hdqrs.

   Temporary Battalion Headquarters M.34.c.8.2. to which place all reports will be sent. (GUNXON POST).

3. **Order of March & Entry into Trenches.**
   "W" Coy. "X" Coy., "Y" Coy., "Z" Coy., H.Q.

   "W" Coy. via LANSDOWN TRENCH.
   "X" " " " "
   "Y" " " LA BASSEE ROAD & HUN STREET.
   "Z" " will detail its Coy. to enter Posts as above.

4. **Starting Point.** Cross Roads CROIX BARBEE leading Coy. to pass Starting Point at 8=30 p.m. Coys. will move by Platoons at 200 yards interval. Guides will meet Companies at THE SHRINE.

5. **Dress.** Men will parade in Greatcoats, with Capes and Waterproof Sheets rolled.

6. **Waterbottles.** Waterbottles will be taken up full.

7. **Rations.** Men will carry Friday's Rations with them.

8. **Sniperscopes, Periscopes, "Very" Pistols, & Steel Helmets.**
   These will be taken over from Battalion in Line. Coys. will detail one Officer to take over on Thursday Afternoon the 18th.

9. **Stretchers.** Coys. will arrange to take their long and short stretchers into the line with them.

10. **First Aid Dressing Station.** First Aid Dressing Station is located at STEWART CORNER S.4.d.4.10.

11. **Ammunition.** O.C. Coys. & Units will see that each man takes 100 rounds into the trenches with him.

12. **Reports and Returns.** The attention of all Unit Commanders is drawn to the revised times of reports circulated to Coys. in FERME DU BOIS Sector. "Z" Coy. to include in Tactical Progress Report that all Posts have been visited daily and found correct or otherwise.

13. **Rounds.** All ranks must move by covered ways beyond road control posts.

14. **Ration Parties.** Coys. will provide their own Ration Parties, Ration Dump & R.E. Dump ST. VAAST.

15. **Taking over Trench Stores.** All Trench Stores will be taken over in daylight, and a receipt given, copy to be retained for reference.

16. **Completion of Relief.** On Completion of Relief O.C. Coys. will notify H.Q. that all men are posted to the places they are to occupy in case of alarm.

17. **Signallers and Bombers.** H.Q. Signallers and Bombers will parade under orders of Signalling & Bombing Officers, and will report at Battalion H.Q. CURZON POST before proceeding to Trenches to take over.

18. **Lewis Guns.** Relief of Lewis Guns, Patrols, Snipers, & Signallers, will take place on the morning of the 18th. Relief to be complete by 7 a.m.

                                                              Captain,
                                                          A/Adjutant,
                       15th. (S) Bn. The Sherwood Foresters.

Issued at

```
Copy No. 1 to O.C. "W" Coy.
         2        "X"  "
         3        "Y"  "
         4        "Z"  "
         5        L.G. Detachment.
         6        Quartermaster.
         7        Bombing Officer.
         8        Signalling Officer.
         9        File.
        10        War Diary.
        11         "    "
```

Operation Orders, No. 15.　　　　　　　　　　　　　　　　Copy No. 11.
By Major F. Vickers,
　　Commdg. 15th. (S) Bn. Sherwood Foresters.　　　24-5-16.

1. **Relief.** The Battalion will relieve the 14th. Gloster Regt. in the Right Sub-sector on the night of the 25th.

2. **Distribution.** Coys. will occupy the identical Front line and Posts as on first tour of duty in the Trenches.

3. **Order of March & Entry into Trenches.**　Y Coy., W.Coy., X Coy., Z Coy., H.Q.

    "Y" Coy. via LANSDOWN TRENCH.
    "W"　"　"　"　"
    "X"　"　"　"　"
    LANSDOWN POST Garrison via LANSDOWN TRENCH, remainder of "Z" Coy. via LA BASSEE ROAD.

4. **Starting Point.** Cross Roads CROIX BARBEE, leading Coy. to pass Cross Roads at 8-30 p.m. and move by Platoons at 200 yards interval, and at least that distance between last Platoon of one Coy. and leading Platoon of another Coy.

5. **Dress.** Men to parade in Greatcoats, capes and groundsheets rolled.

6. **Waterbottles.** Waterbottles to be taken up into the Trenches full.

7. **Rations.** Men will carry Friday's Rations with them.

8. **Sniperscopes, Perispopes, Very Pistols.** These will be taken over from the Battalion in the line. Coys. will detail one Officer to take over on Thursday afternoon the 25th.

9. **Stretchers.** Coys. will take long and short stretchers into the line with them.

10. **First Aid Dressing Station.** First Aid Dressing Station is located at STIRLING CASTLE, S.4.d.4.10.

11. **Ammunition.** O.C. Coys. & Units will see that each man takes 100 rounds into the Trenches.

12. **Reports and Returns.** Reports and Returns as before.

13. **Rounds.** All ranks must move by covered ways beyond xx road control posts.

14. **Ration Parties** Coys. will provide their own Ration Parties. Ration Dump and R.E. Dump ST. VAAST.

15. **Trench Stores.** All Trench Stores must be taken over in daylight, and a receipt given, copy to be retained for reference.

16. **Completion of Relief.** On completion of Relief O.C. Coys. will notify H.Q. by code viz., R.C.

17. **Lewis Guns, Snipers, ~~Bombers~~ Signallers,** Relief of Specialists will take place on the morning of the 25th, relief to be complete by 7 a.m.

18. **Guides.** The Battalion will not require guides.

Issued at 9 p.m.
Copy No. 1. O.C. "W" Coy.
　　　　2.　　　"X"　"
　　　　3.　　　"Y"　"
　　　　4.　　　"Z"　"
　　　　5. L.G. Detchmt.
　　　　6. T.O.
　　　　7. Bombing Officer.
　　　　8. Signalling　"
　　　　9. File.
　　　10. War Diary.
　　　11.　　"　"

　　　　　　　　　　　　　　　　　　　　　　　Captain,
　　　　　　　　　　　　　　　　　　　　　　　A/Adjutant,
　　　　　　　　　　　　　　　　　　　15th. (S) Bn. Sherwood Foresters.

Operation Orders, No. 15.   Copy No. 11
By Lieut-Col. R.W.S.Gordon,
    Cmdg. 15th. (S) Bn. Sherwood Foresters.
                                                    29-5-16.
Map Ref. Bethune Combined Sheet.

1. **Relief.** The 15th. Sherwood Foresters will be relieved by the 14th. Glosters on the night of the 30th.

2. **Bombers, Snipers, Signallers & Lewis Guns.** Bombers, Snipers, Lewis Gunners, & Signallers will be relieved early morning, relief to be complete by 7 a.m. 30th. May.

3. **Order of Relief.** The Battalion will be relieved in the following order :—
    Y, W, X, Z, H.Q.

4. **Route to Billets.** Coys. will move to Billets occupied before at CROIX BARBEE. W & X via LANSDOWNE TRENCH, Y, Z, & H.Q. via LA BASSEE ROAD.

5. **Emergency Coy.** "Y" Coy. will act as Emergency Coy.

6. **Marching Out.** Coys. will not move out until incoming Coy. is properly posted.

7. **Formation.** Coys. will move by Platoons at 200 yards interval, and march independently to Billets.

8. **Cleanliness.** Trenches and Billets must be left clean and tidy. O.C. Coys. to be responsible for this.

9. **Posts.** "W" Coy. will detail garrison for ST. VAAST POST, relief to be completed by 8-30 p.m. "Z" Coy. Platoon formerly in ST. VAAST POST to go to H.Q.
    Lewis Gun Officer will arrange to post one Gun at ST. VAAST POST as before.

10. **Transport.** The Transport Officer will arrange Transport to be at ST. VAAST DUMP at 8-30 p.m. Coys. must arrange to have all surplus stores taken there at about that time.

11. **Trench Stores.** All Trench Stores will be handed over to incoming Unit except Steel Helmets. All these must be taken out. A receipt for all stores in duplicate must be taken from incoming Unit and a copy must reach H.Q. by 2 p.m. 30th. May 1916.

12. **Reports.** On completion of Relief, Coys. will report by phone N.C. and letter of Coy. and on arrival in Billets will detail an Officer to report at H.Q.

13. **Guides.** No Guides will be required.

Issued at 9 p.m.

Copy No. 1   "O.C. "W" Coy.
          2   "X" "
          3   "Y" "
          4   "Z" "
          5   L.G. Officer.
          6   Signalling Officer.
          7   Bombing   "
          8   Transport "
          9   Q.M.
         10   File.
         11   War Diary.
         12   14th. Glosters.

                                    Captain,
                                    A/Adjutant,
                                    15th. (S) Bn. Sherwood Foresters.

First Report on Operations on Night of 30th. May 1916. :-

At 7-20 p.m. enemy commenced an intense bombardment of our front line and Support line, with T.Ms. Rifle Grenades, and guns of all calibres. All Post and communicating trenches were heavily shelled and barrage of H.E. and Shrapnel was placed along the LA BASSEE ROAD and SANDBAG ALLEY.
At 8 p.m. the bombardment ceased slightly for 5 minutes, but was renewed with greater intensity till 10-20 p.m. During the bombardment the enemy entered the trenches but at what time it is impossible to say as considerable distance in the Right Coy. has been smashed down and levelled.
Evidence of the entry of the enemy is found in the presence of bombs, some of which have been recovered intact. As soon as the enemy was perceived a party of the 18th. Lancashire Fusiliers on the Right and a party from one Coy. on the left of the breach worked inwards and re-established connection. Orders were issued as soon as report was received of the breaking of the Line, and a party was sent down from Headquarters and two platoons of the 14th. Glosters were sent down LANSDOWNE TERRACE to re-occupy our line, which was done.
The chief damage done is on our right where bays 10-33 are completely obliterated, the rest of the line being badly breached in many places.
Our Artillery responded at 7-25 p.m. and kept up firing till about 11 p.m. After the bombardment working parties assisted, and two Coys. of the Glosters were organised, all R.E. men were placed in charge and repairs promptly carried out. By 3 a.m. all breaches had been filled in, and in bays 10-33 sufficient earth was thrown up to ensure cover from view.
During the early morning "W" Coy. was withdrawn from the line, and relieved by a Coy. of the 14th. Glosters.
A second Coy. of the 14th. Glosters was distributed along the line to assist in repairing the parapet.
The 18th. Lancashire Fusiliers withdrew to their own line about 2-30 a.m. on completion of the taking over by the 14th. Glosters.
Casualties, I regret, will be very heavy, but the total amount has not yet been ascertained as many men are missing.
Many were blown to pieces and it is feared that several lie under the ruins also some may be taken prisoners, but can only be wounded as when the parapet was breached, orders were issued to withdraw on either flank.
All the 5 Officers in "W" Coy. were wounded, two severely, and one other Officer in "X" Coy. was wounded.
The Casualties will run into 60 or 70.
Full list will be furnished when the roll calls can be obtained.
All recommendations for gallant conduct will be forwarded separately.

31-5-16.

W.A.W.Cellin Capt & Adjt / for. Lieut-Col.
Commdg. 15th. (S) Bn. The Sherwood Foresters

Issued at.

```
            O.C. "P" Coy. Copy No.  1.
                "X"  "    "    "    2.
                "Y"  "    "    "    3.
                "Z"  "    "    "    4.
                R.C. Detmt. "    "  5.
                H.Q.        "    "  6.
                War Diary   "    "  7.
    Major Thelwall          "    "  8.
    Transport Officer       "    "  9.
    Quartermaster           "    " 10.
    O.C. 14th.  )
        Glosters)           "    " 11.
```

Army Form C. 2118

June

15-(S) Bn THE SHERWOOD FORESTERS

Vol 5

XXXV

WAR DIARY or INTELLIGENCE SUMMARY

(Erase heading not required.)

JUNE 1916

54

Place	Date	Hour	Summary of Events and Information	Remarks and references to Appendices
CROIX BARBEE	1st to 9th		In Billets.	
	9th		Relieved 14th Gloucestershire Regt. in Right Sub-Sector Neuve Chapelle Section.	
	9th-16th		In Trenches.	
	16th		Relieved by 12th Royal Sussex Regt.	
LES LOBES	16th-17th		In Billets.	
	17th		Moved to Mt Bernenchon (orders issued verbally to O.C. Coys and units)	
Mt BERNENCHON	17th till 30th		In Billets.	

W. A. L. Collin Capt & O.O/F.
15th(S) Bn The Sherwood Foresters

Operation Orders, No. 17.   Copy No. 12
By Lieut-Col. R.H.S.Gordon,
     Commdg. 15th. (S) Bn. Sherwood Foresters.   8-3-16.

Map Reference.
─────1─────
40,000. Bethune Combined
Sheet & Trench Map Area 1.

1. **Relief.** The 15th. Sherwood Foresters will relieve the 14th. Gloster Regt. in the Right Sub-Sector of the NEUVE CHAPELLE Section during the 9th. inst.

2. **Distribution.** "Z" Coy. will relieve the Right Coy.
   "X" "   "   "   "   "   Centre " } 14th. Glosters.
   "Y" "   "   "   "   "   Left   "
   "W" Coy. will relieve the following Posts.
   LANSDOWN - PORT ARTHUR - NUN STATION - MILLS POST.

3. **Movement & Time.** All Specialists i.e. Lewis Gun Sections, Snipers, Bombers & Signallers will relieve corresponding Specialists 14th. Glosters by way of LANSDOWN & SANDBAG ALLEY C.Ts. Head of each party to be at LANSDOWN POST & NUN STATION at 3 a.m.
   "Z" Coy. & "Y" Coy. will move by LANSDOWN & Covered way respectively to relieve Right and Left Coys. 14th. Glosters Head of Coys. to be at LANSDOWN POST and NUN STATION respectively at 3 a.m.
   "X" Coy. will relieve Centre Coy. 14th. Glosters and will move by LANSDOWN C.T. Head of Coy. to be at LANSDOWN POST by 3 p.m.
   "W" Coy. will relieve Posts at present occupied by 14th. Glosters. Garrison for LANSDOWN POST moving across country, garrisons for remaining Posts proceeding by Covered way and NUN STATION, to be at SANDBAG ALLEY 4 p.m.

4. **ST. VAAST POST.** Garrison for ST. VAAST POST ("Z" Coy.) will move with remainder of Coy. to relief of Right Coy. 14th. Glosters leaving one N.C.O. and two men to hand over to relieving garrison.

5. **Billet Stores.** O.C. Coys. will detail one N.C.O. and two men to remain in Billets and hand over all Stores etc. to incoming reliefs.

6. **Precautions.** All Coys. will take particular care that no concentration of men takes place. Coys. will move by sections at 100 yards interval, and 200 yards intervals between Platoons.
   Every advantage to obtain cover from view must be taken by utilizing hedges where such are available, especially in the open country leading to LANSDOWN POST. Avoidance of beaten tracks is to be observed.

7. **Trench Stores.** Coys. will take over Trench Stores after Relief is complete.

8. **Rations.** All unexpended Rations for day of Relief will be taken up by the men. Rations for the following day will be sent up to DUMP as usual, Coys. furnishing their own Ration parties.

9. **Officers Kit etc.** All surplus Kit of Officers not required in Trenches will be handed over to Q.M. for removal to Q.M. Stores.
   All Kits required for Trenches will be taken to DUMP with Rations.

10. **Waterbottles.** Waterbottles will be taken full.

11. **S.A. Ammunition.** Every man will take 100 rounds S.A.A. with him.

12. **Completion of Relief.** O.C. Coys. will report to HUN STATION "R.C." on completion of Relief.

13. **Command.** Until the entire completion of relief of Battalion, Coys. & Unit will be directly under the orders of the O.C. 14th. Glosters.

14. **Headquarters.** Headquarters will move to HUN STATION at 4 p.m. to which place all reports will be sent.

                                                    Captain & A/Adjutant,
                           15th. (S) Bn. The Sherwood Foresters.

Issued at 2 p.m.

   O.C. "W" Coy. Copy No. 1.
       "X"   2.
       "Y"   3.
       "Z"   4.
   L.G. Officer   5.
   Bombing "   6.
   Signalling "   7.
   Intelligence   8.
   Major Vickers   9.
      " Bartlett 10.
   H.Q.   11.
   War Diary.   12.
   File.   13.
   14th. Glosters. 14.
   Transport Off. 15.
   Q.M.   16.

Operation Orders No. 18.
By Lieut-Col. R.N.S. Gordon,
Commdg. 15th. (S) Bn. The Sherwood Foresters.

FILE   Copy No. 12

Map Ref. __1__ Bethune Combined Sheet,
40,000 & Trench Map Area 1.

15/6/16

1. **Relief.** The 15th. Sherwood Foresters will be relieved by the 12th. Sussex Regt. in the Right Sub-Sector of the NEUVE CHAPELLE Section during the 16th inst.

2. **Detail.** Coys. will be relieved as under :-

    Reserve Coy.   (W) by "S" Coy.   12th. Sussex.
    Right   "   (Z) by "B" "   "   "
    Centre   "   (X) by "C" "   "   "
    Left   "   (Y) by "A" "   "   "

3. **Movements & Times.** All Specialists i.e. L.G. Sections, Bombers, Snipers Signallers will be relieved at 3 a.m. on the 16th inst. and on relief will proceed to LES LOBES
    Right and Left Coys. will be relieved at 6 a.m. and on completion of relief will proceed to Billets at LES LOBES as under :-
    Right Coy. by LANSDOWN C. TRENCH.
    Left Coy. by NUN STREET & Covered Way.
    Centre Coy. & Posts will be relieved at 3 p.m. and on relief will proceed to Billets at LES LOBES as under :-
    Centre Coy. by LANSDOWN C.T.
    Posts by NUN STREET and Covered Way with exception of LANSDOWN POST who will move across open to Billets.

4. **Billets.** Coys. will be billeted at LES LOBES in the same billets as occupied formerly.

5. **Formations.** Coys. on relief will move by sections at 100 yards intervals On arrival at CROIX BARBEE they will move by Platoons.

6. **Cleanliness.** O.C. Coys. will see that all Trenches are left in a state of cleanliness.

7. **Transport.** Transport Officer will arrange for Transport to be at DUMP at 3am O.C. Coys. must arrange for all Stores to be sent up during the night of 15/6/16 to DUMP by 3 am.

8. **Trench Stores.** All Trench Stores will be handed over to incoming Unit except Brigade and Battalion Trench Stores which will be taken out by the Battalion.

9. **Trench Maps.** All Trench Maps in possession of Coys. will be handed over to relieving Unit. Notice to be sent to H.Q. of numbers handed over and numbers of Map area.

10. **Receipts.** A receipt for all Stores (in duplicate) must be taken from Incoming Unit & a copy must reach H.Q. by 9 a.m. on the

11. **Completion Of Relief.** On completion of relief Coys. will report by phone "R.C." and letter of Coy. and on arrival in Billets will detail an Officer to report at H.Q. with usual certificates.

12. **Guides.** Coys. & Units will detail Guides as under, to report at CROIX
BARBEE :-

  Specialists at   3 a.m.   inst.
  Right Coy.   5 a.m.   "
  Left Coy.   5 a.m.   "
  Centre "   2 p.m.   "
  Reserve Coy.   2 p.m.   "

One Guide per Platoon and one per Post will be detailed.

            Capt. & Adjt.
           15th. (S) Bn. Sherwood Foresters.

Issued at

"W" Coy. Copy No. 1.
"X"   2.
"Y"   3.
"Z"   4.
L.G. Officer.   5.
Bombing "   6.
Signalling"   7.
Intelligence   8.
Major Cochran.   9.
H.Q.   10.
War Diary.   11.
File.   12.
T.O.   13.
Q.M.   14.
12th. Sussex.   15.

105th Bde.
35th Division

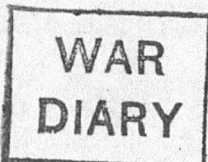

15th BATTALION

NOTTS & DERBY REGIMENT

1st to 31st JULY 1916

Report on Operations 20th JULY.
Operation Orders; Messages etc.

Army Form C. 2118

Original 35 July
10/35

WAR DIARY or INTELLIGENCE SUMMARY

15th. (S) BN. THE SHERWOOD FORESTERS.

JULY 1916.

Vol. 6

Place	Date	Hour	Summary of Events and Information	Remarks and references to Appendices
Mt. Bernenchon	1st. to 3rd.		In Billets, 35th. Division in G.H.Q. Reserve. Entrained CHOCQUES, detrained BOUQUE MAISON, marched to Billets at SUS ST. LEGER.	Operation Orders 19 & 20 and Additions. 1
Sus ST. Leger.	4th. 5th. 6th.		In Billets.	
	7th.		Marched to BEAUVAL.	Op. Order No. 21. 2
Beauval.	8th. 9th.		In Billets.	
	10th.		Marched to BUS LES ARTOIS.	Op. Order No. 22. 3
	11th.		Marched to WARLOY.	Op. Order No. 23. 4
Warloy	12th. 13th.		In Billets. Marched to BOIS du CELESTINS.	Op. Order No. 24. 5
	14th.	8 p.m.	Marched to Grove Town, near BRAY, and bivouaced, Reserve to 9th. Division.	
BOIS de BILLON.	15th.		Marched to BOIS de BILLON - bivouacs. Bivouacs.	
	16th.		Relieved 6th. NORTHANTS in TRENCHES S.E. of TRONES WOOD to immediately W. OF MALTZ HORN FARM. 16th. CHESHIRES on our left flank, 7th. Buffs on our right flank. For tactical purposes under the orders of the 54th. Brigade. 18th. Division.	
Trenches	17th.		Took over Trenches from 7th. Buffs and joined up with the FRENCH on our Right.	
Trenches	18th. 19th.		Rather heavily bombarded, subjected to tear and gas shells.	

6.4

WAR DIARY or INTELLIGENCE SUMMARY

Army Form C. 2118

11 (Contd.) JULY 1916.

(Erase heading not required.)

Place	Date	Hour	Summary of Events and Information	Remarks and references to Appendices
Trenches.	20th.		W & Z Coys. attacked enemy's position in conjunction with French attack on our Right at 5 a.m. Unsuccessful, casualties heavy. 23rd. Manchester Regt. assisted. Relieved at night by 18th. Lancashire Fusiliers, and returned to Bivouac at TALUS BOISE.	Attack Order No.1 Report of Operations & Addenda.
Talus Boise	21st.		In Bivouac.	
Talus Boise	22nd. 23rd. 24th.		Moved to Bivouac on Hill Top near D.H.Q. (MINDEN POST.) In Bivouac. Stood to at 2 a.m. and moved to occupy RESERVE TRENCHES (SILESIA TRENCH).	
Silesia Trench.	25th.		Consolidated and deepened Silesia Trench. Furnished working parties for R.E. "Z" Coy. formed garrison of BRIQUETARIE and made it a STRONG POINT.	
	26th.		"W" Coy. relieved "Z" Coy. at BRIQUETARIE. Remainder of Battalion returned to Dug Outs in Talus Boise.	Operation No. 25.
Talus Boise.	27th.		Resting.	
	28th.		X, Y, & Z Coys. relieved 16th. Cheshire Regt. in DUBLIN TRENCH.	Operation Order No.26.
Dublin Trench.	29th.		Relieved by 106th. Infantry Brigade, and returned to Bivouac near Minden Post.	
Minden Post.	30th.		In Bivouac.	
	31st.		Moved to Bivouac in SAND PIT VALLEY.	

First Report of Operations 20-7-16.

Disposition of Regiment. The 15th. Sherwood Foresters were occupying the Trenches running along Eastern side of TROMES WOOD from Point S.24.c.3.1. to a Point in S.30.C.7.0. thence in a South Westerly direction to a Point in A.5.d.7.9. with an advanced line running in a South Easterly direction from Point A.6.a.4.9. to A.6.c.7.8.

Narrative. In accordance with instructions received in a 105th. Brigade Order No. 38 dated 19-7-16 "Z" Coy. was detailed to assault and obtain possession of enemy's trenches at A.6. Central and "W" Coy. was detailed for the left assault on enemy's trenches at S.30.b.6.1.

First Attack. The Coys. detailed for the assault were in their positions as laid down in orders and at 5 a.m. advanced to the assault in four waves each. From reports received they suffered a good many casualties before the actual time for assaulting having come under severe shelling evidently from the barrage which the enemy at once put up during our intense bombardment.

Right Attack. The first two lines passed over our front line Trenches (which had been evacuated during the bombardment of the enemy's Trenches) and managed to reach MALTZ HORN FARM and the enemy's front line trenches where they came under heavy machine gun and rifle fire from concealed enemy trenches situated behind the enemy's front line. The succeeding two waves who also appear to have got over our front line were also met by this fire and were compelled to fall back on to our front line trenches where they assisted the supporting Coy. of the 23rd. Manchester Regt. who had been detailed to follow up behind the assaulting party to re-occupy our front line and to hold it at all costs.

Left Attack. On the signal for the advance being given four waves moved forward and on topping the rise came in full view of the enemy where they were met by a devastating fire from Machine Guns as far as can be ascertained from concealed positions to the East of MALTZ HORN FARM. From reports received from survivors it appears that the Coy. had suffered severely from the enemy's barrage fire, and owing to the lateness of the time for the attack and the light shining directly on them, they afforded an easy mark for the enemy's fire. As they were unable to proceed further, the survivors, who by this time had become much scattered, proceed to dig themselves in in shell holes and many men who had previously been reported missing eventually found their way back after dark. Reports were furnished to the Brigade stating the failure of both attacks.

Supports. In the meantime two Coys. of the 23rd. Manchester Regt. re-occupied the position originally held by the two Coys. 15th. Sherwood Foresters who had been detailed for the assault and our original line was maintained throughout.

Preparation for second Attack. After the failure of the first attack instructions were received from Headquarters, 105th. Brigade ordering continuation of the attack and stating that Headquarters and two more Coys. of the 23rd. Manchester Regt. were being sent up as reinforcements and also stating that the attack was to take place at 11-35 a.m. after an intense bombardment of enemy's position. Acting under these instructions the Coy. of the Manchester Regt. occupying the right of the line were given orders to evacuate the front line quarter of an hour prior to the bombardment i.e. 10-45 a.m. and take up its assembly position behind the crest of the hill, in A.6.a. and c Central. On arrival of the first of the two new Coys. orders were issued to them to form up behind the attacking Coy. and to follow it "over the Top" and to endeavour to obtain possession of enemy's trenches

trenches and consolidate them. The second new Coy. who only arrived at 11-30 a.m. were given orders to proceed by communication trench and occupy our front line trenches after the attack had passed over, leaving one Platoon in the reserve trench to be used as reinforcements if required elsewhere. At 11-35 a.m. the two Coys. of the Manchester Regt. detailed for the Attack advanced in eight waves and although they again reached the enemy's front line trench, which was reported to be nearly filled in, were unable to hold it owing to the devastating Machine Gun and Rifle fire with which they were met. They were compelled to return to our front line trenches.

During the whole of this time the whole length of trenches occ--upied by us were being subjected to an intense bombardment by enemy artillery of all kinds.

Touch was maintained throughout with the French on our right and shortly after noon a French Staff Officer reported at Battalion Headquarters stating that they had observed signs of the enemy concentrating troops to the East of GUILLEMONT with a view to counter-attacking. I considered the situation at this period to be extremely critical. The men of the Sherwood Foresters who had already occupied the Trenches for four days and had been incessantly subjected to intense bombardment during the whole period, and the remaining men of the Manchesters who had come up into a new part of the line without any knowledge of their whereabouts or the local conditions after a trying forced march, were practically in a state of collapse, especially as the enemy had in addition been sending over considerable quantities of Tear and Chlorine Gas Shells.

Under these circumstances I sent out six special runners to Advanced Brigade Headquarters so as to make certain of some getting through, and at the same time sent up the "S.O.S." signal by rocket.

In the meantime the Officers rallied their men and made all preparations for the expected counter-attack, the Officers of both Regiments taking over definite portions of the line, and preparing for any eventuality.

Reports were furnished to 105th. Brigade stating the conditions of the men and strongly recommending that they should be relieved if possible, the Manchesters being left without any senior Officers, and the Sherwoods with only one effective Officer per Company.

Orders for the relief (which was sanctioned) having been received the movement was carried out, the line being handed over to the 18th. Lancashire Fusiliers on completion of the relief at 1-30 a.m. 21st. inst.

At no time during the whole of the operations was our Front line evacuated except during our intense bombardment of MALTZ HORN FARM and this was done owing to our close proximity to it and for safety purposes on the recommendations of the French Staff.

I wish to bring to notice the work performed by a Coy. of the 17th. Northumberland Fusiliers (Pioneers) under Captain Muir, who during the night of the 19/20th. dug a trench from Strong Point B in S.30.a.8.5. to Arrow Head Copse and who held that position until relieved. By their presence they gave material and moral support to the two Coys. of the Sherwood Foresters on the left of our line, who were suffering severely from four days incessant shelling.

I also wish to bring to notice the conduct of the Officers and men of the 23rd. Manchester Regt. who, arriving at very short notice carried out the second attack with great fortitude and dash and although driven back cheerfully set to work to repair the line and place it in a state of defence in expectation of a counter-attack. I consider the conduct of the Officers and men deserving of high praise especially in view of the fact that they had lost their Commanding Officer and all their senior Officers.

The 105th. Machine Gun Coy. under Major Gordon rendered invaluable assistance and I am greatly indebted to Major Gordon for the useful reports with which he furnished me from time to time regarding the situation.

Also I wish to bring to notice the excellent work of Major Minshall commanding 204th. Field Coy. R.E. who at a critical time volunteered to make a reconnaissance of a position on the right and to ascertain the movements and dispositions of the French Troops with a view to further cooperation. He enabled me to report the actual situation to Brigade H.Q.

I am submitting later names of those who were under my command whom I consider are deserving of further recognition.

Lieut-Colonel,
Commdg. 15th. (S) Bn. Sherwood Foresters.

In the Field.
23-7-16.

Report on Reconnaissance on New Trench GUILLEMONT

– MALTZ HORN FARM.

Carried out by Lieut. K.B. Williamson and 2nd. Lieut. V.K. Haslam 25th.

Siege Battery R.G.A.

These Officers went to ARROW HEAD COPSE and were able to see the Trench well. I attach a tracing which is naturally rough, but is near to correct.

It runs apparently from the place where the trees on the road finish S.30.b.7.3. – passes ARROW HEAD COPSE at about 150 yards, this is within 25 yards of the work and continues as shewn in the tracing to behind MALTZ HORN FARM.

The Trench did not appear to be traversed anywhere and was, as far as could be seen entirely unwired.
The Infantry post in ARROW HEAD COPSE said however they had dispersed parties attending to wire, and the C.O. of the Battalion said a little wire existed behind MALTZ HORN FARM.

A part of the trench shewn from MALTZ HORN FARM enclosure downwards was obtained from the C.O. of this Battalion, whose information (he said) was from photographs and R.E.

That part of the trench seen by the reconnoitring party is from S.30.b.7.3. – A.6.b.0.6.

There is a sap runs out from about S.30.d.1.2. from which the sniping at the corner of our trench opposite is done, where Lieut. West was killed yesterday.

Trench as a whole appears to be shallow and unfinished, but is occupied and manned as lights were sent up from it.

Entry is said to be done from the South rather than the North end.

(Sd.) C.S.S. Curteis, Major R.G.A.
Commdg. 25th. Siege Battery, R.G.A.

HEARSAY FROM INFANTRY.

" German patrols frequent last night patrol of 12 encountered by our own of 5 which withdrew."

REGISTER of MESSAGES

Operations on MALTZ HORN FARM.

July 20th. 1916.

OUT.

Serial No.	Battn. No.	Time	Date.	To Whom.	Purport etc.
1.	S.B.783	12.35 a.m.	20	Bde.	Receipt of O.P. Order 38 & reports arrival of Col. Gordon.
2.	S.B.784	1.5. a.m.	"	"	-do-
3.	S.B.1.	5.7. a.m.	"	"X" Coy. M.	Report Situation.
4.	S.B.2.	5.30 a.m.	"	"Z" S.F.	Report Situation.
5.	S.B.3.	5.40 a.m.	"	"X" Coy.M.	Report Situation.
6.	S.B.4.	5.55 a.m.	"	O.C. 204th.) F.Coy. R.E.)	To move forward and ascertain situation.
7.	S.B.6.	6.8. a.m.	"	Major Cochran	Report Situation.
8.	S.B.7.	6.50 a.m.	"	O.C. Manch.Rgt.	Asking for Officer to report at once.
9.	S.B.8.	6.54 a.m.	"	"Z" Coy.S.F.	To remain bombers being sent up.
10.	S.B.9.	6.46 a.m.	"	Lt. Reynolds	To obtain touch with Lt. Sewell and try and gain objective.
11.	S.B.10.	7 a.m.	"	Major Cochran	Informs preparation of new attack and to send up bombs.
12.	S.B.11.	7.10 a.m.	"	Lt.Clayton Manchesters.	Send half Platoon to reinforce left.
13.	S.B.12.	7.45 a.m.	"	Capt.Rathbone Manchesters.	Giving orders for preparation for second attack.
14.	S.B.13.	8.11 a.m.	"	Capt.Rathbone Manchesters.	Forwarding report of French occupation and to rifle Grenade MALTZ HORN FARM.
15.	S.B.14.	8.40 a.m.	"	- do -	To send bombers forward to assist French in attacking MALTZ HORN FARM.
16.	S.B.15.	8.45 a.m.	"	Lt. Gabriel	To bring up Stokes gun & fire on MALTZ HORN FARM.
17.	S.B.16.	9.50 a.m.	"	Major Cochran	Reporting Situation.
18.	S.B.17.	10 a.m.	"	Brigade.	Reports from French, counter-attack developing on Right.
19.	S.B.18.	10.15 a.m.	"	Brigade	Acknowledges B.M. 20.
20.	S.B.19.	10.30 a.m.	"	O.C. Manch.	Orders for second attack.
21.	S.B.20.	10.43 a.m.	"	O.C. French Regiment.	Reporting zero hour and withdrawal of troops from front line.
22.	S.B.21.	11.15 a.m.	"	Brigade.	Report second attack, no information yet received.
23.	S.B.21a.	12.20 p.m.	"	- do -	Situation critical, report of second attack (16 runners) reorganising & holding front line.
24.	S.B.22.	1 p.m.	"	- do -	Reports situation.
25.c	S.B.23.	1.40 p.m.	"	- do -	Report Situation along all front.
26.	S.B.24.	1.45 p.m.	"	- do -	Reports loss of touch with French.

OUT.

Serial No.	Battn. No.	Time.	Date.	To Whom.	Purport etc.
26.	S.B.24.	1.45p.m.	20	Brigade.	Communication established with left all along front. Asks for medical dressings and requires aid from Bearer Squad.
27	S.B.26.	3.35 p.m.	"	Mjr.Cochran.	Reports Relief XXX in Progress.
28.	S.B.27.	4.35 p.m.	"	Brigade.	Casualty Return.
29.	S.B.29.	5.30 p.m.	"	All Coys.) Manch. &) Sherwoods.)	Orders to move into Rest Bivouac.
30.	S.B.31.	9. p.m.	"	Brigade.	B.M.120 acknowledged.

REGISTER of MESSAGES
Operations on MALTZ HORN FARM.

IN, July 20th. 1916.

No.	Date.	Time of Dispatch.	Arrival.	From Whom.	Purport.
1	20	3.40 a.m.	4 a.m.	"X" Coy.	Reporting Pioneers completed Trench to ARROW HEAD COPSE 3ft. by 18" & cover from earth
2.	"	4.55 a.m.	5.7 a.m.	Lt. Forsyth	Reporting arrival of two Coys. 23rd. Manchester Regt.
3.	"	5.5. a.m.	5.20 a.m.	"Z" Coy.	1st. Line across, heavy fire met.
4.	"	5.40 a.m.	6.5 a.m.	Mjr. Cochran	Reporting Position.
5.	"	6.22 a.m.	6.45 a.m.	Brigade.	Ordering Guides to be sent to BRIQUETARIE.
6.	"	6.30 a.m.	6.58 a.m.	Mjr. Cochran.	Reporting no signs of attack visible and stating position of PIONEER COY.
7.	"	6.41 a.m.	7.50 a.m.	Brigade	Reporting that French state our attack reached trenches but was driven out. Ordered to repeat attack and notify time.
8.	"	7 a.m.	8.15 a.m.	Brigade.	Reporting action of Artillery & wanting to know time arranged for second attack.
9.	"	8.51 a.m.	9.20 a.m.	O.C. 23rd. Manch.	Reporting arrival at BRIQUETARIE.
10.	"	7.45 a.m.	9.50 a.m.	Mjr. Cochran.	Reporting Bombs being sent up.
11.	"	?	10.15 a.m.	2nd. Lieut. Derbyshire.	Reporting being in front trench with Manchesters.
12.	"	10 a.m.	10.50 a.m.	Mjr. Cochran.	Reporting heavy shelling.
13.	"	10.44 a.m.	11.5 a.m.	Brigade.	Zero 11.35 a.m.
14.	"	8.50 a.m.	10.30 a.m.	Brigade.	Reporting arrangements made with French & necessity for gaining objectives.
15.	"	9.45 a.m.	11.5 a.m.	Brigade.	Continuation of instructions and requesting as to inform French as to Zero time.
16.	"	10.15 a.m.	11.22 a.m.	French	Notifying us of orders re attack.
17.	"	10.45 am.	11.35 a.m.	Brigade	Asking for casualties.
18.	"	10.50 a.m.	11.50 a.m.	French.	Reporting evacuation of trenches prior to Artillery bombardment.
19.	"	1.20 p.m.	2.10 p.m.	Brigade.	Ordering to hold line at all costs and consolidate even if attack fails. Relief if possible.
20.	"	1.20 p.m.	2.15 p.m.	Mj. Cochran.	Reporting situation.
21.	"	1.20 p.m.	2.15 p.m.	"	Asking for Stretcher Bearers.
22.	"	1.20 p.m.	2.30 p.m.	French.	Reporting French holding their line.
23.	"	3 p.m.	3.20 p.m.	Mj. Cochran.	Reporting situation and steps taken.
24.	"	2.50 p.m.	3.25 p.m.	Brigade.	Guides to meet relieving Rgt. at HAIR PIN CORNER.
25.	"	10.25 a.m.	4.45 p.m.	- do -	Asking for Casualties.
26.	"	11.55 a.m.	4.45 p.m.	- do -	PIONEERS strengthening wire tonight.
27.	"	4.40 p.m.	7 p.m.	- do -	Ordering touch to be maintained with French.
28.	"	4.45 p.m.	7.45 p.m.	Q.M. S.F.	Reporting arrival of men at Transport Lines.

IN,

No.	Date.	Time of Dispatch.	Time of Arrival.	From Whom.	Purport.
29	20	5 p.m.	7.45 p.m.	Brigade. ~~XXXXXXXXXXXXXX XXXXXXXXX~~	Casualty Return Required.
30	"	5 p.m.	7.45 p.m.	Brigade.	Ordering the Manchesters back to TALUS BOIS.

No.	Date.	Time of Dispatch.	Time of Arrival.	From Whom.	Purport.

REGISTER of TELEPHONE MESSAGES (Verbal) during

OPERATIONS on MALTZ HORN FARM,

July 20th. 1916.

OUT.

No.	Date.	Time.	To Whom.	Purport.
1.	20.	5.59 a.m.	Brigade.	Reporting situation, heavy Rifle and Machine Gun Fire on Right.
2.	20.	6.20 a.m.	"	Reports French in possession of MALTZ HORN FARM. Orderlies not yet returned.
3.	20	6.32 a.m.	"	Informs in possession of all our trenches
4.	20	6.48 a.m.	"	Reports only from Right Attack come through.
5.	20	6.50 a.m.	"	Reports failure of Right Attack.
6.	20	7-30 a.m.	"	Reports further support required before before attack could be recommenced.
7.	20	7.53 a.m.	"	Forwards 19 N.F. Report & Pte. Ward's Statement also Artillery firing short.
8.	20	8.37 a.m.	" "	Reports on store of water etc.
9.	20	11.8 a.m.	"	Reports non-arrival of Manchesters.
10.	20.	12.20 p.m.	"	Situation critical.
11.	20.	3.20 p.m.	"	Reconnaissance shows French Trench unoccupied.
12.	20.	4.25 p.m.	"	Re Relief.
13.	20.	6.50 p.m.	"	Reporting whole Line held & in touch with French.

In.

No.	Date.	Time.	From Whom.	Purport.
1.	20	6.45 a.m.	Brigade	Guides for Manchesters to be sent.
2.	20	6,50 a.m.	"	Order to continue attack & reinforce--ments being sent up.
3.	20	7.30 a.m.	"	Informed of Bombardment.
4.	20	8 a.m.	"	Ordered to report when ready.
5.	20	9.22 a.m.	"	Inquiries re B.M. 90.
6.	20	9-45 a.m.	"	Fixing Zero time and ordered to evacuate Front Trenches.
7.	20	10.57 a.m.	"	Zero 11.35 a.m. Bombardment 11.5 - 11.35 a.m.
8.	20	11.8 a.m.	"	Ordered to send out Guides for Manchesters.
9.	20	12.5 p.m.	"	Ordered to hold line at all costs.

To O.C. Coys. & Units.

with a view to the Battalion being called upon to move, ready to take the field at very short notice, the following arrangements will be at once complied with and Coy. and Unit Commanders will see that all ranks are fully conversant with these orders.

1. **Preliminary Notice.** As soon as Headquarters receive the Brigade Preliminary Notice to prepare for immediate move, notice will be at once sent to Units & Companies by runners with a pre-arranged order.
   On receipt of which Coy. and Unit Commanders will immediately take steps to get their Companies etc. prepared and will despatch an Officer to Headquarters for detailed orders.

2. **Detailed Orders.** Detailed Orders with reference to Concentration Point, Hour of Assembly, Transport etc. will be sent to Coys. as soon as arranged or communicated to the Officer told to report at Battalion Headquarters.

3. **Proceedure on receipt of preliminary Notice.** O.C. Coys. and Units will immediately recall all men away from their Coys. and Units, assemble them and see that they are equipped as laid down in Battalion Orders for light Marching Order. It cannot be too strongly impressed on the men that whilst everything is done to lessen the weight carried by them, the equipment as now authorised is of the utmost importance for their own comfort and safety. The essential points being the necessity of the men having their Iron Rations Complete, the unexpended portion of their rations in the mess tin, entrenching tools, waterproof sheet and cardigan. The frequent occasions of men not taking biscuits because they do not like them and expecting bread in lieu must be checked, and all ranks must understand that once on the march, bread issues will be stopped the exception and biscuits the rule.
   All articles i.e. greatcoats, personal property etc. not laid down in the authorized establishment will be immediately packed in the men's packs, placed in sacks, labelled and collected in the Coy. Store Depot. to be brought to the Battalion Salvage Depot if time permits. Each Coy. will then be inspected and report sent to Headquarters that the Coy. or Unit is ready to move.
   In order to get the men accustomed to turning out quickly and correctly Coys. and Units will have one inspection daily of all their men, completely equipped for a sudden move, with all their excess articles placed in their packs.

4. **Officers Kits.** Officers will see that their personal kit is reduced to the scale laid down 35lbs. and that all surplus is got rid of, or ready packed and labelled so as to be collected in the Salvage Depot.

5. **Officers Mess.** O.C. Coys. will arrange for a cradle to be built on the front limber of the cookers to take a small amount of food and mess tins for themselves. It is recommended that a small case containing only absolutely only necessary articles be always kept in readiness, so as to be available in case of a sudden move.

6. **Deficiencies.** O.C. Coys. and Units will see that every endeavor is made to complete all deficiencies in their Company and that all ranks be warned that in future any articles lost will be made good by the men themselves.

7. **1st. Line Transport.** On receipt of orders to move, the Transport Officer will immediately have all horses harnessed and sadled. Horses for Cookers will be immediately despatched to Companies. Pack Mules will be loaded and despatched to Companies and the Transport Officer will see that Drivers of Cookers and Pack Mule Loaders are completed in every way in their equipment.
   Limbers for S.A.A. Bombs and tools will be immediately loaded, the teams be harnessed ready to hitch up.
   Water Carts will be immediately filled and sent to Coys. to have water bottles filled, and then filled again. Maltese Cart will be sent to Battalion Aid Station and loaded. Mess Cart will be sent to Battn. H.Q.

All picketting gear etc. will be collected and placed on limbers and all personnel of Transport will stand to fully equipped. Chargers will be saddled and equipped with picketting gear etc.

8. **2nd.Line Transport.** No.1 Baggage wagon will be immediately prepared and sent round Coys. to collect Officers Kit, commencing with "X" Coy. No.2 Baggage wagon will load with Q.M.Stores and be then sent to Battn.H.Q. for Signalling Stores and Office Stationary. All Transport Animals will carry a feed of corn.

9. **Q.M.Stores.** The Quartermaster will arrange for all rations being issued to Coys.and Units if not already done so, or for them to be placed on the supply wagon. All stores necessary for the march or move will be loaded on No.2 Baggage wagon.

10. **Surplus.** All Surplus Stores will be collected and labelled and if time permits will be sent to the Battalion Salvage Dump.

11. **Salvage Details.** 2nd. Lieut.Snape and the men already detailed will immediately proceed to collect all surplus stores of the Battalion at the Battalion Salvage Dump, and make a list of them, and hand them over to the Brigade Salvage Officer. On completion of their duty they will make arrangements to rejoin the Battalion, Receipts will be taken for all articles handed over.

12. **Signallers.** When Coys. are ready to move instruments will be disconnected and packed, and all signallers will report to Headquarters with their instruments. The Signalling Officer will detail squads ready to proceed, after the march has commenced, to any Unit detached from the Battalion.

13. **Bombers.** Headquarters Bombers will parade under the Bombing Officer and will be available for distribution of bombs to Coys. if required.

14. **Pioneers.** Pioneers and Sanitary Squad will parade under the orders of the Quartermaster.

15. **Scouts.** Scouts and Snipers will parade immediately at Headquarters under the orders of the Intelligence Officer who will be furnished with all available information and who will instruct them as to the Route etc of the move.

16. **Battalion Runners.** will be under the direct orders of the Adjutant, and will parade at Headquarters.

17. **Band.** All instruments will be immediately returned to the Quartermasters unless otherwise ordered, and the band will automatically become stretcher bearers, and act under the orders of the Medical Officer. If the instruments are allowed to be taken, stretchers will be carried in the Maltese Cart.

18. **Medical Officer.** The M.O. will make arrangements for all men unable to march leaving them in charge of a N.C.O. and informing Field Ambulance of their position and number of men requiring to be evacuated.

19. **Sandbags.** In the event of the move being preparatory to taking up a position for an attack, each man will be issued with two sandbags to be tucked under the belt, Sandbags have been indented for and on arrival will be issued to Companies.

20. **Lewis Guns.** The Lewis Gun Section will parade under the orders of the Lewis Gun Officer and will fall in complete with Limbers loaded.

21. **General.** Only by constant practice of the above orders can Coys. and Units turn out quickly, a saving of an hour may mean the saving of many men's lives and positions gained, and every endeavour must be made to make every one conversant with the orders issued, so so that each man knows his work and the quickest way of doing it. Co-operation is essential, and Coy. and Unit Commanders will detail men to carry out the necessary duties.

In the Field.
24-6-16.

Lieut-Col.
Commdg. 15th. (S) Bn. Sherwood Foresters.

Copies to:-
O.C. Companies.
    L.G.Officer.
    Intelligence Officer.
    Bombing   "
    Signalling   "
    Transport   "
    Qr.Mr.
    Major. Cochran.
    2nd.Lieut.Snape.
    Medical Officer.
    Headquarters.

War Diary
Copy No. 10

Operation Order No 21
by
Lieut. Col. R. M. S. Gordon
Commdg 15th (S) Bn. Sherwood Foresters.
6/7/16.

1. **MOVE** — Brigade will move tomorrow by road to BEAUVAL.

2. **PARADE** — Bn. will parade tomorrow ready to move off from Starting Point at 7.15 a.m.

3. **STARTING POINT** — 400x clear of the Village of Sus St. LEDGER on the road to TUIlle

4. **ORDER OF MARCH** — H.Q. Y. W. Z. X. L.G. 1st Line Transport.

5. **DRESS** — Field Service Marching Order.

6. **BAND** — Parade as such between W and Z Coy's

7. **ROUTE** — TUIlle — LUCHEUX — S. of GROUCHES — DOULLENS — BEAUVAL.

8. **BILLETING PARTY** — Lt. MacHUTCHEON and 2 N.C.O.s will report to Bde. H.Q. LUCHEUX tomorrow 7th at 6-45 A.M.

9. **BILLETS** — All Billets will be left clean.

10. **DINNERS** — Will be cooked en route and served on arrival in New Billets

11. **REPORTS** — To head of Bn.

Issued at 5 P.M.
Llewellin. Capt. + Adjt.
15th Sherwood Foresters

Copies to:-
H.Q. 105th Bde. No. 1.
W Coy. " 2
X " " 3
Y " " 4
Z " " 5
L. Gun Officer " 6
Transport Officer " 7
Quarter Master " 8
Bn. H.Q. " 9
War Diary " 10
File " 11

"OPERATION ORDER Nº 23   Copy Nº 2
BY
LIEUT-COL R N S GORDON
CMDG 15TH SHERWOOD FORESTERS
                                            10.7.16.

1 DESTINATION :- The Bn will move tomorrow
                 by Route March to WARLOY
2 STARTING POINT :- MAIN GATE
  TIME   9.25 a.m.
3 ORDER OF MARCH :- HQ. W.X.Y.Z. L.G.Sect. 1st LINE TPT.
4 DRESS :-   FIELD SERVICE LIGHT MARCHING ORDER
5 KIT.   Officer's Kits to be at Q.M's Stores by 7 AM.
6 BAND.   Will parade as such.
7 STRETCHERS   Will be carried by Companies
8 BILLETS.   Must be left thoroughly clean & tidy
9 LOADING PARTY   2 Men per Coy. under L/C. MITCHELL
                   to load lorries & proceed with them.
                   Details will be issued later.
10 REPEATS   To Head of Battalion
  Issued at 6.45 pm   Wawtullin Capt & Adjt
  Copy Nº 1 to Bde   15/Sherwood Foresters
       - 2 - War Diary
       - 3 - File
       - 4 - H.Q.
  Verbally to O.C. Coys. L.G.Sect. T.O, Q.M,

OPERATION ORDER Nº 24 Copy Nº 1
BY
LIEUT-COL R.N.S. GORDON
Cmdg 15TH SHERWOOD FORESTERS
⑤
12.7.16.

Destination 1. Bn will proceed by Route March to HEILLY.

Starting Point 2. Bn Headquarters.

Time 3. 7.35 pm.

Order of March 4. HQ. Z. Y. X. W. L Gun 1st Line Tpt.

Rear Party. 5. O.C. W Coy will detail party of 1 Officer, 1 Sgt and 10 Men to collect ~~stretchers~~ stragglers.

Band 6. As such.

2nd Line Tpt. 7. March in rear of 16 Cheshires.

Billets 8. To be left clean.

Route 9. BAISIEUX — FRANVILLERS

Reports 10. Head of Column.

Issued verbally at 7 pm
Copy Nº 1   War Diary.   Wanselli Capt & Adjt.
  —   2   File.   15/Sherwood Foresters
  —   3   Y Coy.

52

War Diary No 1.

Papers in Connection with
Operations on MALTZ HORN FARM.
July 20th. 1916.

※※※※※※※※※※※※※

(1) Report of Operations.
(2) Brigade Orders No. 38.
(3) Attacks Orders No. 1.
(4) Report of Reconnaissance.
(5) Register of Messages.
(6) TRENCH. MAP. MONTAUBAN. $\frac{1}{20,000}$.

③ War Diary! Copy No. 9

Operation Orders, N° 22. 9-7-16.
By Lieut-Col. R.H.S. Gordon,
Commdg. 15th. (S) Bn. Sherwood Foresters.

Map Ref. 1/100,000. Sheet 11.

1. **Destination.** The Battalion will move tomorrow to BUS-LES-ARTOIS by route march.

2. **Route.** BULEUX - TERRAMESNIL - SARTON - THIEVRES - AUTHIE.

3. **Order of March.** H.Q., W., X., Y., Z., L.G. Section, 1st. Line Transport.

4. **Starting Point & Time.** Bottom of Church Steps at junction with MAIN STREET. Time :- 7-15 a.m. "X" Coy. will line along RUE NEUVE on the South and join in behind "W" Coy. "Z" Coy. will line along RUE NEUVE on the North and join in behind "Y" Coy. Transport will join in behind L.G. Section.

5. **Dress.** Field Service Light Marching Order.

6. **Packs.** All Packs will be collected in Sacks at Q.M. Stores by 5am.

7. **Officers Kit.** All Officers Kit will be at Q.M. Stores by 5 a.m.

8. **Band.** Will parade as such at Headquarters at 7 a.m.

9. **Stretchers.** All Stretchers will be carried by Companies.

10. **Billets.** Coy. Commanders will see that all Billets are left in a clean condition.

11. **Loading Party.** Coys. will detail two men per Coy. under L/Cpl. Mitchell "X" Coy. to load lorries at Q.M. Stores to report there at 6 a.m. preference being given to men unable to march, who will travel in Lorries.

12. **Reports.** To head of Battalion.

Issued at 10-15 p.m.

O.C. "W" Coy. Copy No. 1.
     "X"   2.
     "Y"   3.
     "Z"   4.
L.G. Section,   5.
Q.M.   6.
T.O.   7.
H.Q.   8.
War Diary.   9.
File.   10.
105th. Bde.   11.

Wanstellin Capt & Adjt
Lieut-Colonel,
Commdg. 15th. (S) Bn. The Sherwood Foresters.

Operation Orders No. 19.
By Lieut-Col. R.N.S. Gordon,
Commdg. 15th. (S) Bn. The Sherwood Foresters.

Ref. Map.
$\frac{1}{100000}$. Sheet 5A. & 11.

28-5-16.

1. The 35th. Division may be required to reinforce the 3rd. Army.

2. All Baggage proceeding by Baggage Wagon will be at Q.M. Stores by 3 p.m. and loaded by 5 p.m. Guard of 2 N.C.Os. and 4 men will accompany.

3. All available Trench Stores will be taken, and loaded under orders of Q.M. Greatcoats and Packs will be carried by men. Extra Stores will be dumped at Battalion Dump (Orderly Room) by 10 p.m. tonight.

4. Transport as already detailed will proceed by road.

5. Concentration Point. Road Junction South of G in OBLINGHEM. 15th. Sherwoods on ROBECQ-BETHUNE ROAD behind 15th. Cheshires Transport.

6. Route. BETHUNE - FOUQUIERES - BRUAY - OURTON - LA COMTE - HOUVELIN.

   Destination. BAILLEUL AUX CORNAILLES.

   Time - 9-15 p.m. for Head of Column.

7. The remainder of the Battalion will be ready to proceed by Tactical Train at 6 hours notice at CHOCQUES.

8. From tomorrow until ordered to entrain, all Units will be supplied direct from the Supplyv Column.

Captain & Adjutant,
15th. (S) Bn. The Sherwood Foresters.

War Diary 1.

Operation Orders, No. 35.20
By Lieut-Col. R.N.S. Gordon,
Commdg. 15th. (S) Bn. Sherwood Foresters.

Map Ref. $\frac{1}{100,000}$ 2-7-16.

Sheet 5A. & 11.

1. <u>Movement.</u>   The Battalion will move by train 3-7-16.

2. <u>Starting</u>   "Z" Coy. H.Q.   -   4-20 a.m.
   <u>Point & Time.</u>

3. <u>Order of</u>   H.Q. Z, W, Y, X.
   <u>March,</u>

4. <u>Route.</u>   ROBECQ - BETHUNE ROAD - CHOCQUES.

5. <u>Transport.</u>   Transport   ) under command of Lieut. Moore parade outside
                           L.G. Section   ) Transport Lines ready to move at 6-15 a.m.
                                            to arrive at CHOCQUES by 8 a.m.

                           Lewis Gun Section will furnish brakesmen and loading party.

6. <u>Cookers.</u>   Cookers will be fetched from XXXXXXX Coys. by 3-30 a.m.

7. <u>Reports.</u>   Reports to head of Battalion.

8. <u>Band.</u>   Band will parade as such between W and Y Coys.

9. <u>Billets.</u>   Billets must be left in a thoroughly clean condition. O.C.
                           Coys. will furnish reports that this has been done.

Issued at 11 p.m.   Ivan Mellin Capt & adjt for   Lieut-Col.
                                     Commdg. 15th. (S) Bn. Sherwood Foresters.

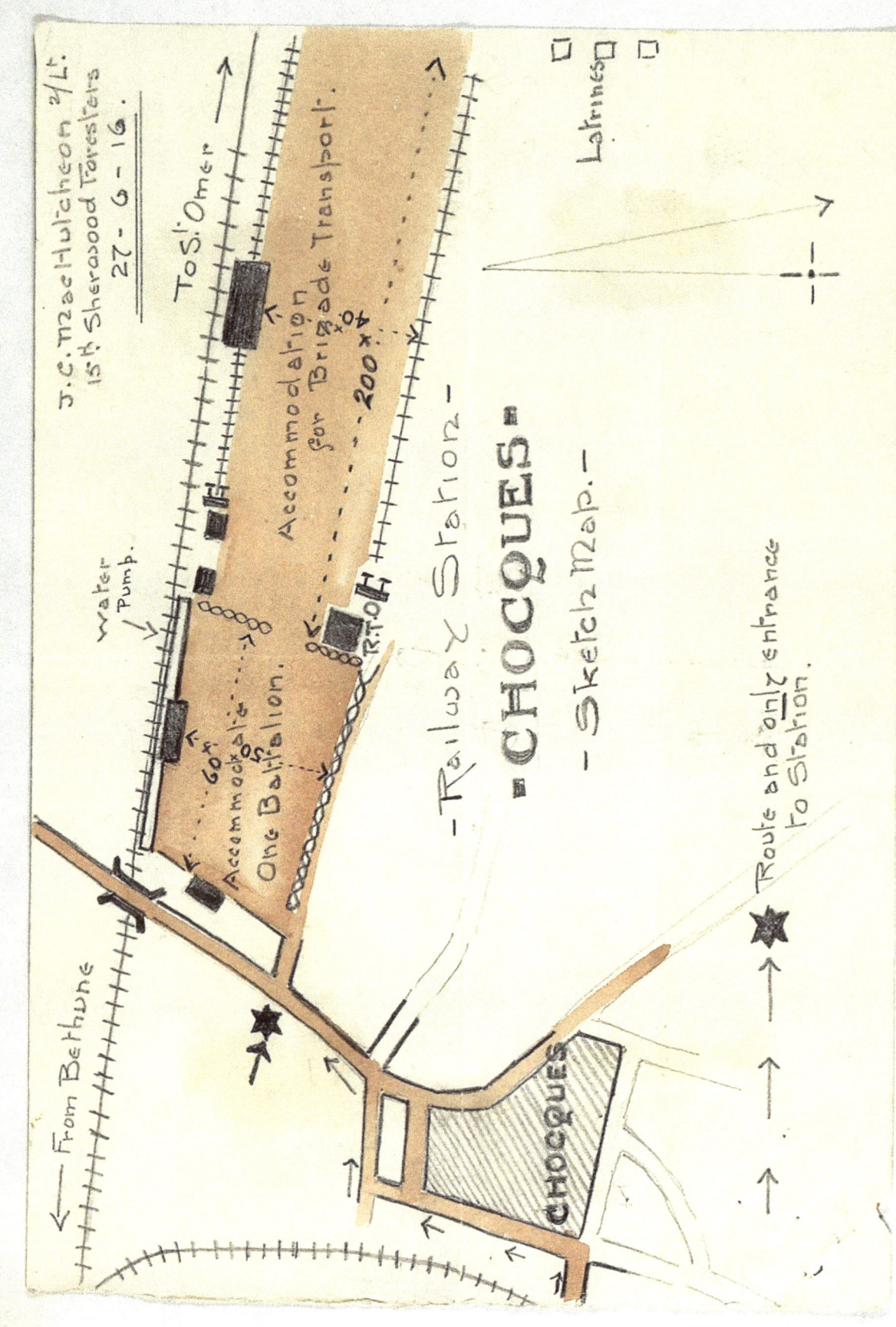

Operation Orders, No. 26.
By H.P.G. Cochran,
Commdg. 15th. (S) Bn. Sherwood Foresters.

Ref. Trench Map MONTAUBAN   28-7-16.
1/20,000

1. **Relief.**   The Battalion, less "W" Coy., will relieve the 16th. Cheshire
                    Regt. in DUBLIN TRENCH tonight.

2. **Order of**   Y, X. Z.   H.Q.
   March.

3. **Time.**   Leading Platoon "Y" Coy. to be clear of Battalion Area by
                    8-45 p.m. Five minutes interval between Companies, 100 yards
                    between Platoons.

4. **Transport.**   Two S.A.A. carts, two tool carts, one maltese cart, with
                    Battalion Bombers under R.S.M. will be parked on the same
                    ground as when we occupied SILESIA TRENCH.

5. **Officers'**   will be stacked by Transport park by 8 p.m.
   Baggage.

6. **Watercarts.** will be brought filled to Ammunition Dump.

7. **Disposition.** "Y" Coy. and "Z" Coy. will occupy "DUBLIN TRENCH on left
                    of BRIQUETARIE - MARINCOURT ROAD, "X" Coy. on right of road.

8. **Reports.**   Reports to Battalion H.Q. CASEMENT TRENCH as soon as Relief
                    is complete.

9. **Communication.** Communication by telephone to be established with
                    Advanced Brigade Headquarters.

10. **Trenches.**   All Trenches and Dug-outs at present occupied by the
                    Battalion to be left thoroughly clean.

Issued Verbally to
O.C. Coys. at 6 p.m.
                                                        Adjutant,
                                              15th. (S) Bn. Sherwood Foresters.

Copy No. 1. War Diary.
        2. File.
        3. H.Q.
        4. 105th. Brigade.

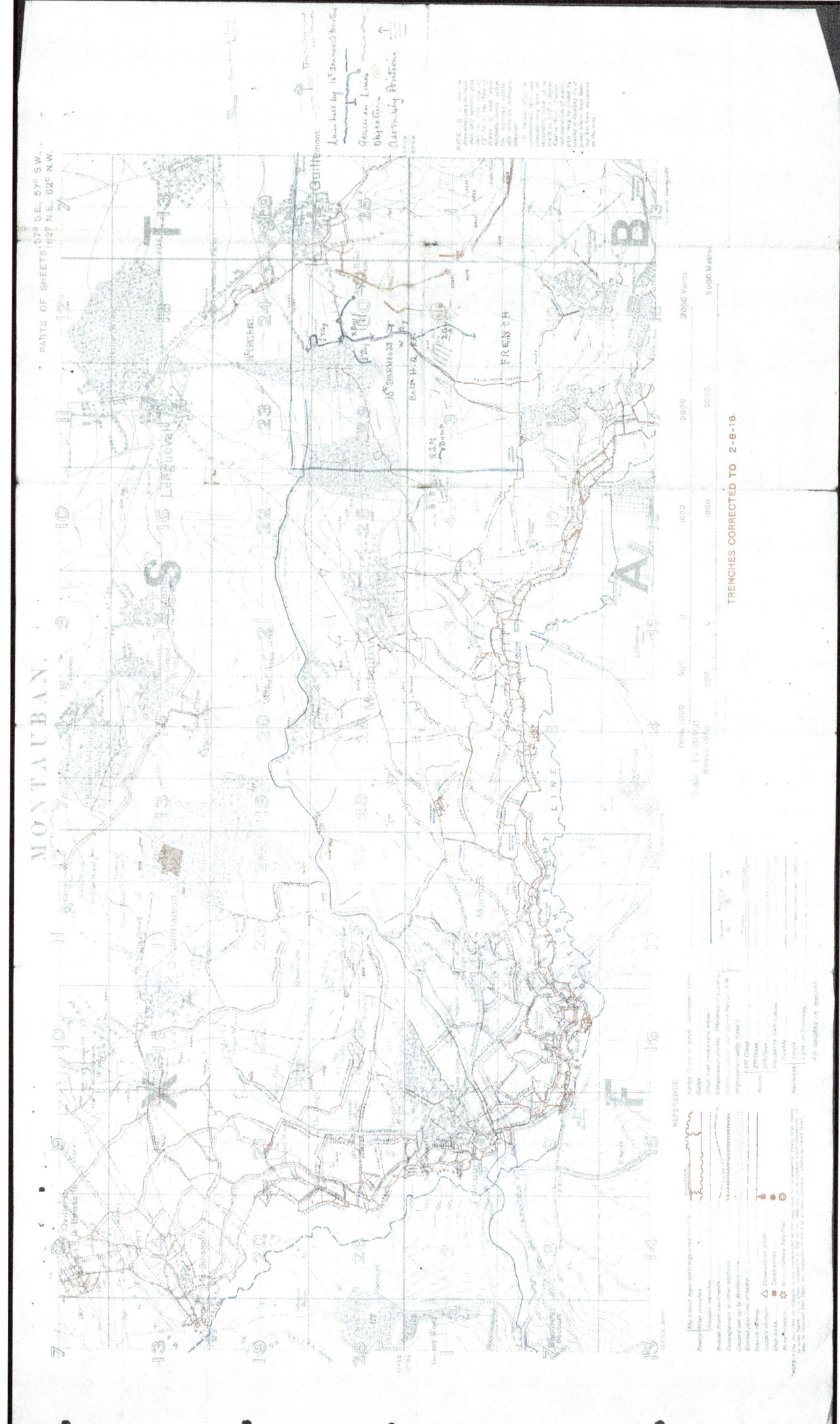

TRENCH MAP.

MONTAUBAN.

Scale 1:20,000.

7. **W.Coy** W.Coy will remain in its present position as GARRISON of BRIQUETERIE STRONG POINT until further orders.

8. **BDE.HQ:-** Will remain in its present position. An Advanced BDE.HQ. will be established at the BRIQUETERIE

9. **TRENCHES:-** The trenches at present occupied by the Battalion will be thoroughly cleaned up this morning, latrines properly filled in and all Rubbish and Refuse buried deep. O.C Coys will render to Bn HQ at 1.30 p.m a certificate to the effect that this has been done.

10. **SALVAGE:-** All ammunition, grenades, equipment etc, which do not belong to this battalion will be dumped at Bn HQ by 12 NOON

Issued at 8 AM

Copy No 1 — WAR DIARY
        2 — FILE
        3 — HQ
        4 — W. Coy
        5 — X Coy
        6 — Y Coy
        7 — Z Coy
        8 — TPT OFFICER
        9 — Quarter Master

WaW Crellin Capt
& Adjt
15 SHERWOOD FORESTERS

OPERATION ORDER No 25 Copy No
BY.
MAJOR. H. P. G. COCHRAN   **Z**   3
CMDG 15TH (S) BN THE SHERWOOD FORESTERS.
REF:- TRENCH MAP MONTAUBAN
    1/20000   26.7.16

1. RELIEF:- THE 15TH SHERWOOD FORESTERS, less
   "W" Company holding (BRIQETERIE STRONG POINT)
   will relieve the 23RD MANCHESTER REGT
   in TALUS BOISE
2. MOVE:- Companies will move in the
   following order, an interval of 100 yards
   being kept between platoons and 5
   minutes interval between Companies
   HQ., Z., X., Y,
3. TIME:- HQ. Coy will move off at 2.0 PM
4. DINNERS:- Cookers should be here with
   Dinners at 12.30 PM
5. TRANSPORT:- Transport will remain in its
   present position with the exception of
        2 G.S. limbers (SAA)
        2 Tool Carts,
        1 Maltese Cart
   which will follow the Battalion to TALUS BOISE
6. TOOLS:- Tools will be collected and handed over to
   the Regt Sgt Major who will see that they
   are loaded on to the Tool Limbers, by
        12 NOON.

SECRET.
                                                  Copy No. 8.

        105th. (Infantry) Brigade Order No. 38.
        Map GERMAN 2nd. Line from LONGUEVAL
Ref. to MAUREPAS 1/10.000.   19-7-16.

1. In conjunction with Operations which are being carried out by the French Army the 105th. Infantry Brigade has been ordered to attack and hold the German trench running from MALTZ HORN FARM (A.6.Central) to S.30.b.6.0.

2. This Trench from S.30.b.6.0. to S.30.d.3.0. will be shelled tonight & will be heavily bombarded from 4.25 a.m. to 5 a.m. at which hour the Artillery will lift and form a barrage from T.19.c.0.round the SOUTH WEST of the town of GUILLEMONT, and down the valley to ANGLE WOOD.

3. The attack will be carried out by the 15th. Sherwood Foresters.
One Coy. in four waves will attack from the South West of ARROW HEAD COPSE forming up at right angles to a Trench which is being dug from Strong Point B (S.30.a.9.5.) to ARROW COPSE.
One Coy. in four waves will attack from our new trench just South of MALTZ HORN FARM against the enemy trenches about A.3. Cent. each Coy. will have Bombing Squads ready on its inner Flank ready to Bomb inwards along the trench between the two points of attack. Care must be taken to bomb out the sap running out of the enemy's trench at S.30.d.1.2. These bombing squads will be accompanied by Rifle Grenadiers as laid down in Standing Orders for Attack. Each Coy. will be accompanied by its Lewis Guns.
The Pioneer Coy. will assist the left attack in consolidation, and the 204th. Field COY. R.E. will provide a section to assist the Right attack.

4. The O.C. 15th. Cheshire Regt. will send one Coy. to be in support to be at the BRIQUETARIE at 2 a.m. where a guide will meet it.
The Officer commandong the Coy. will report at H.Q. 15th. SHERWOOD FORESTERS, S.30.c.6.2. as soon as possible after receipt of this order.

5. One Coy. PIONEER BATTALION has been ordered to report to O.C. 15th. SHERWOOD FORESTERS at Strong Point A, S.30.a.5.4. at midnight. It should at once commence to dig a trench from Strong Point B to ARROW HEAD COPSE, which can be continued to the enemy's trench when captured. It will construct a Strong Point at the junction of this trench and the enemy's trench, and will otherwise help in consolidating the left of the line and wiring it. A R.E. Officer will point out the line, and will inform the O.C. COy. where stores can be obtained.

6. A section, R.E., and two Officers will report to O.C. 15th. SHERWOOD FORESTERS and will assist in consolidation on the right of the line.

7. <u>Communication.</u> The O.C. 15th. SHERWOOD FORESTERS will communicate by telephone direct to BDE. H.Q. as long as the wire stands. A Bde. Staff Officer and an Artillery Officer will be at the BRIQUETARIE in case the line brakes between BRIQUETARIE and BDE. H.Q. the O.C. 15th. SHERWOOD FORESTERS will telephone to the BRIQUETARIE and the information will be passed on by Visual or other means.
In case the line breaks between the Battalion and the BRIQUETARIE Communication must be made by runner, whence the message will be telephoned on.
Other Battalions will pass any information they may obtain.

8. <u>Machine Guns.</u> The O.C. Machine Gun Coy. will report to O.C. 15th. SHERWOOD FORESTERS and will assist in consolidating and repelling a counter-attack by Machine Gun fire.

Issued at 9-50 p.m.   (Sd.) G. de C. Glover, Captain,
                                                      Brigade Major.
                        105th. (Infantry) Brigade.

Attack Orders No. 1.
　By Lieut-Col. R.N.S. Gordon,
　　Commdg. 15th. (S) Bn. Sherwood Foresters,

Copy no. 1.

19-7-16.

Map References

$\frac{1}{20,000.}$
MONTAUBAN TRENCH MAP
$\frac{1}{10,000.}$
German 2nd. Line LONGUEVAL-MAUREPAS.

1. **Intention.** 15th. Sherwood Foresters will attack and occupy the enemy's Trenches from MALTZ HORN FARM (A.6.Central.) to ARROW HEAD COPSE (S.30.b.6.0.)
Two Coys. 23rd. Manchester Regt. will be in support on our Right and a Coy. of the 19th. Northumberland Fusiliers (Pioneers) will assist in consolidating the enemys trench when captured on our left. A section 204th. Field Coy. R.E. will assist in consolidating enemy's trench when captured on our right. The attack will be carried out by "W" and "Z" Coys.

2. **Information.** The enemy are known to be occupying a line of trenches running north and south from S.30.b.6.4. to A.6.d.3.7. with a sap running in a westerly direction at S.30.d.2.4. MALTZ HORN FARM is also supposed to be occupied as sniping has been observed from it. Indications of wire have been observed along the front of the enemy's line, but it is not considered strong.

3. **Objectives.** Right Attack "Z" Coy.
The enemy's trenches running from A.6.d.2.8. to A.6.b.2.4. This will be immediately converted into a stronghold after capture. Bombing squads will then proceed down enemy's trench in a Northernly direction and join up with the Left Attacking Party.
Left Attack "W" Coy.
The enemy's trenches from S.30.b.6.0. to S.30.d.4.7. and on capture will be immediately formed into a stronghold. Bombing Squads will then proceed in a Southernly direction along enemy's trench and join up with the Right Attacking Party.
Pioneer Coy.
One Coy. 19th. NORTHUMBERLAND FUSILIERS (Pioneers) will dig a Communication Trench during the night 19/20. July from STRONG POINT B S.30a.8.5. to ARROW HEAD COPSE and on capture of enemy's trenches will continue the Communication Trench to the captured position constructing a STRONG POINT at the junction of this and the enemy's trenches and otherwise help in consolidating the left of the line and wiring it.
Section 204th. Field Coy. R.E.
will follow up the Right Attack and on capture of enemy's trenches and convert the trench between Points A.6.d.2.8. and A.6.b.2.4. into a STRONG POINT, assist in consolidating the remainder of enemy's trenches and place MALTZ HORN FARM into a state of defence.

4. **Machine Guns.** The O.C. 105th. M.G. Coy. will detail two VICKERS GUNS to accompany the RIGHT ATTACKING PARTY and ONE VICKERS GUN to accompany the LEFT ATTACKING PARTY. On reaching enemy's trenches these guns will immediately take up positions from which they can cover the new front to afford protection to the parties consolidating the line. Every endeavour will be made to get the guns under cover and in protected positions.

5. **Lewis Guns.** LEWIS GUNS will be under the orders of the Coy. Commanders and will be utilised to the best advantage in giving covering for especially with a view to a counter-attack, particular

5. **Lewis Guns.** (Contd.)

attention being paid to the flanks.

6. **Supports.** Two Coys. of the 23rd. MANCHESTER REGT. will act as Supports and after the Attack has started occupy the trenches held by "W" and "Z" Coys. 15th. Sherwoods.   One Coy. from A.6.c.7.8. to A.6.a.4.9. with one platoon in reserve in old fire trench.   One Coy. from A.6.a.4.9. to S.30.c.5.7. "Y" and "X" Coys. SHERWOOD FORESTERS will occuoy their present positions and "Y" Coy. will guard the left flank of the attack with Lewis gun and Rifle fire.   "X" Coy. will furnish carrying parties for the Left Attack and the Right Coy. 23rd. MANCHESTER REGT. will furnish carrying parties for the RIGHT ATTACK.

7. **Method of Attack.** Each Coy. will attack in four waves at 50 yards interval between waves and two yards interval between men. Details of waves as laid down in BDE. & BATTN. STANDING ORDERS for an ATTACK.

8. **Assembly Points.** "Z" Coy. will assemble in Dead Ground behind our present Front Line Trenches in A.6.a.& c.
"W" Coy. will assemble in Dead Ground in S.30.a.& c.
Troops to be in position by 3-45 a.m. O.C. Coys. will report to Battn. H.Q. that this is done.

9. **Hour of Attack.** The Attack will commence at 5 a.m. All watches to be synchronized.

10. **Direction.** RIGHT ATTACK. with its left on MALTZ HORN FARM.
LEFT ATTACK with its left on a line passing through the Southern Edge of ARROW HEAD COPSE due East.

11. **Dumps.** AMMUNITION.
(1) STRONG POINT "A" S.30.a.5.4.
(2) NORTH END of HAIR.
PIN TRENCH   A.5.d.7.9.
(3) COMPANY DUMP   S.30.c.5.4.
(4)   "   "   A.6.a.2.7.

ENGINEER STORE DUMP.

(1)   A.5.d.7.9.
(2)   S.30.c.6.3.

RIFLE GRENADE & BOMB DUMPS.

(1)   S.30.a.5.4.
(2)   A.5.d.7.9.

12. **1st. AID POSTS.** will be located at :-

(1) STRONG POINT "A" S.30.a.5.4.
(2) HAIR PIN CORNER A.5.d.7.9.
to which all wounded men will be directed.

13. **Water.** Reserve WATER SUPPLY is stored at S.30.c.5.4.

14. **Prisoners.** Will be sent immediately to A.6.a.4.9.

15. **Communications.** Communications from Coys. to H.Q. will be by Runners and from there onwards by phone and visual.
Coys. on the flanks will see that touch is maintained with Units on their Flanks and if necessary will be prepared to send information to ADV. BDE. H.Q. (A.4.b.Central) direct if unable to do so through Battalion Hdqrs.

16. **Reports.** Will be furnished regularly to Battn. H.Q. A.6.a.4.9. stating progress.

17. **Artillery Barrage.** An intense bombardment of the enemy's trenches will be made from 4 a.m. - 5 a.m. at which hour the Artillery will lift and form a barrage round S.W. of GILLEMONT and down the Valley to ANGLE WOOD.

18. **DRESS.** Each man of the attacking Coys. will carry 3 sandbags and 100 rounds S.A.A. The equipment and organisation of Platoons will be as laid down in BDE. & BATTN. STANDING ORDERS.

Issued at 12 M.N. verbally & dictated to all concerned.

Cavallin.
Captain,
Adjutant,
15th. (S) Bn. Sherwood Foresters.

Copy No. 1. War Diary.
2. " "
3. File.
4. 105th. Bde.

To O.C. Coys. & Units.

War Diary.

In continuation of instructions already circulated with reference to moves, the following instructions will be noted and attached

Moves will come under two headings :-
1. By road entirely, in which case orders already issued will hold good the Division being prepared to march within 9 hours

2. If required to move parially or wholly by rail, the move may come under either of the following headings :-
    (a) Tactical Move.
    (b) Modified strategical move.
    (c) Complete " "

In case (a) an Infantry Bde. with a proportion of its Transport can move by each set of 3 tactical Trains. The first two trains taking the personnel of two Battalions each. The 3rd. Train takes the Transport detailed in Table B (attached) The remaining Transport will follow either by road or rail as may be detailed in subsequent orders.

In case (b) Infantry Bdes. and certain Divl. Troops in 1st. 19 Trains in Table A (attached) move by rail. Remainder of Div. by road.
All Units who entrain take with them their complete Transport.

In case (c) The whole Division moves by rail according to Table A.

As soon as the hour of zero is announced by G.H.Q. all units are then able to ascertain from Table A, the hour of departure of their train, by adding the number of hours of their Train departure to the zero hour as announced by G.H.Q.   e.g. The Battalion's train time is 13 hrs. D.H.Q. zero hour is announced at 8 p.m. consequently time of departure of Battn's train would be 9 a.m. the following morning.
Infantry will send Transport and a strong loading party to report to R.T.O. at their entraining station 3 hours before time of departure. Remainder to arrive at Station 1½ hrs. before time of departure.
The Battalion entraining Station will be "CHOCQUES".

SUPPLY ARRANGEMENTS.   Troops will in all cases move with one day's iron rations on the man, and the unexpended portion of the current day's rations on the man or in the 1st. Line Transport.   Troops in training in afternoon should have the following rations in addition to the day's rations in the supply Vehicles with the Train.
Supply Vehicles with the Train will move full and entrain with its Unit. Baggage section will also entrain with Units.

25-6-16.
                Lieut-Col.
          Commdg. 15th. (S) Bn. Sherwood Foresters.

PROGRAMME OF ENTRAINMENT.   TABLE A"

Train No. & Hour of Departure.	Serial No.	Station "B" CHOCQUES.
14 13.00	24. 26.D. Section 104. M.G. Coy.	15th. Sherwoods.

NOTES :- ALL TRAINS TYPE COMBATTANT, unless PARC is shown after the Train No.

TABLE "B".

Table showing Troops to travel by Third Tactical Train.

UNIT.	Officers.	O.R.	Horses.	G.S. Limbd. Wagons.	2 Wheeled Carts.	Notes for Battalion use.
Lewis Guns, 4 Battalions, MG.Sections Complete.	4	120	16	8	-	1 Officer, 30 men 4 Mules. 2 L.G. Limbers.
S.A.A. (1 Limbered Wagon per Battn.	-	4	8	4	-	1 Driver, 2 Mules, 1 Limber.
Tools (1 Limbered Wagon per Battn.)	-	4	8	4	-	1 Driver, 2 Mules, 1 Limber.
Chargers. (3 per Battn.)	-	12	12	-	-	3 Grooms, 3 Horses.(C.O. 2nd. in C. & Adjt.)
Cookers & Mess Carts. 4 Ens.(4 Cookers & 1 mess Cart per Bn.	-	20	36	-	16	5 Drivers, 8 H.D's. 1 Mule. 4 Cookers, 1 Mess Cart.
Medical Personnel (Part Personnel & 1 Maltese Cart per Bn.)	4	8	4	-	4	1 M.O. 1 Orderly, 1 Driver, 1 Mule 1 Maltese Cart.

Personnel. i.e. Cooks, Brakesmen etc. belonging to above detailed Transport will accompany the Battalion in the preceding Train. Remainder of Transport (both personnel and animals) not above detailed will proceed to destination by road or by a later train as may be ordered.

To O.C. Coys. & Units.

The following additions are made to Move Orders :-

As it is not yet known what intervals between Tactical Train will be kept it is imperative that Unit Commanders should be prepared.

Transport must arrive at Station 3 hours before departure of its Train. Billeting Party will arrive at Station in order to catch the first train. This Battalion, which is under orders for second train will arrive 1½ hours previous to departure.

The Station may either be CHOCQUES or FOUQUEREUIL. In the event of the latter the roads will be (Sheet 5a.) ROBECQ -BETHUNE ROAD - CHURCH 300 yards W. of L in VENDIN-LES-BETHUNE - ANNEZIN - STATION (1 Mile N.E. of FOUQUEREUIL.

In order to give time to Transport to reach their destination Cookers must be in a constant state of preparedness, and the rations handy to place immediately on the Cookers.

Officers Mess Kit must be such that it may be loaded without the least delay.

The Mess and Maltese Cart when not in actual use will be kept alongside the H.Q. Mess and the Battalion Aid Post, so that the loading of them may proceed forthwith in the event of an alarm.

"Z" Coy. will detail one Officer and 20 men to go with Transport & L. Gun Section as loading party.

2-7-16.   Captain & Adjt.
                                    15th. (S) Bn. The Sherwood Foresters.

To O.C. Coys. & Units.

Companies and Units will be prepared to move very early tomorrow morning.

All grocery rations will be distributed and cookers loaded with meat rations for tomorrow.

Fires will be laid ready to light when orders given.

Officers Mess Kit will be packed tonight and loaded on to Cookers.

As far as is known first train will start 5-30 a.m. 3rd. July.

Detailed orders will follow.

2-7-16.

Captain,
Adjutant,
15th. (S) Bn. Sherwood Foresters

105th Brigade.
35th Division.

1/15th BATTALION

NOTTS & DERBY REGIMENT

AUGUST 1916

Army Form C. 2118

WAR DIARY
or
INTELLIGENCE SUMMARY
(Erase heading not required.)

Instructions regarding War Diaries and Intelligence Summaries are contained in F. S. Regs., Part II. and the Staff Manual respectively. Title Pages will be prepared in manuscript.

VOL 7

15th SHERWOOD FORESTERS

AUGUST 1916.

I

7.4
J.D.

Place	Date	Hour	Summary of Events and Information	Remarks and references to Appendices
BOIS de TAILLES	1st		Move to Camping ground at BOIS de TAILLES	1. ORDER No. 27
	2nd		Camp	
	3rd		Camp	
do	4th		Camp. All transport moved to MOLLIENS VIDAME	2. ORDER No. 28
	5th		Battn. entrained at MERICOURT; detrained SALEUX	3. ORDER No. 29
	6th		Arrived at MOLLIENS VIDAME	
MOLLIENS VIDAME	7th		Billets	
	8th		Billets	
	9th		Billets. All transport moved to THE CITADEL	4. ORDER No. 30
	10th		Battn. moved with 13th Corps Reserve. Entrained HANGEST-S-SOMME; detrained at MERICOURT and moved to bivouac ground at THE CITADEL.	5. ORDER No. 31
	11th			
	12th			
	13th			
THE CITADEL	14th		Camp. Supply working parties for R.E.	
	15th			
	16th			
	17th			
	18th			
	19th			

Army Form. C. 2118

WAR DIARY
or
INTELLIGENCE SUMMARY

(Erase heading not required.)

15th SHERWOOD FORESTERS

AUGUST 1916

Place	Date	Hour	Summary of Events and Information	Remarks and references to Appendices
TALUS BOISE	20th	—	Battalion moves to OLD BRITISH LINE near TALUS BOISE. "W" Coy. moves up to trenches by BDE H.Q. in CHIMPANZEE TRENCH.	OP. ORDER No. 32
	21st	—	In O.B.L. Furnish working parties for other Battns. of the BDE.	
	22nd	8 p.m.	Relieve 18th LANCS. FUSILIERS in MALTZ HORN TRENCHES.	ATTACK ORDER No. 2.
TRENCHES	23rd		In occupation of MALTZ HORN TRENCHES. Heavily shelled during day. Raid newly taken place on enemy position at 5 p.m. Report of Operations & preparation. Objct but cancelled owing to inferior Artillery preparation. Objct of discovering enemy's strength however ascertained.	7 Addenda
	24th	10.30 p.m.	Battalion relieved by 2nd LEINSTER REGT. Very heavy shelling during relief. Move to bivouacs near BILLONWOOD.	OP. ORDER No. 33
BIVOUACS	25th		In bivouacs. Resting.	
BIVOUACS	26th		Relieved by 1st NORFOLKS, 15th BDE. and move to reserve area in SANDPIT VALLEY.	OP. ORDER No. 34
SANDPIT VALLEY	27th		Camp.	
BOIS de TAILLES	28th		Move to BOIS de TAILLES	OP. ORDER No. 35
	29th	—	Camp. All transport moves by road to PROUVILLE.	OP. ORDER No. 36

Army Form C. 2118

WAR DIARY
or
INTELLIGENCE SUMMARY

(Erase heading not required.)

13th SHERWOOD FORESTERS.

AUGUST 1916

Place	Date	Hour	Summary of Events and Information	Remarks and references to Appendices
	30th		Battn. less transport, entrains at HEILLY to move into 3rd Army Area	12 Op. Order No 37
	31st		Return in CANDAS; march to PROUVILLE. Battn. marches, with transport, to M billets in GROUCHES.	13 Battn. Orders 30/8/16

Rudge Lieut Col

Comdg. 13TH (SERVICE) BATT. SHERWOOD FORESTERS

Copy No. 1

Operation Orders, No. 21
By Lt.-Col. R.M.S. Gordon,
Commdg. 15th. (S) Bn. Sherwood Foresters.

Ref. Sheet 62D. N.E. 1/20,000.   1-8-16.

1. **Move.** The Battalion will move to BOIS DES TAILLES NORTH (K.12.a. and c) tonight.

2. **Route.** SAND PIT - TRACK SOUTH of MEAULTE running through E.18.c.; E.17.d.; and E.23.b.; (not marked on the Map) -Point about E.23.a.8.8. - thence along main Double Telegraph Post Road to Cross Roads K.6.d.8.8. - thence by track SOUTH WEST to BIVOUAC GROUND.

3. **Order of March.** H.Q. Z. X. Y. W. 1st. Line Transport, & Baggage Wagons.

4. **Time.** 6-45 p.m.

5. **L. Guns.** Proceed with Coys.

6. **Officers Kit.** to be stacked at Q.M. Stores by 5-30 p.m.

7. **Cleanliness.** The Bivouac Ground now occupied by the Bn. is to be left thoroughly clean. O.C. "Z" Coy. will detail one N.C.O. and 20 men to remain behind after the Battalion has moved off to clean up any rubbish which may have been overlooked by the Bn. 2nd. Lt. B. Snape will be in charge of this party which will not leave the Camp until it has been passed clean by an Officer of the Bde. Staff.

8. **Reports.** Reports while on the move to head of Battn.

Issued at 4-30 p.m.

Copies to   No. 1 War Diary.
            2   "   "
            3 File.
            4 "W" Coy.   W.A.W. Crellin, Capt. & Adjt.
            5 "X" "   15th. (S) Bn. Sherwood Foresters.
            6 "Y" "
            7 "Z" "
            8 T.O.

Operation Order No. 8   Copy No. 8
By Lieut-Col. R.N.S. Gordon,
    Commdg. 15th. (S) Bn. Sherwood Foresters.
                                                4-8-16.

Ref. Map 62.D. N.E. 1/20,000.
    Sh. AMIENS 1/100000.

1. **Move.** The Battalion will move to new Billeting Area on 4th. and 5th.inst.

2. **Transport.** All Transport, including Cookers, Watercarts, and Officers' Chargers, will concentrate at SOUTH END of DAOURS on evening of the 4th. The Head of Brigade Transport Column to pass starting Point (K.11.d.7.5.) at 2 p.m.

3. **Dinners.** All Dinners are to be served and Cookers ready to move by 1-30 p.m.

4. **Water.** All Waterbottles will be filled by 12 noon. Men must be warned to conserve their water, as no further opportunities for filling waterbottles may occur for several days. After all Waterbottles have been filled the watercarts will refil.

5. **Tools.** All Tools to be returned to the Limbers at once.

6. **Officers Kits.** All Officers Kits will be dumped by the Baggage Wagons ready for loading by 12-30 p.m. Officers Mess Kits will be loaded in Cookers by 1-30 p.m.

7. **Lewis Gun Carts.** Lewis Gun Carts will accompany T.M. Battery and march with them. The full eight teams will accompany carts.

8. **Pioneers Tools.** The Pioneers will retain 6 shovels and 3 picks to fill in, and will carry these tools with them.

9. **Battalion.** The remainder of the Battalion will move by train on the 5th. inst. Detail orders will be issued later.

Issued at 9 a.m.

Copies to "W" Coy. No. 1.
           "X"   2.
           "Y"   3.
           "Z"   4.
           H.Q.   5.
           L.G.   6.
           T.O.   7.
           War Diary. 8.
           File.   9.

                                        2nd. Lieut.
                                        A/Adjutant,
                                        15th. (S) Bn. Sherwood Foresters.

Operation Orders No. 29. Copy No. 6
By Lieut-Col. R.N.S.Gordon,
    Commdg. 15th. (S) Bn. Sherwood Foresters
                                                            5-8-16.

Ref. Map. AMIENS. 1/100,000.

1. <u>Move.</u>   The Battalion less the Advanced Party, will proceed by train to new Billeting Area at MOLLIENS VIDAME today.

2. <u>Starting Point & Time.</u> The Battn. will form up in Mass on the Parade Ground ready to march off at 2-45 p.m. and will proceed to entraining station at MERICOURT.

3. <u>Order of March.</u>   H.Q., W., X., Y., Z..

4. <u>Band.</u>   Band will parade as such at the head of the Column.

5. <u>Stretchers</u> Stretchers to be carried by Coys.

6. <u>Water Cart.</u> All Waterbottles will be filled before 2-30 p.m. and the Water Cart will then proceed to the Lines of the 14th. Glosters and report to the Officer of the 14th. Glosters under whose charge it will remain.

7. <u>Detraining Station.</u> The Battalion will detrain at SALEUX, and march to the Billets via CLAIRY - PISSY - SEUX - BRIQUEMESNIL.

8. <u>Camp.</u>   The Camp will be left in a thoroughly clean condition. All tent ropes will be slackened and curtains rolled up. All refuse will be burned in the Incinerators outside the wood.

9. <u>Reports.</u> Reports to the head of the Column whilst on the march, and to Battalion H.Q. at MOLLIENS VIDAME on arrival at destination.

Issued at 10 a.m.

Copies to :-

    "W" Coy. No. 1.
    "X"   2.
    "Y"   3.
    "Z"   4.
    H.Q.   5.   2nd. Lieut.
    War Diary. 6.   A Adjutant,
    File.   7.   15th. (S) Bn. The Sherwood Foresters.

Operation Orders No. 30.
By Lieut-Col. R. N. S. Gordon,
Commdg. 15th. (S) Bn. Sherwood Foresters

Copy No. 6

8-8-16.

1/100,000.   AMIENS Sheet.

1. **Move.**   Battalion will move to the 13th. Corps Area on Aug. 9th. & 10th.

2. **Transport.**   On Aug. 9th. all Transport including Cookers, Watercarts, all whelled vehicles & horses will move by road via BRIQUEMESNIL -FERRIERES - SAVEUSE to VECQUEMONT and DAOURS.

3. **Starting Point.**   1¼ miles EAST of BRIQUEMESNIL.

4. **Time.**   8-5 a.m.

5. **Breakfasts.**   All Breakfasts must be served and Cookers ready to move by 6 a.m.   A Lorry will be provided to carry Officers Mess Kit and four dixies per Coy.

6. **Officers Kits.**   Officers Kits will be dumped by the Baggage wagon ready for loading by 5-30 a.m.

7. **Lewis Guns.**   Lewis Gun Carts of the Battn. drawn by the L.G. Teams will accompany the T. M. Battery and march with them.

8. **Petrol Tins.**   All Petrol Tins will be collected and stacked on the Water Carts at once.

9. **Q.M's. Personnel.**   The whole of the Q.M's. personnel (less R.Q.M.S. & Pioneers) will accompany the Transport tomorrow.

10. **Battalion.**   Entraining Orders for the remainder of the Battalion will move on the 10th. and will be issued later.

Issued at 7-45 p.m.

Copies to:-
W Coy   No. 1.
X "   " 2.
Y "   " 3.
Z "   " 4.
H.Q.   5.
War Diary   6.
File   7.

2nd. Lieut.
A/Adjutant,
15th. (S) Bn. The Sherwood Foresters.

Operation Order No. 31.   Copy No. 6
        By Lieut-Col. R.N.S. Gordon,
           Commdg. 15th. (S) Bn. Sherwood Foresters.
                                                      10-9-16.

Ref. 1/100,000. AMIENS.   Sheet 62D. 1/20,000.

1. <u>Move.</u>   The Battalion will move today to bivouacing ground near the CITADEL at F.21.b.5.4. by road and train.

2. <u>Entraining Station.</u>   HANGEST.

3. <u>Detraining Station.</u>   MERICOURT.

4. <u>Route to Entraining Station.</u>   Main Road via RIENCOURT - SOUCES.

5. <u>Route to Bivouacs.</u> Tracks passing through D.6.c.4.5., K.2.d.5.0. K.10.a. K.6.c.

6. <u>Starting Point & Time.</u> South end of MOLLIENS VIDAME at 12-30 p.m.

7. <u>Order of March.</u> H.Q. W., X., Y., Z..

8. <u>Band.</u>   Band will parade as such.

9. <u>Lewis Gun Boxes.</u>   L.G. Boxes and Dixies will be collected at Battalion H.Q. ready to load on Lorries at 9-30 a.m. Two men will be detailed to accompany lorries.

10. <u>Reports.</u>   Reports to head of Column.

11. <u>Billets.</u>   O.C. Coys. are responsible that the CITADEL and grounds are left perfectly clean.

Issued at 8-45 a.m.

Copies to :-

    O.C. "W" Coy. No. 1.
         "X"   2.   2nd. Lieut.
         "Y"   3.   A/Adjutant,
         "Z"   4.
         H.Q.   5.   15th. (S) Bn. Sherwood Foresters.
    War Diary.   6.
    Files   7.

Operation Order No. 32.
By Lieut-Col. R.N.S. Gordon,
Commdg. 15th. (S) Bn. Sherwood Foresters.

Copy No. 8

19-3-16.

1. **Move.** The Battalion will move tomorrow to O.B.L. at A.9.d.

2. **Starting Point & Time.** Citadel- 7 a.m.

3. **Route.** MINDEN POST - SOUTH END OF TALUS BOIS - O.B.L.

4. **Order of March.** X.Y.W.Z. H.Q.

5. **Formation.** Coys. will move by Platoons at 100 yards interval, 10 minutes interval between Coys. and Units.

6. **L.G. Carts.** L.G. Carts will accompany Coys. and will be drawn by their respective Coy. teams.

7. **Transport.** Cookers, Tool Carts, & Mess Cart will proceed to a point to be selected behind the lines. Horses and personnel to return to the Transport Lines.

8. **Water.** The Transport Officer will arrange for constant supplies of Water to be brought to the Trenches.

9. **Breakfasts.** Breakfasts tomorrow will be at 5-30 a.m.

10. **Cleanliness.** O.C. Coys. and Units will see that the Camp is left spotlessly clean.

11. **Sick.** Men certified Sick by the M.O. and details will return to the Transport Lines.

12. **Reconnaissance.** O.C. Coys. will detail an Officer to report to Capt. Urellin at 6 a.m. to allot areas for Coys.

13. **Officers Kit.** All Officers Kits & Coy. surplus Kit will be collected in front of H.Q. Mess by 7 a.m. The T.O. will arrange to remove these to the Transport Lines.

14. **Dress.** Field Service Marching Order. 3 sandbags per man to be carried. Waterbottles to be carried full.

15. **Battalion Headquarters.** Battalion Headquarters will close at the CITADEL at 8 a.m. and will open at the O.B.L. at 9 a.m.

Issued at 9 p.m.

Copies to :-

Copy No. 1. H.Q.
2. "W" Coy.
3. "X" "
4. "Y" "
5. "Z" "
6. T.O.
7. L.G.O.
8. War Diary.
9. File.

2nd. Lieut. A/Adjt.
15th. (S) Bn. Sherwood Foresters.

Papers in connection with

Operations on MALTZ HORN TRENCHES

August 23rd. 1916.

Copy of 105th. Brigade Orders No. 48, d/- 23-8-16.

Report of Operations. 23-8-16.

Register of Messages.

Attack Order No. 2.

SECRET-

105th.(INF.) BRIGADE ORDER NO.48.

COPY NO 8.

Ref. Map Sh. GUILLEMONT 1/20000.   20-8-1916.

1. The Brigade has been ordered to secure the strong point about S30.b.7.2.tonight.
   If opportunity occurs it will secure as much of the Trenches running from that point to the ORCHARD(T.25.c.½.8.)as possible. Otherwise, these Trenches will be attacked tomorrow in a combined operation.

2. The Heavy Artillery is bombarding the strong point and these Trenches and also the Trench running from the strong point to T.25.c.4.9. from 12 noon to 6p.m, and with greater intensity from 6p.m.to 7p.m.

3. During this period front line Trenches will be cleared to a distance of 250 yds. ARROW HEAD COPSE need not be cleared.

4. At 7p.m. the Divisional Artillery will form a Box Barrage from S.30.b.8.7. to road junction at T.25.a.8.8., thence along road to T.25.c.4.9.,and thence along Trench to strong point at S.30.b.7.2.
   It will also shell at intervals the line of the two trenches from the strong point to the ORCHARD, ceasing to do this at zero minus 5. At this hour the barrage on the trench from T.25.c.6.9. to strong point will not come furthur West than S.30.d.9½.9½. The remainder of the barrage will continue.

5. At zero, two Stokes Mortars at the second Barrier S.30.d.4.0.,will fire for three minutes rapid at the strong point and Trenches West and East of road about S.30.b.7.8. and at zero plus three, the Raiding Party detailed by O.C. 16th.CHESHIRES will leave the first Barrier and rush the strong point. This party will have a large proportion of Bombers and Carriers as well as Bayonet men, and will, after securing the strong point, bomb its way up the trenches on both sides of the Road towards the ORCHARD, being careful to clear all dug-outs.
   It will be followed by a consolidating party assisted by R.E., who will at once make good the strong point, and then consolidate the rest of the trenches after.
   A Party of bombers and supports will be detailed to bomb along the trench towards T.25.c.4.9.
   If it reports no opposition the Artillery will be requested to cease its barrage on this trench, and the party will push on and establish strong points at S.30.d.9½.9½. and at T.25.c.4.9.

6. **TRENCH MORTARS.**
   In addition to the two Trench Mortars at the second barrier two trench mortars will fire from a position about S.30.b.5.4. and form a barrage across the two trenches alongside the road and along the communication trench about S.30.b.7.8. These T.Ms. will cease fire on a signal to be arranged between O.C. 16th. Cheshire Regt. and the O.C. T.M. Battery. In addition, 4 Stokes T.Ms. will fire from a point near the TRONES WOOD - GUILLEMONT and form a barrage across the trenches at their junction with the road, (S.30.b.9.7½.). These will commence fire at zero plus three, and continue in sharp bursts with slow fire between until ordered to stop by O.C. 16th. CHESHIRE REGIMENT.

7. **M.G. COY.**
   The O.C. 105th. M.G. Coy. will detail two guns to fire from a position near the first barrier to sweep the ground east of the trenches to be attacked, and particularly to deal with the corner of trenches about T.25.a.8.4.

(2)

He will also detail two guns to fire along the TRONES WOOD - GUILLEMONT ROAD and form a barrage about S.30.b.9.7½. These guns will be prepared to move up to this point if the whole length of the two trenches is captured, and will cross fire with the guns at the First Barrier to prevent counter-attack.
The guns are under the command of the O.C. 16th. Cheshire Regt.

8. **CONSOLIDATION.**
In addition to consolidating the Strong points mentioned in para 5 the O.C. 16th. CHESHIRE REGT. will make arrangements to dig a communication trench along the TRONES WOOD - GUILLEMONT ROAD and join it to the furthest point North reached in the trenches attacked.
He will also arrange to join up the strong point at S.30.b.7.2. with the First Barrier, and if points S.30.d.9½.9½. and T.25.c.4.9 are reached will endeavour to join hands with the 104th. (INF.) BDE.

9. **R.E.**
The O.C. 204th. Field Coy. R.E. will detail a party to assist in the consolidation.

10. **Medical Arrangements.**
Medical Arrangements are as follows :-
  1. Collecting Post at junction of CASEMENT TRENCH and BRICQUETERIE ROAD.
  2. Main Dressing Station just South of Main PERONNE Road in A.21.a.
  3. Walking Wounded to BROMFAY FARM.

11. The hour of Zero will be notified separately.

12. All watches will be synchronized at BDE. H.Q. at 6 p.m.

13. **RELIEF.**
The O.C. 14th. Gloster Regt. will be ready to carry out the Relief of the 16th. CHESHIRE REGT. if circumstances permit.

14. **CARRYING PARTIES.**
The O.C. 15th. CHESHIRE REGT. will provide such carrying parties as are detailed from Brigade H.Q.

15. **REPORTS.**
O.C. 16th. CHESHIRE REGT. will report the situation at frequent intervals to ADV. BDE. H.Q. in CHIMPANZEE TRENCH, using runners if the telephone breaks down. Visual signalling will be established for use in emergency.

(Sd.) G. de C. Glover, Capt.
Brigade Major.
105th. (Infantry) Brigade.

Issued at 2-15 p.m.

Copies to :- No. 1 G.O.C.
2 B.M.
3 S.C.
4 35th. Div.
5 16th. Chesh.
6 14th. Glos.
7 15th. Chesh.
8 15th. Sher.
9 105th. M.G. Coy.
10 105th. T.M. Battery.
11 204th. Field Coy. R.E.
12 Diary.
13 104th. (Inf.) Bde.
14 72nd. " "
v15 R.F.A.
16 -do-

REPORT OF OPERATIONS AUGUST 23rd. 1916.

Disposition of Regiment. 15th. Sherwood Foresters were occupying the trenches East of ARROW HEAD COPSE. Two Companies in the Front Line, one in Support and one in Reserve.

Narrative. In accordance with 105th. Brigade Order No. 48 dated 23-8-16 a raiding party as detailed in Battalion Attack Orders No. 2 dated 23-8-16 was detailed under command of Lieut.Hodgkinson. Zero hour was fixed at 5-30 p.m. and all arrangements were perfected and the men for the assaulting parties were in their places ready for the signal.
At 5-27 p.m. a telephonic message was received at Battalion H.Q. from Brigade H.Q. postponing Zero hour quarter of an hour. As this was impossible Brigade H.Q. was notified and attempts were made to stop assault. The men however, had already moved into their jumping off positions prior to the arrival of the notice of postponement and were met with Machine & Rifle fire at the same time the enemy threw bombs into our trenches causing several casualties.
Owing to the contradictory orders and the knowledge that the enemy was prepared to receive an attack the raiding party was ordered to stand fast, and at 6 p.m. the operations were cancelled.

Lieut-Colonel,
Commdg. 15th. (S) Bn. The Sherwood Foresters.

RECEIPT.

No.	Time.	Purport.	From Whom.	Remarks.
1 O.P.	5-55 p.m.	Report from Lt. Hodgkinson.	Lt. Hodgkinson.	Runner.
11 O.P.	6-15 p.m.	Lt. Hodgkinson asks for more Bombers.	Capt. Crellin.	Runner.

DESPATCH.

No.	Time.	Purport.	To Whom.	Remarks.
1.	5-56 p.m.	Postpone Operations.	Capt. Crellin.	Runner.
11.	6 p.m.	Cancel Operations.	Capt. Crellin.	Runner.
111.	6-15 p.m.	No further attempts to be made.	Capt. Crellin.	Runner.

Telephone

RECEIPT.

No.	Time.	Purport.	From Whom.	Remarks.
1T	5-27 p.m.	B.M. phones postpone zero by ¼ hour.	B.M.	phone.
2T	5-33 p.m.	B.M. reports too late to stop Operations mentioned in 1T.		
3T	5-54 p.m.	G.O.C. ask information.		
4T	6 p.m.	B.M. orders operations to be cancelled.		

Telephone

DESPATCH.

No.	Time.	Purport.	To Whom.	Remarks.
1 T	5-27 p.m.	Reported impossible but would do my best and send round immediately 2 watches compared and found correct at 5-32 p.m.		
2 T.	5-54 p.m.	Reports information as received in 1 T. and 2 T Receipt and 1 T Despatch.		
3 T.	6 p.m.	Reports Lieut. Hodgkinson message to Bde.		

Attack Orders No. 2.
By Lieut- Col. R.N.S. Gordon,
Commdg. 15th. (S) Bn. Sherwood Foresters.   Copy No. 7.

Ref. Trench Map 1/10,000. 35th. Div.   23-8-16.

1. **Intention.** An attempt will be made in conjunction with the 14th. Glosters to seize enemy's STRONG POINT at S.30.b.7.2. and the enemy's trench running from that point as far as S.30.b.9.1.

2. **Preparation.** A Howitzer battery is bombarding this part of enemy's line from 11 a.m. and will cease fire at zero hour. At zero hour Stokes Mortar Battery will fire on the trenches running N. from the enemy's STRONG POINT and 100 yards North of it. Machine guns will open indirect fire during the bombardment, on the South side of GUILLEMONT. Ten minutes after zero Field Batteries will place a barrage from S.30.b.9.7. to T.25.a.2.7. to T.25.a.4.1.

3. **Assault.** The assault will be carried out as under :- 2 bombing squads of "Z" Coy. will advance from points S.30.d.8.9. and S.30.d.7.8. and will rush the enemy's trenches immediately in front of them.
The Right Bombing Party will seize a point in enemy's trenches at S.30.b.9.1. and form a block.
The Left Bombing Party will bomb down XXX towards the enemy's strong point until they meet the bombing party of the GLOSTERS. These bombing parties will be provided with flags and will indicate their positions by waving their flags.
A consolidating party consisting of 2 Lewis Gun Sections of "Z" Coy. and 20 men of "Z" Coy. and 20 men of "W" Coy. will immediately follow over and consolidate the line gained, particular attention being paid to turn the point S.30.b.9.1. into a Strong Point. This Consolidating Party will not advance until it appears that the bombing party has entered the enemy's trenches. The Right Bombing Squad will be supplied with a tape which it will unroll behind it so as to act as a guide to the Consolidating Party. A Communication Trench will be immediately commenced from both ends of the tape to join up with our present front line, following the line of tape laid down by Bombers.
If the assault is successful the positions gained must be held at all costs.

4. **Dress & Equipment** Parties will proceed over equipped as laid down in Battn. Standing Orders. The Consolidating Parties will carry Tools, Food and Water. Each Man will carry in addition 2 bandoliers S.A.A. and Spare bombs.

5. **Assembly Positions.** O.C.Z & W Coys. will see that a short time before zero they push their men as near to the jumping off places as possible.

6. **Front Line.** As soon as the Assaulting Parties have commenced to move Y & X Coys. will resume their former positions in the front line to give assistance in case the assaulting party is driven back, or in view of an enemy counter attack.

7. **Reinforcement.** O.C. "Z" Coy. will have the remainder of his Coy. in readiness to move forward if required. O.C. "W" COY. will have the remainder of his Coy. in readiness also.
All Coys. will stand to, fully equipped.

8. **Advanced Headquarters** Advanced Headquarters will be situated at the junction of JACKSON TRENCH and GUILLEMONT - MALTZ HORN ROAD (at Point S.30.d.4.5.) All reports will be sent there.

9. **Time.** Zero hour will be notified later (about 4-30 p.m.) All watches will be synchronized.

10. <u>Tools etc</u>.   O.C. Coys. will see that their men are equipped with Tools, Ammunition etc.

11. <u>Digging Party</u>.   O.C. "Y" Coy. will furnish a digging party to commence work on the new Communication Trench as stated above, immediate-ly it is perceived that the assault is successful, and will also establish a dump of Bombs, S.A.A. and Lewis Gun Magazines in readiness to rush across if necessary.

12. <u>Command</u>.   The Assaulting Party will act under the direct orders of Lieut. Hodgkinson.

13. <u>Bombing Party</u>.   Bombers will devote particular attention to any Dug-outs they may see and must satisfy themselves that they leave no one armed in them, behind them.

A.M. Forsyth
2nd. Lieut.   A/Ad.
15th. (S) Bn. Sherwood Foresters.

Issued at 2 p.m.

Copy No. 1.   "W" Coy.
      2.   "Z"
      3.   "X"
      4.   "Y"
      5.   Glosters.
      6.   105th. Bde. H.Q.
      7.   File.
      8.   H.Q.
      9.   War Diary.

Operation Orders No. 33.
By Lieut-Col. R.N.S. Gordon,
Commdg. 15th. (S) Bn. Sherwood Foresters.

8 Copy No 1

1. **Move.** The Battalion will be relieved tonight by 2nd.   23-8;-16.
Leinster Regt.

2. **L.G.** Lewis Gunners will load their Guns & Equipment in the Carts at
Bde. H.Q. and move off under the orders of Lieut. Moore.

3. **Relief.** "A" Coy. 2nd. Leinsters relieve "X" & "Y" Coys. Each Coy. will
send two guides to meet incoming Coy. at SUNKEN ROAD where track
joins in Point S.30.c.6.1. at 9-30 p.m. The relieving Coy. will
move by JACKSON TRENCH and divide into two, half Coy. proceeding to
"X" Coy. on right, and half Coy. proceeding to "Y" Coy. on left.
B Coy. 2nd. Leinster Regt. will relieve "W" Coy. 4 Guides to meet
incoming Coy. at same point S.30.c.6.1. at 8-30m p.m.
Coys. on relief will proceed by shortest route to Coy. area near
BILLON WOOD at A.19.d. central.
"Z" Coy. will move independently after the relief of "W" Coy. and
to be clear of the junction of MALTZ HORN TRENCH and JACKSON TRENCH
by 9-30 p.m.

Coys. will notify Bn. H.Q. when clear of JACKSON TRENCH.

In the event of this afternoon's operations being successful a
special party 2nd. Leinsters will relieve the Garrison independently.

"X" Coy. will have two guides at H.Q. at 9 p.m. to show the way.
Transport Officer will arrange to have all Watercarts removed
from Brigade Headquarters. He will arrange for one G.S. Limber
to take tins and stores back.
Coys. will see that their men are completely equipped. There is
enough equipment lying about to equip double the number of men in
the Battalion.
Men must be warned that no excuse will be taken for having
deficiencies.

Movements from JACKSON TRENCH should be made across the open
avoiding main roads.

4. **Route.** STANLEY DUMP - DUBLIN TRENCH - BRIQUETERIE MAIN ROAD across country
to MERICOURT MAIN ROAD - CAMP.

Issued at 5-30 p.m.

2nd. Lieut.   A/Adjt.
15th. (S) Bn. Sherwood Foresters.

Copies to :-
No 1. H.Q.
2. "W" Coy
3. "X"
4. "Y"
5. "Z"
6. T.O.
7. L.G.O.
8. War Diary
9. File

Operation Orders No, 34
By Lieut-Col. R.N.S. Gordon
Commdg. 15th (S) Bn. Sherwood Foresters.

Copy No. 8

Ref. Map 1/20,000 62d.N.E.

26-8-16.

1. **Move.** Battalion will move to SAND PIT VALLEY today in relief of the 15th. Infantry Brigade.

2. **Route.** via CITADEL.

3. **Time.** Parade ready to march off at 11-15 a.m.

4. **Order of March.** H.Q., W., X., Y., Z., and portion of 1st. Line Transport.

5. **Lewis Guns.** Lewis Guns will proceed with their respective Coys.

6. **Officers Kits. etc.** Officers kits etc., to be stacked at a point on the right of "W" Coy's Field Kitchen, ready for loading by 10-45 a.m.

7. **Band.** Bandsmen will parade with their Coys, as stretcher bearers.

8. **Transport.** Field Kitchens, Water Carts and Mess Cart will accompany the Battalion. The Transport Officer will arrange to have the horses for these vehicles, and Officers chargers at the Camp by 10-45 a.m. The remainder of the Transport and the Q.M's Department will move at 2 p.m.

9. **Cleanliness.** O.C.Coys. are responsible that the Bivouac Ground now occupied by the Battalion is left thoroughly clean.

10. **Reports.** Reports while on the Move to head of the Battalion.

Issued at 8 a.m.

Copies to :-

No. 1 O.C. "W" Coy.
    2   "X" "
    3   "Y" "
    4   "Z" "
    5   H.Q.
    6   T.O.
    7   File.
    8   War Diary.

A.M. Forsyth. 2nd.Lieut.
A/Adjutant.
15th. (S) Battn. Sherwood Foresters.

Operation Orders No 35   Copy.
By Lieut-Col. R.N.S.Gordon,
Commdg. 15th. (S) Bn. Sherwood Foresters.

Ref. Map. $\frac{1}{20.000}$ Sheet 62d.N.E.   28-8-16.

1. <u>Move.</u>   The Battalion with Transport will move to BOIS de TAILLES NORTH this afternoon.

2. <u>Route.</u> SAND PIT-south of MEAULTE running through E.18.d. E.18.c. E.23.b. E.23.a.8.5. thence along Main Road through E.30.a. & c - Cross Track in K.6.d.8.7. thence to destination.

3. <u>Time.</u>   Battalion will parade on parade ground ready to march off at 1-30 p.m.

4. <u>Order of March.</u>   H.Q. W. X. Y. Z. Transport.

5. <u>Cleanliness.</u>   The Camp will be left spotlessly clean, with tent curtains rolled up and ropes slackened. All Bivouacs must be removed, & all boxes piled on the west of the tents.

6. <u>Dinners.</u>   Dinners will be served not later than 12 noon.

7. <u>Reports.</u>   Reports, while on the move, to head of Battalion.

Issued at 11 a.m.

Copy No. 1. "W" Coy.
        2. "X"
        3. "Y"
        4. "Z"
        5. H.Q.
        6. T.O.
        7. L.G.O.
        8. War Diary.
        9. File.

2nd. Lieut.
A/Adjutant,
15th. Sherwood Foresters.

Operation Orders No. 36
By Lieut-Col. R.N.S.Gordon,
Commdg. 15th.(S) Bn. Sherwood Foresters.

Copy No. 5.

Ref. Map.62d.N.E. & AMIENS sheet.   28-8-16.

1. **Move.** The Transport and all Horses will move to the New Area to-morrow.

2. **Time.** 11-15 a.m.

3. **Route.** Route to be notified later.

4. **Lorries.** A Lorry is being provided for the transport of Lewis Guns and spare Kit.
   8 Lewis Gun Carts complete with wheels, will be stacked in the Lorries. The remaining four drawn by mules will proceed with the Transport.

5. **Field Kitchens.** Field Kitchens will proceed with transport and be accompanied by two Cooks per Coy.

6. **Dixies etc.** Two Dixies and two frying Pans per Coy. and a small portion of Officers Mess Kit will be retained.
   A quarter of a lorry will be provided for the transport of these on the 30th.

7. **Officers Kit.** Officers Kit to be loaded by 10-45a.m. Officers may retain a Blanket and Ground Sheet which will be carried in the Lorry on the 30th.

8. **Q.M's Dept.** The whole of the Q.M's Dept. will accompany the Transport.

9. **Lewis Guns.** 2 Lewis Gunners per Coy. will proceed with the Transport and 2 more per Coy. will accompany Capt. Crellin on the Moter Lorry to act as Billeting Party.

10. **Move.** The remainder of the Battalion will proceed by Tactical Train on the 30th. time to be notified later.

Issued at 9 p.m.

Copy No. 1   O.C. "W" Coy.
         2   "X" "
         3   "Y" "
         4   "Z" "
         5   H.Q.
         6   T.O.
         7   L.G.O.
         8   War Diary.
         9   File.

A.M. Forsyth. 2nd.Lieut.
A/Adjutant.
15th. (S) Bn. Sherwood Foresters.

Operation Orders No 37.   Copy No.
    By Lieut-Col. R.N.S.Gordon,
        Commdg. 15th. (S) Bn. Sherwood Foresters.
                                                                    29-8-16.

1. **Move.** The Battalion less advance party will move by train early to-morrow
   Morning to PROUVILLE.

2. **Entraining Station.** HEILLY.

3. **Route.** MORLINCOURT-VILLE-TRENX-Mericourt-HEILLY.

4. **Starting Point.** MORLANCOURT ROAD.

5. **Time.** Battalion will Parade ready to march off at 1-15 a.m.

6. **Advance Party.** An Advance Party under 2nd. Lieut. Johnson will proceed to
   HEILLY in advance of the Battalion to prepare tea for the Battalion.
   They will take with them the Lewis Gun Carts, Bicycles and Dixies.

7. **Lorries.** A quarter of a lorry is available for Officers Kits and Coy.
   Frying Pans. These will be loaded at once.

8. **Waterproof Sheets.** Inview of probable rain men will parade with their
   waterproof sheets carried over the left shoulder.

9. **Reports.** Reports to head of Battalion.

Issued at 1-30 p.m.

Copies to No 1. All Coys.
         2. War Diary.
         3. File.

                                                    2nd. Lieut.
                                                    A/Adjutant.
                                            15th. (S) Bn. Sherwood Foresters.

Battalion Orders,
 By Lieut-Col. R.N S.Gordon,
  Commdg. 15th. (S) Bn. Sherwood Foresters.

30-8-16.

Part 1.

1. <u>Duties</u>. Orderly Officer tomorrow :- Lieut. A. Moore.
   Next for duty :- 2nd. Lieut. B. Snape.
   Coy. on Duty :- "W" Coy.

2. <u>Orders</u>. No Battalion Orders were published on the 28th. and 29th. Aug.

3. <u>REvielle</u>. Revielle tomorrow 6-30 a.m.

4. <u>Breakfasts</u>. Breakfasts 7-30 a.m.

5. <u>Move</u>. Battalion will move to Billets in GROUCHES tomorrow.

6. <u>Transport</u>. All 1st. Line Transport will accompany the Battalion.

7. <u>Time</u>. Parade ready to march off at 9-30 a.m.

8. <u>Starting Point</u>. Cross Roads just North East of Battalion Headquarters.

9. <u>Order of March</u>. H.Q. W. X. Y. Z. Transport.

10. <u>Band</u>. Band will parade as such at the head of the column.

11. <u>Officers' Kits. etc</u>. All Officers Kits. etc. must be loaded by 8-30 a.m.

12. <u>L.G. Carts</u>. L.G. Carts, drawn by mules, will proceed with their respective Coys.

13. <u>Billeting Return</u>. Billeting Returns must be handed into Orderly Room by 10 p.m. tonight.

14. <u>Sick</u>. Sick Parade tomorrow will be at 7 a.m.

                                    A.M. Forsyth, 2nd. Lieut. A/Adjt.
                              15th. (S) Bn. Sherwood Foresters.

Operation Orders NO. 40 ~~3~~   COPY NO. 9
By Lieut-Col. R.N.S. Gordon, Comdg.
15th. (Service) Bn. The Sherwood Foresters.

3-8-16.

1. **Relief.** The Battalion will relieve the 6th. LIECESTER'S in "J" Sector of the Line tonight.

2. **Guides.** 16 Platoon Guides from the 6th. Leicester's will report to Battalion H.Q. at 6-45 p.m.

3. **Order of Relief.** "Y" Coy. will relieve "C" Coy. of the Leicester's
"Z" " " " "B" " " "
"X" " " " "D" " " "
"W" " " " "A" " " "

"Y" Coy. will occupy the left of the line (J.2.93/95 inclusive
"Z" " " " " the right of the line (J2.89/92 ")
"X" " " " " Support Line.
"W" " " be in Reserve in Britannia Works.

4. **Order of March.** Z Coy. Y Coy. X Coy. W Coy. H.Q. Coy.

5. **Route.** On Arrival at The CANDLE FACTORY "Z" Coy. will proceed to the Line via JULY AVENUE C.T. The Remainder of the Battalion in the order given, via AUGUST AVENUE C.T.
Coys. will move by Platoons with 3 minutes interval between Platoons.

6. **Lewis Guns.** Lewis Guns and Teams, under the Orders of Lieut. MOORE, will meet guides at CANDLE FACTORY at 11 a.m. and will proceed to the Front Line.

7. **Signallers, etc.** 3 Signallers per Coy. and 3 H.Q. Signallers, under Sgt. Moore; and the Bombing Corporal, will meet Guides at the CANDLE FACTORY at 11-30 a.m. The R.S.M. will accompany this party, and will take over Battalion Trench Stores and details from the 6th. LEICESTER'S.

8. **C.Q.M.S., Storeman, etc.** All C.Q.M.S's., Storeman, Cooks, Pioneers, and Shoemakers will proceed with Headquarters, as far as the CANDLE FACTORY, where accommodation for their respective duties will be found.

9. **Taking Over.** One Officer per Coy., accompanied by his runner, will meet guides at the CANDLE FACTORY at 3 p.m. and will proceed to the H.Q. of their respective Companies, in the Line to take over Trench Stores.

10. **Runners.** H.Q. runners will be formed into three groups. The first group will be accompanied at the Runners post at G.16d4.8, the remaining two groups staying at Battalion H.Q.

11. **Fatigues.** Company in Reserve will furnish all fatigues and carrying parties. The O.C. Coy. will detail one Platoon for each Coy in the Line to carry rations, etc.

12. **Drinking Water.** "Y" Coy. will obtain their drinking water from tanks in SEPTEMBER AVENUE, the support Coy. also obtaining their water from the same tank. "Z" Coy will obtain water from FORESTIER REDOUBT, and "W" Coy from supplies in their own post.

13. **Rations.** The Transport Officer will arrange to bring the Rations up to the CANDLE FACTORY at a stated time each night.

14. **Returns.** It is imperative that returns should reach Battn. H.Q. punctually whilst the Battalion is in the Line. Company Commanders will be notified what returns are required, with time stated.

15. **Officers' Kits.** All Officers' Kits to be at Battn. H.Q. by 4 p.m. and Officers' Mess Kits by 6-30 p.m.

16. **Reports.** Reports on completion of relief to Battalion H.Q.

Issued at 12 noon.

Copies To
No. 1 H.Q. Coy.
     2 "W" "
     3 "X" "
     4 "Y" "
     5 "Z" "
     6 Captain Crellin
     7 T.O.
     8 L.G.O.
     9 War Diary.
    10 File

                          2nd. Lieut. A/Adjutant,
15th. (Service) Battn. Sherwood Foresters.

43   6   27/8/16

Operation orders by
Major W. A. W. Grellis,
15th. (S) Battn. The Sherwood Foresters.

No 6 copy

The Battalion will be relieved by PUMP on the 28th. inst. in the following order:-

    W Coy relieved by X Coy PUMP about 7-30 a.m.

    X "   "   " W "   "   "   7-45 a.m.

    Z "   "   " Z "   "   "   9-0 a.m.

    Y "   "   " Y "   "   "   9-0 a.m.

One guide per platoon and Lewis Gun Teams will report to the Adjutant at 6-45 a.m.

All movements out will be by platoons at 5 minute intervals as follows :-

W Coy via MAY AVENUE, BRITTANIA WORKS, CANDLE FACTORY.

X Coy via JULY AVENUE.

Z Coy via most direct route.

Y Coy via AUGUST AVENUE.

H.Q. Coy via AUGUST AVENUE to HOTEL de l'UNIVERSE.

One guide per Coy will be furnished by pump to conduct leading platoon for W and X Coys to DEAF and DUMB ASYLUM.

Platoons moving into ARRAS will proceed in single file close under cover of the houses, the centre of the road has on no account to be used.

Coys will report to the Adjutant by runner when relief is complete.

All Trench Stores will be correctly inventoried and handed over to incoming unit and receipts taken.

Trenches, dugouts, saps, etc., to be will be left scrupulously clean, latrines to be emptied. No loose ammunition or bombs will be left lying about.

All Very Pistols and Periscopes will be taken out be Coys.

Battalion Headquarters will be at the HOTEL de l'Universe.

Transport. Orderly Room boxes, Officers kit and Mess Boxes of H.Q. W and X Coys., requiring conveyance to ARRAS will be dumped at CANDLE FACTORY by 8-30 p.m. this evening. Coys must arrange any other kit or stores to ARRAS. One man per company will be sent in charge of and coys accompany stores to Arras.

The Quartermaster will arrange to bring Officers Valices of H.Q., Y and Z Coys to the HOTEL de L'UNIVERSE this evening where they will be dumped and handed over to Sgt Smith H.Q. Coy.

Sgt Master Cook will arrange to send four dixies each from W and X Coys and one from H.Q. Coy to ARRAS. These dixies will be handed over to the R.S.M. at 8 p.m. this evening. Two cooks per Coy and two for H.Q. Coy. will be detailed to proceed to the DEAF and DUMB ASYLUM with Transport this evening.

Contd.

    Coy. Quarter-Master-Sergeants of W and X Coys. will be at the DEAF and DUMB ASYLUM not later than 6-30 am to take over Billets from PBSP.

                                        2nd. Lieut. A/Adjutant,
         16th. (S) Battn.
                          THE SHERWOOD FORESTERS.

Issued at 3-15 P.m.

No 1 Copy 2t Mr
    2 - W Coy
    3 - X Coy
    4 - Y.
    5 - Z.
    6 - File
    7 - War Diary
    8 - H Qr
    9 - L.90

Operation Orders,
    By Lieut-Col. R.N.S. Gordon,
        Commdg. 15th. (S) Bn. The Sherwood Foresters.

Copy No. 9

31-8-16.

Ref. Map Sheet LENS. 1/100,000.

1. **MOVE.** The Brigade moves to ARRAS by march route Sept. 2nd.; takes over the line Sept. 3rd. and all four Battalions are in the line Sept. 4th.
   The Battalion will move to WANQUETIN by bus tomorrow from LUCHEUX.

2. **STARTING POINT.** Junction of the GROUCHES ROAD with the main DOULLENS-GROUCHES ROAD.

3. **TIME.** 2-30 p.m.

4. **ORDER OF MARCH.** H.Q. Z. Y. X. W.

5. **BAND.** Band will parade as such.

6. **TRANSPORT.** Transport will move to WANQUETIN by road starting at 7-30 a.m. It will join the Brigade Transport at LUCHEUX.

7. **OFFICERS KITS ETC.** Officers Kits, etc., must be loaded on the Transport by 7 a.m.

8. **DIXIES.** Two Dixies per Coy. will be retained for cooking the Dinners, and will be carried by Coys.

9. **BREAKFAST.** Breakfast must be served before the departure of the Transport.

10. **Q.M's. DEPT.** The Q.Ms. Dept. with the exception of any men whom the Quartermaster Sgt. may detail to go with the Transport, will proceed by bus with the Battalion.

11. **COOKS.** Two Cooks per Coy. must accompany the Field Kitchens.

12. **L.G. CARTS.** Lewis Gun Carts will proceed with the Transport.

Issued at 10-40 p.m.

Copies to :-
No. 1. "W" Coy.
    2. "X" "
    3. "Y" "
    4. "Z" "
    5. H.Q. "
    6. T.O.
    7. L.G.O.
    8. Q.M.
    9. War Diary.
    10. File.

2nd. Lieut. A/Adjutant,
15th. (S) Battn. The Sherwood Foresters.

Army Form C. 2118

V OC 8

WAR DIARY
or
INTELLIGENCE SUMMARY
(Erase heading not required.)

15th SHERWOOD FORESTERS

SEPTEMBER 1916

Instructions regarding War Diaries and Intelligence Summaries are contained in F.S. Regs., Part II. and the Staff Manual respectively. Title Pages will be prepared in manuscript.

Place	Date	Hour	Summary of Events and Information	Remarks and references to Appendices
	1st		Battn. less Transport, marches to LUCHEUX; Transport conveyed by Mot.T.	1 OP ORDER No. 38
WANQUETIN	2nd		Transport to WANQUETIN. Reconnaissance of line by C.O. and Company Commanders. Battn. marches to Billets in ARRAS.	2 OR.ORDER No. 39.
	3rd		Relieve 6th LEICESTERS, 110th BDE, in J2 Sector of the line. 16th CHESHIRES on our right; 15th CHESHIRES on our left.	3 OR.ORDER No. 40
	4th			
	5th			
	6th			
	7th		In the Trenches	
	8th			
	9th			
	10th			
	11th			
	12th			
	13th			
TRENCHES	14th		Raid by the 15th CHESHIRES on our Lft. Diversionary movements along our Battn. front.	4 OP. ORDER No. 41
TRENCHES	15th		Operation by the 104th BDE on our right. Diversionary feint on our Brigade front	OP.ORDER No. 42.
	16th		In the trenches	84
	17th			

Army Form C. 2118

WAR DIARY
or
INTELLIGENCE SUMMARY

(Erase heading not required.) 15th SHERWOOD FORESTERS

SEPTEMBER 1916

Place	Date	Hour	Summary of Events and Information	Remarks and references to Appendices
	18 19 20 21 22 23 24 25 26 27		In the trenches.	
	28th		Relieved by 14th & 15th GLOSTERS, Bn. moved to RESERVE. "W" and "X" Coys in RESERVE BILLETS in ARRAS. "Y" Coy (less 1 PLATOON) in BILLETS in ST. NICHOLAS. 1 PLATOON "Y" Coy in BOSKY REDOUBT. "Z" Coy — 2 PLATOONS NICHOLLS REDOUBT. — 2 PLATOONS FORESTIER REDOUBT.	6 OP. ORDER No 43
	29th 30		Furnished Working Parties for R.E. W.O.W. Crellin Major Comdg. 15th Batn. Sherwood Foresters	

Operation Orders No. 39   2   Copy No. 8
By Lieut-Col. R.N.S. Gordon, Commdg.
The 15th. (Service) Battn. Sherwood Foresters.

2-9-16.

Ref. Map 1/100,000 LENS Sheet.

1. **Move.** Battalion will move to ARRAS today and will relieve a battn. of the 110th. Infantry Brigade on 3rd. Sept. 1916.

2. **Starting Point.** Junction of Roads at BRICQUETERIE 1½ Kil. East of WANQUETIN.

3. **Time.** 7-15 p.m.

4. **Route.** WARLUS - DAINVILLE - ARRAS. After passing WARLUS an interval of 5 minutes will be kept between Coys.

5. **Order of March.** H.Q. Z. Y. W. X.

6. **Band.** Band will parade as Stretcher Bearers. Instruments to be handed into the Q.M's Stores today.

7. **Transport.** Cookers and Baggage Wagons will proceed to ARRAS with the Battn. and will dump their loads in ARRAS. They will then return being clear of DAINVILLE before dawn. All Brigade Transport will probably be parked at AGNEZ-LES-DUSSANS. Further instructions re this will be issued later.

8. **Relief.** On the evening of the 3rd. inst. the Battalion will relieve the 6th. LIECESTER'S in the Line. Sixteen Platoon Guides from the 6th. Liecester's will report to Battalion H.Q. about 6-45 p.m. At 7 p.m. the Battalion will move to the line, an interval of 3 minutes being kept between Platoons. All trench stores will be handed over to Coys. by the 6th. Liecester's.

9. **Cooking.** As proper Cook-houses exist in the line and in the billets, all Cooking will be done in there and the Field Kitchens will return to the Transport Lines after the Dixies and Frying Pans have been dumped in ARRAS.

10. **Officers' Kits,** etc., must be loaded by 5-30 p.m.

11. **Q.M's. Stores** and Personal will remain with the Transport.

Issued at 12 noon.

Copies to -
No. 1 "W" Coy.
    2 "X" "
    3 "Y" "
    4 "Z" "
    5 "H.Q."
    6 "T.O."
    7 "Q.M.S."
    8 "War Diary"
    9 "File"

2nd. Lieut. A/Adjutant,
15th. (S) Battn. Sherwood Foresters,

Operation Orders. No. 41   Copy No.
By Lieut-Col. R.M.S. Gordon,
Commdg. 15th. (S) Bn. Sherwood Foresters.

SECRET.   14-9-16.

Ref. Map 51B. N.W. 3.

1. **Intention.** A Raid will be carried out by the Battalion on our left at a time to be notified later.

2. **Preparation.** Artillery will co-operate by placing a Box Barrage on all sides of the point of entry.

3. **Diversions.** Other diversions to detract the enemy's attention have been arranged.

4. **Instructions.** Lewis Guns situated in sub-sectors 95, 94, & 93 will fire on enemy's trenches opposite craters care being taken that no gun fires North of a line drawn from G.12.a.5.1. - G.12.a.6.8.
Time 0.15 onwards.
Lewis Guns in other subsectors will sweep enemy's parapet opposite them and rifle fire will be directed straight to the front from 0 onwards until end of operations.

5. **Zero Hour.** Zero will be notified later.

6. **Watches.** Watches will be synchronized. O.C. Coys. will send a representative to Battalion Headquarters at 4-30 p.m. for this purpose.

7. **Equipment.** All Ranks will stand to at their Battle positions fully armed and accoutred half an hour before Zero and will not Stand Down until notified from Battalion Headquarters.

8. **Lines of Communication.** Under no circumstances will men be permitted to leave their positions. C.Ts. must be kept absolutely free for special purposes.
Sentries will be posted at ends of C.Ts. with orders to X arrest any man disobeying this order.

9. **Reports.** To Headquarters.

10. **Rations.** As the Transport have received orders not to arrive until a late hour, rationing parties will not be sent to the Candle Factory until after the Stand Down.

Issued at 11 a.m.

Copies to :-

O.C. "B" Coy. Copy No. 1.
    "S" "   "   "   2.
    "T" "   "   "   3.
    "Z" "   "   "   4.
    H.Q. "   "   "   5.
    L.G.O.   "   "   6.
    File   "   "   7.
    War Diary   "   "   8.

                            A.M.Forsyth   2nd. Lieut.
                                          A/Adjutant,
                                15th. (S) Bn. The Sherwood Foresters.

Operation Orders No. 45   Copy No. 7
By Lieut-Col. R.N.S.Gordon,
Commdg. 15th. Sherwood Foresters.

SECRET.
Ref. Map. ARRAS 1/10,000.   15-9-16.

1. The 104th. Inf. Bde. will raid the enemy trenches in the neighbourhood of Square G.24. tonight.

2. In order to cause a diversion the 105th. Inf. Bde. will co-operate by bringing concentrated fire to bear on G.18.a.3.1. and G.6.c.5½.1. from 2-30 a.m. on the 16th. inst. The 15th. SHERWOOD FORESTERS will sweep enemy front opposite with Lewis Gun and Rifle Fire.

3. In the event of a Gas Attack taking place in the 105th. Bde. Area as mentioned in the 105th. Bde. Letter No. G.31.dated 14-9-16 ZERO hour will be notified and the programme mentioned in para 2 of this order will be carried out from Zero plus 1.55 to ZERO plus 2.5.

Issued at 7 p.m.
Copies to :-

Copy No. 1 "W" Coy.
  "   "   2 "X"
  "   "   3 "Y"
  "   "   4 "Z"
  "   "   5 H.Q.
  "   "   6 L.G.O.
  "   "   7 War Diary.
  "   "   8 File.

                                  Wnd. Lieut.
                                  A/Adjt.
                         15th. Sherwood Foresters.

Army Form C. 2118

WAR DIARY
or
INTELLIGENCE SUMMARY
(Erase heading not required.) 15th SHERWOOD FORESTERS

OCTOBER 1916

Instructions regarding War Diaries and Intelligence Summaries are contained in F.S. Regs., Part II. and the Staff Manual respectively. Title Pages will be prepared in manuscript.

Place	Date	Hour	Summary of Events and Information	Remarks and references to Appendices
ARRAS	1st		Bn in RESERVE Furnished Working Parties for R.E.	O.P. Order No 44
	2/3/4/5		do do	
	6th		Relieved 11th Glos'ter Regt in J II Sub Sector.	
	7/8/9/10/11		In Trenches.	
	12/13	4pm	Combined shoot by Artillery and T.M.s. on wire opposite CUTHBERT CRATER.	
	14/15/16		Trenches	
	17	3.30pm	Combined shoot by Artillery and T.M.s on wire opposite CUTHBERT.	9.4 a.m.
	18/19/20/21/22		In Trenches	

Army Form C. 2118

WAR DIARY
or
INTELLIGENCE SUMMARY

(Erase heading not required.) 15th SHERWOOD FORESTERS.

OCTOBER 1916

Place	Date	Hour	Summary of Events and Information	Remarks and references to Appendices
Ref Map 57B.N.W.3	23 24		In the Trenches	
	25	8 P.M.	Regained out a Raid on Enemy Trenches at G.12.a.55.45 One Prisoner was taken and a great amount of damage done to Enemy Trenches. Report. Narrative	1 Op. Order No 45 2 Op. Order No 45 3 Narrative
	26 27 28 29 30 31		In the Trenches.	

Rutherford
Lieut Colonel
Commanding 15th Sherwood Foresters

Operation Orders No. 43   Copy No. 1
By Major W.A.F. Grellin,
    Commdg. 15th. (S) Bn. Sherwood Foresters.

SECRET.

                                                           5-10-16.

1. Relief.   The 15th. Sherwood Foresters will relieve the 14th. Gloster Regt.
             in J.11. Sub-sector on 6th. inst. as follows :-

             Sherwood   Gloster   Take   Leave
             Foresters.   Regt.   Over.   present
                                                                       position
                                                                       at.

             "W" Coy. will relieve "W" Coy.   in SUPPORT LINE   7 a.m.
             "X" "   "   "X" "   in BRITANNIA   7-30 a.m.
                                                 WORKS.
             "Z" "   "   "Z" "   in J.11.89 -   8 a.m.
                                              J.11.92.
                                              (both inclusive)
             "Y" "   "   "Y" "   J.11.93 - J.11.95. 8-30 a.m.
                                              (both inclusive)

             H.Q. Coy.   "   "   H.Q. "   in H.Q. Dug-outs   7 a.m.
             L. Guns will relieve independently under arrangements to be made
             by L.G. Officers concerned.

2. Route.   "W" Coy. will use JULY AVENUE.   "X" Coy. will use AUGUST AVENUE.
             "Y" Coy. will use AUGUST AVENUE. "Z" Coy. will use JULY   "
             H.Q. Coy. will use AUGUST and SEPTEMBER AVENUES.
             H.Q. Coy. will carry out relief by detachments. e.g. Signallers
             complete, Bombers complete, etc. Relief to be completed by
             10-30 a.m.

3.   O.C. "W" and "X" Coys. will arrange to have any articles e.g.
             Officers Kits, Mess Kits etc. stacked at the Guard Room, HOTEL
             de L'UNIVERS before 7 p.m. tonight.
             Anything which is not so stacked will have to be carried by hand
             to the Trenches.

4.   "W" and "X" Coys. will keep four DIXIES per Coy. back for
             Breakfast on 6th. inst. remainder, under charge of one Cook per
             Coy. will be stacked at H.Q. Guard Room by 7 p.m. tonight.
             The R.Q.M.S. will arrange to have the Meat and Vegetables Ration
             of the Battalion taken direct to the CANDLE FACTORY tonight.

5. Surplus Kit. All Officers Surplus Kit etc. will be stored in the Battalion
             STORE ROOM in the CONVENT by 6-30 a.m.

6. Advance Parties.   O.C. Coys. will arrange to send an Advance Party of
             one Officer and one N.C.O. per Coy. to take over Trench Stores
             etc. The taking over must be done very carefully and must be
             completed before the arrival of the incoming Coy. One copy per
             Coy. of A.F.W. 3405 will be rendered to Orderly Room not later
             than 6 p.m. 6th. inst.

7. Blankets. All Blankets will be collected in bundles of ten, clearly
             labelled, and stacked at Battalion STORE ROOM at the CONVENT
             by 6 a.m. 6th. inst.

8. Formation. Coys. will move by Platoons in single file at 3 minutes
             interval between Platoons. Troops moving through ARRAS must
             be kept well in against the houses.

9. Reports. On completion of Relief Coys. will immediately report by runner
             to Battalion ORDERLY ROOM in AUGUST AVENUE.

10. **Cleanliness.** Before vacating present positions, O.C. Coys. will take steps to ensure that BIVOUACS, BILLETS, and surroundings occupied by their Coys. are left clean and tidy. Latrines will be emptied and dis-infected, also Drains and refuse pits.

11. **Billeting Certificates.** Billeting Certificates to reach Orderly Room by 4 p.m. 5th. inst.

Issued at 8 a.m.

```
Copy No. 1.    File.
  "    "  2.    War Diary.
  "    "  3.     "    "
  "    "  4.    "W" Coy.
  "    "  5.    "X"  "
  "    "  6.    "Y"  "
  "    "  7.    "Z"  "
  "    "  8.    M.O.
  "    "  9.    R.Q.M.S.
```

[signature] 2nd. Lieut.
A/Adjutant,
15th. (Service) Battalion,
The Sherwood Foresters.

SECRET.

15th. (S) Battn. The Sherwood Foresters.

OPERATIONS.

Special Instructions for Intelligence Party.

To follow behind Clearance Parties and confine themselves to the Collection to material and documents of enemy dead. Shoulders straps, caps, cartridges and rifles, are all means of identification. Documents are to be found in tail pockets of dead. Identity discs to be removed from dead. Each man to have a strong Clasp Knife to cut off shoulders badges and cut identity disc cords. To estimate number of dead if any; damage to wire, trenches and dug-outs, caused by our fire; and any information that can be observed relative to the construction and up-keep of trenches. To be under the direct orders of O.C. raid. One man will be attached to the R.E. Party, and act under orders of O.C. demolition party.

Operation Orders No 44 Copy No 5
By Lieut Col R.M.S Gordon
Commanding 15th Bn Sherwood Foresters
Field 24-10-16

Map Ref
51B. N.W.
Square G.12.

1. OBJECT   The 15th SHERWOOD FORESTERS will Raid
enemy trenches about G.12.a.65.40 on the
night of Oct. 25th and will endeavour to
(a) Capture prisoners.
(b) Destroy suspected mine shaft
     about G.12.a.65.50.
(c) Obtain material
(d) — — identifications.

2. INFORMATION   All information with reference to
enemy wire, gaps, No mans Land,
prominent objects, are contained in
special memoranda already issued.

3. COMPOSITION   As already detailed. Special
   OBJECTIVES   memoranda showing men told off to
   AND DUTIES   parts of enemy trench. Parties as
                 detailed will be led by 2nd Lieut's
                 K... Y... Son [...]

4. EQUIPMENT
   ARMS ETC

5. EQUIPPING
   STATION

6. TRAFFIC All traffic except for Raiding Party along JULY and AUGUST AVENUES will be suspended from 7 p.m. till the return of Raiders. O.C. Coys concerned will post sentries to see that this Order is strictly carried out.

7. SPECIAL DUTIES The O.C. Left Company will detail two Runners at point of departure to direct or carry on any message to Advanced H.Q. from O.C. Raiding Parties.

8. DEMONSTRATION The remainder of the Battalion will stand to during the Raid and will remain so until notice from H.Q. is sent to O.C. Coys. O.C. Coys in front line will assist by demonstrating with Lewis Gun, Rifle & Rifle Grenade fire during the time laid down for the Raid. Particular care being taken that no man fires in the direction of the Raiding Party.

9. ARTILLERY A Heavy Artillery barrage will enclose the Area selected for the Raid.

10. RETURN OF RAIDING PARTY All men detailed for Raiding Party will on return to our line proceed immediately to BRITANNIA WORKS where the Covering Party will join Hurworth Company.

11. ZERO HOUR Zero Hour will be communicated later.

12. SYNCHRONIZATION OF WATCHES All watches will be synchronized. Coys will send a representative to Battn HQ at 5pm 26th inst for this purpose.

13. SIGNALS The following signals have been arranged:-
Expiry of time limit
Two Red Rockets fired together and repeated after one minute interval and again after one minute interval.
Recall signal at point of entry
Sounding of horn or bugle.

14. DURATION OF RAID The time limit for the duration of Raid has been fixed for 0.45.

15. CONGESTION OF TRENCHES O.C. Coys will see that front line immediate support and support line are kept absolutely clear for the free passage of Raiding Parties.
All Ranks will be on fire steps.

16. MOVEMENT OF RAIDING PARTY TO RENDEZVOUS Parties detailed for Raid will proceed to their rendezvous in order with the exception of special party.

Party	Start Hour	Route	Time	Arrival about or Assembly Point
Special Party	Lance Corp Mackey	TURK AVENUE T.S. LINE C.T. C.T.a 20.11 C.T.a 25.26 RIGHT WIRE PASSAGE	0.65	RIGHT CAMOUFLET
Right Squad	do	ACCRA C.T. T.S. LINE C.T. C.T.c 13.16 C.T.c 20.22 CENTRE WIRE PASSAGE	0.65	CENTRE CAMOUFLET
Left Squad	do	ACCRA C.T. T.S. LINE C.T. LEFT WIRE PASSAGE	0.65	LEFT CAMOUFLET

PARTY	START FROM	ROUTE	TIME	RENDEZVOUS OR ASSEMBLY POINT
Clearing Party Right Squad	CANDLE FACTORY	JULY AVENUE I.S.LINE - C.T. G12a.20.16. G12a.26.20	-0.55	Front line with leading man opposite RIGHT WIRE PASSAGE
Centre Squad	-do-	AUGUST AV. I.S LINE - C.T G12a.12.26 G12a.20.20	-0.55	Front line with leading man opposite CENTRE WIRE PASSAGE
Left Squad	-do-	AUGUST AV.	-0.55	Front line with leading man opposite LEFT WIRE PASSAGE
DEMOLITION PARTY R.E.	-do-	AUGUST AV I.S LINE	-0.50	Head of C.T at G12a.20.30. but not to move forward till centre clearing party are through wire passages.
INTELLIGENCE PARTY	-do-	JULY AV I.S.LINE	-0.50	Head of C.T at G12a.20.25 but not to move forward till right clearing party are through wire passages.

17) **COVERING PARTY** The Covering Party will be equipped and assemble in BRITANNIA WORKS prior to the start of remainder of Raiding Party & will not move up to their rendezvous in I.S. LINE until remainder have cleared RESERVE LINE.

RIGHT COVERING PARTY will move by JULY AV. to I.S. LINE in such formation that the leading man is resting on C.T. G12a.20.16.

LEFT COVERING PARTY will move by AUG. AV. to near I.S.LINE in such formation that the leading man is resting close to CLARENCE CRATER

18. **SILENCE** Absolute quietness is to prevail, no talking, smoking or striking matches is to be allowed. It is essential that the Raid should be sudden & swift, and Coy Comdrs must impress up on all Ranks the necessity of carrying out these Orders.

19. **RATION PARTIES** Rations will be sent up to the Coy after the completion of the operations when the stand down is given from H.Q.

20. **REPORTS** Advanced Battn H.Q. will be situated in the new cockloum AUGUSTAV just below junction of Support Line & AUGUSTAV.

21. **DRESSING STATION** An advanced Dressing Station will be established in T.S. LINE.

22. In the event of the enemy attempting to follow up behind of Raiding Party after the Return or during the night O.C. Coys must see that the men remain particularly on the alert & any movement on the part of the enemy to be at once met by steady & particular by Lewis Gun & Rifle fire.

Copies

No 1 — Brig
2 — X
3 — Y
4 — Z
5 — TM
6 — Hawthorn
7 —
8 — 105th Bde
9 —
10 — 35th Divn S.S.
11 — 10th Cheshire
12 — " Gloster

J. Johnson 2nd Lieut
Adjutant
10th R. Welsh
Fusrs

To 105th. (Infantry) Brigade.

Forwards herewith, in duplicate -

(a) Report on Operations on night of the 25th. October.
(b) Special Report of Sergeant Peacock, 204th. Field Company, R.E.
(c) Name and Regiment of German Prisoner.
(d) List of Articles found on prisoner, and material and arms taken from enemy's lines.

Ruspon

Lieut - Col., Commanding
The 15th. (S) Battalion, The Sherwood Foresters.

Trenches
26-10-16.

15th. (S) Batta. The Sherwood Foresters.

Report of Operations on Night of 25th. October 1916.

Map Ref.
1:10,000
Square G.12 A
& Photos.

Orders.
1. In accordance with instructions laid down in 105th. Bde. letter G/30, dated 17th. Oct. Preparations were immediately taken to organize and train men for carrying out the raid on enemy's trenches at G12a.60.40.

Preparations.
2. Careful reconnaissances of our own lines, condition of "No-Man's-Land", state of enemy's wire were made and patrols were out every night, so that as many men possible could acquaint themselves with the going and actual conditions of the ground they were to work over. The work of the two flanking scouts (Ptes. Rhodes and Hinton) were of great usefullness and they carried out their investigations and made reports which proved of immense value. The officers and men for the various parties were selected and it is particularly satisfying for me to record that in nearly every case the men willingly came forward and volunteered for the different parties, not only from the two Companies selected, but from the whole Battalion. As, however, it was necessary to detail where possible units, as a whole, all those who volunteered could not be selected. Arrangements having been made by the 105 Brigade for the special training at the 35th. Divisional School for the bombing squads, and later for the Clearing squads, and Intelligence party, the men selected for these parties were withdrawn from the line and the training carried out through proved of immense value and contribute largely to the success of the raid.

Composition.
3. The raiding party were detailed as under :-

(a) A bombing party of one Officer and 31 men, divided into three squads as under :-

1 N.C.O. in Command
2 Bombers
2 Carriers
2 Bayonet Men
2 Rifle Grenade Men
1 Spare man

10 X 3 = 30

The whole party under 2nd. Lieut. Warburton who was accompanied by his runner, making a total of one Officer and 31 men.

(b) A Clearing party of one Officer and 30 men, divided into three squads as under :-

1 N.C.O. in Command
6 Bayonet men
3 Bombers

10 X 3 = 30

The whole party under 2nd. Lieut. Dunn who was accompanied by 2 Spare Bayonet Men, One Spare bomber and one runner, making a total of one Officer and 34 men.

Composition. Contd.

3. (c) A Demolition Party furnished by the 204th. Field Coy.
R.E. and Comprising of one N.C.O. and 6 men, total
7 men.

(d) An Intelligence party of 10 men including one attached
to R.E. Party as runner.

(e) A Covering Party of 2 Officers, 2nd. Lieut. Judge and
2nd. Lieut. Swallow, and 42 N.C.O's. and men in 2
squads, each squad consisting of 1 Officer 2 N.C.O's
18 Rifle Men, and one Lewis Gun team (4 men) total
2 Officers and 42 men.

In addition 2 scouts were detailed to guide by means of
tapes laid across "No Man's Land" from our line to the
point of entry. These two men of whom mention has already been made, were detailed to keep in advance of the
bombing squads, and lead them to the point of entry by
confining them within the area enclosed by the tapes.

The whole raiding party was under the orders of 2nd. Lieut.
Dunn.
Other men were detailed in our lines at various points as
control men and runners, were stationed near point of
departure, to assist in directing and delivering of any
orders that arrived from raiding party.

Battalion Arrangements 4. All orders with regard to the organisation,
and Orders.   training, equipment, arms, special duties, rendezvous
orders affecting the remainder of the Battalion etc., were
issued separately, and are attached to this report.

Narrative. 5. Parties as detailed in orders having been equipped at the
Candle Factory, proceeded to their assembly positions
without incident and were reported all so rect by 7.30
p.m. without, apparently, the movement being noticed as
no fire of any description was opened on them. From the
statements collected from the various party leaders, which
were taken down immediately on the party's return to Battalion Headquarters, the course followed by the different
parties were as follows:-
The three bombing parties started crawling forward from
their assembly positions, punctually at -8.15, but owing
to the darkness and extremely bad going in "No-Man's-Land"
due to the several days wet weather, and also to the
broken nature of the ground from the result of the previous
bombardments. The rate of progress was extremely slow.
Two parties, however, managed to keep ouside the tapes,
which was hoped would be the means of keeping them straight,
and resulted in only one party actually reaching the cut
in enemy's wire aimed at and which was reported very well
done. The centre party which was to advance, numbered to
the left and finding themselves to the left of the artillery
barrage, and being fired on, returned to our own lines,
bringing all wounded and one killed with them. The right
party in the same manner to the right and after reaching
enemy's wire, and were unable to find the opening, moved to the left, but arrived too late, or at any rate.
Left bombing party was the only one to arrive at the point
aimed at and was of considerable value. 2nd. Lieut.
Warburton who was in charge of the bombers and also under
the centre party, after seeing his party back apparently,
attempted to join the others. He is, I regret to say,
missing at time of writing, though parties are still out
searching for him. One flanking parties report as follows:
Right party followed bombers and got too far to the right
and lost touch with bombers. Under 2nd. Lieut. R.
however, they made their way into the trenches, and came

Narrative, Contd, 5.

across a party of Germans clustered in the trenches. They
fired on them and the enemy were observed moving backwards.
As the time limit had expired 2nd. Lieut. Dunn, considered
it best to return slowly, especially as he had no bombers
with him.
The Centre Clearing Party hit off the point of entry and
assisted in clearing the trenches according to the orders
issued to them.
The Left Clearing Party also hit off the gap in the wire,
but further to the left, and with them rests the honour of
capturing the prisoner who was obtained in the enemy's dug-
out itself, the three men being :-

   Pte. Wharton, the leader of the party.
    "   Jefferies, bayonet man.
    "   Newton, Bomber.

The prisoner was the only one in that particular dug-out.
The Demolition Party of R.E's. gained entry into the trenches
and their work appears to have been well done.
The report of Sgt. Peacock, the leader of the party is
attached.
The Intelligence party also gained entry into the trenches
and have given me the following :-

Gap in Enemy's wire, well cut and easy to get through.
Enemy's trenches badly damaged by our shell fire, where
undamaged about 10 feet deep, strongly revetted with many
frames close together with braces well fixed over head on
both sides, brushwood and expanding metal revettments.
Ground seemed firm much covered with earth from the
bombardment, bottoms dry. One dug-out seemed on fire
from A.P. Bomb, saw a few dead in trenches, but nearly
completely buried. The party were unable to get any
documents, but one rifle, one bayonet, and portions of
equipment brought back. The Covering parties went out
according to programme, and they again, in extending, managed
to wonder outwards too far, their two ends near the enemy's
wire getting too far apart instead of drawing closer as
was hoped. Thinking to a certain degree, minimising their
field of fire. 2nd. Lieut. Dunn, who was in Command of
the raiding party has given me the following information in
his report.

The movement forward started at the time fixed. The party I
was with i.e. the right clearing party managed to get too
much to the right, but managed to make entry into the
trenches. Owing to the bombers going astray, the organising
was not as arranged. Owing to the dense clouds of smoke,
drifting along the trench caused by (P.S.K. Bombs) it was
impossible to get touch on the left. The men who got in
were immediately re-organized in the best way we could, and
we worked down to the right, a small party of the enemy were
seen and one bomb was thrown by them which did not explode.
We fired on them and they immediately bolted along their
trench. As the recall signal had already gone I considered
it adviseable to withdraw my party, which was done. The
enemy's trenches were badly damaged. Going in "No-Man's-
Land was very heavy, and difficult, owing to the wet and
broken condition of the ground due to the bombardments
which accounted for the late arrival at the trenches. 2nd.
Lieut Dunn was wounded, slightly in the face.

contd.

4

The observations gathered from all sources were as follows:-

The preliminary arrangements for the assembly of the various parties worked well, and all the men were in position two minutes before Zero Hour without being noticed.
The forward movement was simultaneous, but the time taken to get across "No-Man's-Land" was greatly underestimated, owing to the bad going, and the men had only started getting busy in the enemy trenches when the recall signal was given, as arranged.

The failure of two of the bombing squads to make the point of entry interfered considerably with the organization of the whole raid, and was partly responsible for the failure of the results hoped for.

Owing to the damage done to the trenches, it was very difficult to follow out the lines as practised.

The use of "P" bombs caused a considerable volume of smoke in the trenches, and hindered the operations, several of the men were overcome with gas from the H.E.T. Bombs, which filtered into the trenches.

The following incidents collected from men may be of interest. Lieut. Dunn's party report that the enemy they fired on were wearing gas masks.
Pte. Rhodes, the left tape man reports, that as he was working forward he noticed 5 Huns in a shell hole outside their wire. He threw two bombs at them, and on his return counted 4 dead. An attempt is being made to verify this and will be reported later on. He also reports that while waiting for the bombardment to start, he distinctly saw Huns in front of their wire, and that at the moment of the first shell falling they ran back through their own wire.

The enemy's retaliation consisted chiefly of 4.1's, and were directed on the right company, top of VINE and AVENUES, and on J 5 sub-sector.
A battery of 10.5 d' Hms seemed to be firing on PAIRE.
10.5 d' Hms from direction of LOOS on J 5 sub-sector.
Promiscuous shrapnel from a northerly direction along front. Rifle and machine gun fire, very little. Lights from areas outside barrage.
Red lights fired at 9.11 p.m. which went up all along the line, and from well behind the enemy's support line.
Enemy sent up two rockets, breaking into red and green stars about 9.17 p.m.
T.Ms and shrapnel were fired intermittently until shortly after 2 a.m. (30th.) from which time everything remained quiet up to time of despatch.

The casualties, I regret to state, are heavy.

	Officers	Other Ranks.
Killed	1	6
Wounded	1	15
Missing	2	8

It is hoped to trace the missing other ranks, search parties being still out.

Communication with Brigade Headquarters was efficiently throughout, and all phases during the operation notified immediately on receipt of same.

(5)

Contd.

I am sending under separate letter all names of men, which
have been brought to my notice for conspicuous good work.
The men engaged in the raid were despatched to ARRAS,
for a good night's rest as soon as they reported.

Trenches

26-10-16.

Rutproom.

Lieut-Colonel, Commanding,
15th. (Service) Battalion, The Sherwood Foresters.

From H.P.J. Peacock, Sgt.
   I/C of R.E. Raiding Party.

To O.C. 15th. (S) Bn. The Sherwood Foresters.

Sir

I beg to report that I met the centre Clearing Party, and proceeded with my party to the German Lines.   Owing to the delay in getting into the enemy's front line, we had not time to make a systematic search for the suspected mine.

On our arrival, we discovered a deep dug-out (about 30 feet) in which were two of the enemy, on being ordered to come out they refused, and as there were none of the Clearing party in this section of the trench, we threw down a "P" Bomb, and blew in the entrance, in the meantime another section of our party in search of the mine shaft, found five more of the enemy in a dug-out who they promptly bombed, and informed the Intelligence Party; not being successful in finding the mine, we used our explosives in doing as much damage as possible.

We arrived at the enemy's line when the red lights for return were sent up, but remained there about 20 minutes, as a party we can account for at least seven of the enemy.   Before returning word was passed round that the left party had gone in, so we had then to return.   On the way back we took the wrong direction, but eventually struck a gap near CUTHBERT CRATER, and reached our line at 9.55 p.m.   Party reported safe. We picked up one bomber gassed, and one of the Covering Party wounded slightly, the gassed man (from smoke bombs) had practical recovered on our return.

Condition of German Line, etc.

Our artillery had smashed up the wire very satisfactorily, and passage through was comparatively easy.   The front line trench was very deep (about 11 feet) and well revetted with hurdles, and in some places, with wire and angle iron pickets.   Ammunition boxes were of iron, but empty.   Dug-outs about 30 feet deep. Blankets to frames badly fitted.   No machine gun emplacements were discovered in the front line.   The wire was about 40 feet thick in two series, with knife rests and footballs, or gooseberries in between, of hoop irons, covered with barbed wire.

S/d

H. P. J. Peacock,

Sergeant, R.E.

Name of Prisoner Captured by the 15th. Sherwoods.

Ogefreiter

Franz Fleischer,

Fusilier Rasgt 90 1 Batl,

3 Rouez F Fuf Davifion.

List of Trophies captured.

1 Field Dressing   )
1 letter   )
1 piece of ribbon   )   On Prisoners.
1 pay book   )
1 note book   )

1 Bayonet

1 Smoke Helmet Case

1 Entrenching tool and part of equipment

1 Rifle.

SECRET.

15th. (S) Battn. The Sherwood Foresters.

OPERATIONS.

Special Instructions for Bombing Party

COMPOSITION 1. The Bombing Party will consist of 1 Officer, 3 N.C.O's, and 27 men, divided into 3 squads, each squad to consist of

    1 N.C.O. in charge.
    2 Bayonet Men.
    2 Throwers.
    2 Carriers.
    2 Rifle Grenadiers.
    1 Spare man.

The squads will be designated as

    Right Bombing Squad
    Left   "   "
    Centre "   "

DUTIES - 2. **Right Bombing Squad.**

On obtaining entry of enemy's trenches to work along enemy's front line as far as G12a.75.30, as close to artillery Barrage as possible, and prevent enemy from approaching point of entry. To establish blocks where possible to force enemy, if he attemps to approach, into the open. On the time limit expiring, or before if special signal is given, to retire to point of entry, and return to our own lines.

Centre Bombing Squad.

As above, but to work north, along enemy's front line trenches as far as G.12a.60.50, and proceed down communication trench as far as G.12a.85.40, as close to artillery barrage as possible.

Left Bombing Squad.

As above but to work north, along enemy's front line trenches as far as G.12a.63.58, as close to artillery Barrage as possible

Equipment. None.

Arms. N.C.O. Rifle and Bayonet
          10 rounds in Magazine.
          20 rounds in pockets of coat.
          2 Mills Bombs in pocket of coat.

Bayonet Men. - DO -

Throwers. Knobkerrie.
          12 Mills Bombs in bucket.

Carriers. Knobkerrie.
          24 Mills bombs in 2 Buckets.

Rifle Grenadiers. Rifle with Cup attachment.
          12 Mills Rifle Grenades in waistcoat.

Spare Man. Rifle and Bayonet.
          10 rounds in magazine.
          20 rounds in pockets of coat.
          2 Mills bombs in pocket of coat.

Contd.

    <u>Wire Cutters</u>.   Each squad will be given as many wire cutters as can be obtained.

    <u>Order of Progress and retirement</u>.   As being practised at Divl. School.

    <u>Order of Return</u>.   Centre Bombing Squad folowed by flanking squads.

15th. (S) Battn. The Sherwood Foresters.

Special Instructions for Clearing Party.

COMPOSITION.
The Clearing party will consist of

- 1 Officer.
- 3 N.C.O's.
- 30 men.

divided into three squads, each squad to consist of

- 1 N.C.O. in charge.
- 6 Bayonet men.
- 3 bombers.

Each squad to be divided into three sections of

- 1 Bomber
- 2 Attendant Bayonet Men.

In addition three spare men (Two bayonet men and one bomber) to remain with the Officer Commanding.

Squads to be designated.

- Right clearing squad.
- Centre " "
- Left " "

DUTIES.
Right Clearing Squad. To follow up close behind right bombing squad along enemy's front line to and from point of Entry to Junction with bombing squad. To capture or despatch any enemy who may come out of dug-outs. To throw M.S.K. and "P" Bombs into any dug-outs that may be found to protect bombing squad in front, and take as prisoners, any enemy who may try to leave dug-outs. To watch for and drive back any enemy who may attempt to come across the open from their Support Lines. To cover retirement of bombing squads.

Centre Clearing Party. As above, but to follow centre bombing squad up C.T. leading to G12a.85.40, to cover the work of the demolition party round suspected mining shaft at G12a.60.50.

Left Clearing Party. As for right clearing party, but following along enemy's front line trench, in conjunction with left bombing squad.

EQUIPMENT AND ARMS.
N.C.O. Rifle and bayonet.
10 rounds in magazine.
20 "   in pockets of jacket.
2 Mills bombs.

Bayonet Men. - DO -

Bombers. Knobkerrie.
Electric Lamp.
6 M.S.K. Bombs.
6 "P" Bombs.

DUGOUTS.
In the small space being raided it is not anticipated that the dug-outs will number more than four, and giving two outlets to each, the number of sections are such as to give a guard over each.

Contd.

<u>Order of progress and retirement.</u>   As being practised at Divl. bombing school.

<u>Order of return.</u>   Centre followed by flanks.

Map Reference:-　　　　　　　　　　　　　　　COPY NO.
51B. S.W.3.
Square G.12.

OPERATIONS.

ORGANIZATION OF RAID IN ENEMY TRENCHES IN G.a.12 CENTRAL.

OBJECT. (1). To enter enemy's trenches between G.12.a.70.32. and
G.12.a.60.45. and

    (a). Take Prisoners.

    (b). Discover and damage mine-shafts suspected about
G.12.a.65.50.

    (c). Capture Material.

    (d). Obtain identifications and documents.

INFORMATION. (a). **WIRE.** Estimated 50 yds. width; low trip wire 10 yds.;
(2).   entangled wire on stakes interspersed with
knife-rests (laid end on) up to 5 - 6 ft. high,
reaching almost to enemy's parapet.
No previous openings or lanes have, as yet,
been observed, but suspected, but suspected
openings closed by hinged bars near Sap at
G.12.a.70.32. Considerable amount of loose
wire in front of trip wire.

    (b). **SAPS.** North sap running S.W. to N.E. at G.12.a.60.45,
length 25 - 30 yards from trench, enclosed by
wire.
South Sap running S.W. to N.E. at G.12.a.70.32,
length 20 - 25 yards from trench, enclosed by
wire.

    (c). **NO MAN'S LAND.** Good. Generally free from shell-holes
until close to enemy's wire. Grass and
thistles long and clinging.

    (d). **PROMINENT OBJECTS.** Line of three Craters giving
direction of our lines. Three camouflets
forming semi-circle between CLARENCE and
CUTHBERT CRATERS.
Old Sap running East into NO MAN'S LAND from
our lines for 200 yards, commencing South
side of CUTHBERT.

                                                        Offs. OR's

COMPOSITION. (a). Bombing Party in three squads of 1 N.C.O.
(3).   and 9 men each.
Squad to consist of 2 bayonet men;, 2 Throwers;
2 Carriers; 2 Rifle Grenadiers; 1 spare man
1 N.C.O. The whole party under 2/Lt.
WARBURTON..1...30.

    (b). Clearing Party in 3 squads of 1 N.C.O. &
9 men each.
Squad to consist of 6 Bayonet Men; 3
Grenadiers; 1 N.C.O. ; 3 spare men
(1 Grenadier - 2 Bayonet Men) to accompany
O. C. The whole under 2/Lt. DUNN............1...33.

    (c). Demolition Party furnished either by N.Z.
TUNNELLING COY., or 204th. FD. COY. R.E.,
strength as arranged by O. C.

(2).

Offs.   OR'S

COMPOSITION. (CONTD.)
(3).

(d). Intelligence Party of 6 specially trained men
to search for documents and material from
dead, and to estimate number of enemy dead
and damage to trenches caused by our fire.   6

(e). Covering Party of two squads of 2 N.C.O's.
and 13 men (Bayonet men) and 1 Lewis Gun
Team (6 men) each. Each party under command
of an Officer.
North party under 2/Lt. SWALLOW.
South   "   "   "   . JUDGE...........2.......42.

The whole Raiding Party to be under the orders of
2/Lt. DUNN.

GENERAL DUTIES. (a). To obtain entry into enemy's trenches, cutting wire,
(4).   if not accomplished by T. M. fire, and work down
trenches and establish blocks, as shown on attached
map.
To prevent enemy from approaching Raiding Party.
To cover retirement of Clearing Party, and, on
completion of Raid to return to Point of Entry, and
return to our lines.

(b). To follow up immediately behind Bombing Squads, and
deal with dug-outs, or any men who may come out of
dug-outs behind Bombing Squads. To capture prisoners
and immediately pass them back to our lines. To
collect material for identification, and to remove any
M. G's. that may be in enemy's lines. To assist
Bombing Squads, and cover them if driven back.

(c). To search for, and destroy, enemy's mine-shafts, and
M. G. emplacements.

(d). To search for material and documents from enemy dead.
To make note of construction and condition of enemy
trenches. To estimate numbers of enemy dead, and
damage to trenches and surroundings.

(e). To protect flanks of Raiding Party, and to cover their
retirement. To guide all men of Raiding Party on
their return. To assist wounded, and to bring in
killed, if possible. To pass prisoners back to our
lines.

SPECIAL INSTRUCTIONS. Will be issued separately to each party, giving every
(5).   detail, and information that can be further obtained.

DRESS.   (6).   Field Service Uniform. Cap. Warm under-clothing,
Cardigans, Gloves, etc. Buttons to be dirtied. Faces
and hands also.

EQUIPMENT. (7).   None. Riflemen to carry one bandolier, or rounds in
clips in their pockets.
Grenadiers to have waistcoats to carry bombs.

WIRE-CUTTERS.   As many heavy wire-cutters as can be obtained will be
(8).   issued to Bombing Squads.

ARMS.   (9).   (a). BOMBING SQUADS.

P. T. O.

(3).

ARMS. (9). (a). BOMBING SQUADS.

Bayonet Men........Rifle & Bayonet.........2 bombs.
Throwers............Knobkerrie...............12 "
Carriers............   "   ....12 " (?)
Rifle Grenadiers...Rifle & Bayonet....12 grenades.

Indent

(b). Bayonet Men........Rifle & Bayonet.........2 bombs.
Grenadiers..........Knobkerrie.....M.S. 6 Stink Bombs.
                                   P   6 Mills   "

(c). As arranged.   C.

(d). I.t.l.? ?ce......Rifle & Bayonet.

(e). Bayonet Men........Rifle & Bayonet.
Lewis Gun Teams. As laid down, and 10 magazines.

AMMUNITION. (10).
Each rifleman will carry 50 rounds S.A.A. in bandolier, or 14 packets of P. S. Jacket.

COVER TO BAYONETS. (11).
Each man with fixed bayonet will have a sand-bag placed over his bayonet, and tied below muzzle of rifle to prevent glitter and fouling of rifle.
Sand-bags to be darkened.
Sand-bags to be cut in half lengthways, and resewn.

GAS HELMETS. (12).
To be carried pinned to the shirt in the "alert" position.

IDENTIFICATION. (13).
All identifications to be removed from all clothing Arms, and equipment.
Identification discs to be removed from the person and deposited at Battalion H. Q. All letters, documents, and papers to be taken off every man of Raiding Party.

TOKENS. (14).
Each man will be supplied with a small token shewing which party he belongs to, and will be numbered serially. These tokens will be collected immediately a man ~~returns~~ reenters our line, and will be the means of ascertaining that men have returned.

ASSEMBLY POINTS. (15).
Party A. 3 Camouflets. G.12.a.30.35. - 30.20.
  "   B. Front Line.   G.12.a.20.38. - 25.20.
  "   C. Top of C.T.   G.12.a.20.20.30
  "   D. " " "   G.12.a.20.20.
  "   E. I. S. Trench. G.12.a.10.38. - 18.15.

FLANK PROTECTION. (16).
In addition to Covering Party in No Man's Land, Lewis Gun and rifle fire from Front Lines.

PRISONERS. (17).
To be immediately sent back under escort to Bn. H. O. C. Left Coy. will have men detailed in readiness to take over prisoners, and escort them back. 2 men to each prisoner.

CASUALTIES. (18).
To return immediately to point of entry, help to be given by Covering Party only in case of severe wounds. Under no circumstances is the Raiding Party to be delayed by wounded until the completion of Raid when any help will be given to the removal of wounded, and dead, if any.

(4).

CASUALTIES. (18). (CONTD.)

Communications to Regtl. Aid Post will be opened from both JULY and AUGUST AVENUES.

COMMUNICATIONS. (19). Communication Trenches will be opened up between I.S. Line and Front Line as already detailed, so as to avoid crowding.
JULY and AUGUST AVENUES to be kept free of all traffic until completion of Raid. Support and I.S. Lines to be kept as free as possible.

COUNTER-ATTACKS. (20). In case enemy counter-attack, whole line stand-to, and carry-on as laid down in Defence Scheme. Reserve Coy. at BRITANNIA WORKS to be ready to move at moment's notice.

SIGNALS. (21). A special signal for recall will be notified later to Raiding Party.

REPORTS. (22). To Advanced H. Q. at T. M. Dug-out, top of AUGUST AVENUE, which will be in direct communication with Battalion H. Q. and Brigade H. Q.
If possible, a line will be run out to enemy's parapet.

ZERO HOUR. (23). To be notified later.

ARTILLERY PROGRAMME.
(24). Will be communicated separately.

STARTING POINTS (25). Parties to be in position as detailed in Order 15 -
& SUBSEQUENT   0.10.
MOVEMENTS OF
DIFFERENT PARTIES.

PARTY.	NATURE OF PARTY.	RENDEZVOUS.	MOVE TO.	TIME.
A	Bombing Squads. Rifle Squads Centre " Left "	S. CAMOUFLET) C. ") N. ")	Point of Entry. 0.12.a.62.40	Plus 0.15 0.20 enter plus 0.20
B	Clearing Party. Right Sqd. Centre " Left "	Front Line.	(a) S CAMOUFLET) C ") N ") (b) Point of Entry.	Plus 15. Plus 0.17. following immediately behind A.
C	Demolition Party.	Head of C.T. 0.12.a.20.30.	(a) O CAMOUFLET (b) Point of Entry.	Plus 17. Plus 19. following

(25). (CONTD.)   (5).

PARTY.	NATURE OF PARTY.	RENDEZVOUS.	MOVE TO.	TIME.
C	(CONTINUED)		(b) Point of Entry.	Plus 19 following immediately behind B Party.
D	Intelligence Party.	Head of C.T. G.12.a.20.20.	(a) S. CAMOUFLET.	Plus 0.17.
			(b) Point of Entry.	Plus 0.19. following immediately behind B Party.
E	Covering Party.		(a)	
	R. Squad.	I. S. Line.	By S. C.T. to front line, & thence to S. CAMOUFLET.	Plus 0.17.
	R.L.G.Team.			
			(b) Extend from S. CAMOUFLET across NO MAN'S LAND facing SOUTH. L.G.Team to take up position in S. CAMOUFLET.	Plus 0.20.
	L Squad.	I. S. Line.	(a) By N.C.T. to front line & thence to N. CAMOUFLET.	Plus 0.17.
	L.L.G.Team.			
			(b) Extend from N. CAMOUFLET across NO MAN'S LAND facing North. L.G.Team to take up position in S. CAMOUFLET.	Plus 0.20.

CHANNELS OF RETURN. (26). Direct between CLARENCE and CUTHBERT CRATERS to Front Line, and thence by JULY and AUGUST to BRITANNIA WORKS. Raiding Party to move steadily, and not loiter and talk.

DURATION OF RAID. (27). 25 minutes from Plus 0.20 to Plus 0.45.

WIRE-CUTTING. (28). Any wire found intact to be cut immediately, so as not to block forward movement.

PASSAGES THROUGH WIRE. (Overleaf).

PASSAGES THROUGH OUR WIRE. (29).	Three passages will be cut through our wire from the front line, one leading to each of the camouflets.
GUIDING TAPES. (30).	Guiding tapes will be laid in front of wire to camouflets. Two specially picked men will accompany Bombing Squads one on each flank, and will unroll Engineer Tracing Tapes out to the Point of Entry. Parties should keep within these lines to avoid losing direction.

Army Form C. 2118.

15 H. SHERWOOD FORESTERS WAR DIARY

NOVEMBER 1916.

INTELLIGENCE SUMMARY
(Volume 10)

(Erase heading not required.)

Instructions regarding War Diaries and Intelligence Summaries are contained in F. S. Regs., Part II. and the Staff Manual respectively. Title Pages will be prepared in manuscript.

Place	Date	Hour	Summary of Events and Information	Remarks and references to Appendices
ARRAS	1st		In trenches T.M. Sub sector. ARRAS.	
	2nd	4 PM	Bombardment of T.D. Sub sector by Enemy Heavy T.M's	
		9 AM	Heavy T.M. attack but medium T.M & Rifle Grenades were employed until 1 PM.	
		1 PM	The Heavy T.M. again commenced causing considerable damage to Front line & Support Trenches. At 4 PM.	
		4 PM	Our Artillery & T.M's in a combined operation effectively silenced the Enemy. — Situation Normal during the nights 2 – 3rd.	
	3rd	5 AM	Relieved by 14th GLOSTER REGT. and proceeded to RESERVE Billets in ARRAS & REDOUBT LINE.	1 + 41
	4th		Resting in RESERVE Billets	
	5th 6th 7th 8th		RESERVE BILLETS Furnishing Working Parties under R.E. supervision	10.Y. E.Y.

1/15th SHERWOOD FORESTERS WAR DIARY
INTELLIGENCE SUMMARY
NOVEMBER 1916

Army Form C. 2118.

Place	Date	Hour	Summary of Events and Information	Remarks and references to Appendices
ARRAS	9th		RESERVE BILLETS - Furnishing working Parties under R.E. supervision	
	10th			
	11th		Relieved 14th GLOSTER REGT in N II Sub sector	2 Bgd Order No 48
	12		In the trenches	
	13		" "	
	14		" "	
	15		" "	
	16		" "	
	17		" "	
	18		" "	
	19		" "	
	20		" "	
	21		" "	
	22		" "	
	23		" "	

Page III 15th SHERWOOD FORESTERS

Army Form C. 2118.

WAR DIARY
or
INTELLIGENCE SUMMARY

NOVEMBER, 1916

(Erase heading not required.)

Instructions regarding War Diaries and Intelligence Summaries are contained in F. S. Regs., Part II. and the Staff Manual respectively. Title Pages will be prepared in manuscript.

Place	Date	Hour	Summary of Events and Information	Remarks and references to Appendices
ARRAS	24		In the Trenches	
	25		Enemy Bombarded FRONT LINE & Immediate SUPPORT LINE throughout the day. Heavy & Medium T.M. Aerial Torpedoes & Rifle Grenades were used for this Bombardment	
	26	2 am.	Enemy made a Raid on our Trenches and succeeded in gaining entry into our trenches, but were promptly driven out. Enemy suffered very heavy casualties.	3 Report on Raid
	27		Enemy very Quiet. Relieved by 14th GLOSTER REGT and went over to BDE RESERVE BILLETS in ARRAS and REDOUBT LINE	4 O.P. Order No. 49
	28		Resting in RESERVE BILLETS.	
	29		RESERVE BILLETS furnished Working Parties under R.E. Supervision.	
	30			

1st December 1916

Nilson
Lieut Colonel
Comdg 15th S.Bn Nottsherwood Foresters

Operation Orders, by 9046
Lieut-Col. R.N.S. Gordon, Commdg.,
15th. (S) Battn. The Sherwood Foresters.

1-11-16.

1. **Relief.**   The Battalion will be relieved by the 14th. GLOSTERS on the 3rd. Inst.

"X" Coy. GLOSTERS will leave BOSKY REDOUBT and ST. NICHOLAS at 6-30 a.m. and move by JULY AVENUE to the relief of "X" Coy. SHERWOODS.

On relief "X" Coy. SHERWOODS will move three Platoons by MAY and one Platoon by AUGUST AVE. Coy. Headquarters and three Platoons will be stationed in ST. NICHOLAS and one Platoon in BOSKY REDOUBT.

As soon as "X" Coy. GLOSTERS pass BRITANNIA WORKS "W" Coy. SHERWOODS will side-step and relieve "W" Coy. GLOSTERS in FORESTEERS and NICHOLS REDOUBT.

"W" Coy. GLOSTERS will then move by JULY AVENUE, and proceed to relieve "Y" Coy. SHERWOODS. On relief "Y" Coy. SHERWOODS will return by AUGUST AVENUE to the Convent in ARRAS.

"Y" Coy. GLOSTERS will move at 7-30 a.m. and take over BRITANNIA WORKS.

"Z" Coy. GLOSTERS will move at 8 a.m. and proceed by JULY AVENUE, and relieve "Z" Coy. SHERWOODS, who will return by MAY AVE. direct to the Convent in ARRAS.

O.C. Lewis Guns will make arrangements with the Lewis Gun Officer GLOSTERS to relieve at the same time as Companies.

Headquarter Coy. will be relieved by Headquarter Coy. GLOSTER at 9-20 a.m.

2. **Stores etc.**   In connection with above, reliefs O.C. "W" and "X" Coys. will each detail an Officer and N.C.O. to take over Stores etc. from GLOSTERS. All taking over must be completed before the time due for the GLOSTERS to move.

O.C. "Z" Coy. will detail and Officer and N.C.O. to proceed to the Convent, and take over Billets and Stores from the GLOSTERS.

Particular care must be taken in handing and taking over Stores etc. Receipts must be obtained on A.F.W. 3405 for all Stores handed over

Issued to

1. "W" Coy.
2. "X" "
3. "Y" "
4. "Z" "
5. "H.Q."
6. War Diary
7. " "
8. Glosters.
9. L.G.O.
10. T.O.
11. File.

2nd. Lieut., A/Adjt.,
15th. (S) Battn. The Sherwood Foresters.

Copy No. ____

Operation Orders, by No 44
    Lieut-Col. R.M.S. Gordon, Commdg.,
    The 15th. (S) Battn. The Sherwood Foresters.

2-11-16.

1. **Relief.**   The Battalion will be relieved tomorrow by the 15th. GLOSTER REGT. The relief will be carried out per operation Orders issued yesterday.
All movements will be by Platoons at three minute intervals. Platoons moving into ARRAS will proceed in Single File and keep well under the cover of the houses, the centre of the road is on no account to be used.

2. **Guides.**   O.C. letter "X" Coy. will detail four guides, one per Platoon to meet letter "X" Coy. GLOSTERS, to lead in the relieving Platoons. These guides will be at Junction of JULY AVENUE and BRITANNIA WORKS at 6-25 a.m.
O.C. "Y" Coy. will detail four guides to meet "Y" Coy. GLOSTERS. Guides to be at Junction of JULY and BRITANNIA WORKS at 6-35 a.m..
O.C. "Z" Coy. will detail four guides to meet "Z" Coy. GLOSTERS at the W end of JULY AVENUE at 8 a.m.

3. **Trench Stores.**   All Trench and area Stores will be correctly inventoried on A.F.W. 3405, and handed over to incoming unit. Great care must be taken in checking stores etc. before handing over. Signature of Officer taking over will be obtained on A.F.W. 3405. One signed copy of A.F.W.3405 will be handed in to Orderly Room by 12 noon 3rd. inst.

4. **Sanitation etc.**   All trenches, dug-outs, saps etc. will be left scrupulously clean. No articles of clothing, tins, food, etc., lying about. Latrines to be emptied and well disinfected.

5. **Bombs, S.A.A. etc.**   Loose S.A.A. and Bombs must not be left lying about in the trenches. All bombs will be thoroughly cleaned and oiled previous to being handed over.

6. **Transport.**   Orderly Room Boxes, Officers' Kit and mess Boxes of H.Q. "Y" and "Z" Coy. will be dumped at the Candle Factory by 7-45 p.m. tonight 2nd. inst. The cook Sgt. will arrange to dump all the Cooking Utensils of H.Q. "Y" and "Z" Coys. at the same time and place. The Stores etc. for the Convent and HOTEL de l' UNIVERS will be stacked separately under the supervision of the R.S.M.
One N.C.O. or man per Company will be detailed to accompany these Stores to ARRAS. The cooks of H.Q., "Y" and "Z" Coy. will also proceed with these stores.
The receptacles used for carrying the soup to the line tonight must be returned to the Candle Factory immediately the soup has been issued.

7. **Breakfasts.**   Breakfasts will be served under Company arrangements on completion of relief.

8. **Billets.**   Company Quarter-Master Sgts. of "Y" and "Z" Coys. will be at the Convent not later than 6-30 a.m. to take over Billets. Sgt. Canner will take over Billets at HOTEL de l'UNIVERS for Headquarter Coy.

9. **Reports.**   O.C.Coys. will report by runner to the Adjutant when relief is complete.

10. Battn. H.Q.   Orderly Room will close at 9-30 a.m. and open at
                    HOTEL de l'UNIVERS at 10-30 a.m.

   Issued to -

   1.   "W" Coy.
   2.   "X" "
   3.   "Y" "
   4.   "Z" "
   5.   "H.Q."
   6.   War Diary.
   7.   "   "
   8.   106th. Bde.
   9.   L.G.O.
   10.   T.O.
   11.   File.
   12.   Glosters.

                                    signature Johnson
                                                2nd. Lieut., A/Adjt.
             15th. (S) Battn. The Sherwood Foresters.

SECRET.

Copy. No. 6

Operation Orders, No.48,
By Lieut-Col. J.F. Clyne.
Commdg. 15th. (Service) Battn. The Sherwood Foresters.
9-11-16.

1. **Relief.** The Battalion will relieve the 14th. GLOSTER REGIMENT in J.2.sub-sector on 11th. inst.
Ltr. "Z" Coy. will leave the CONVENT at 6-30 a.m. and proceed via JULY AVENUE to relieve Ltr. "X" Coy. GLOSTERS in front line J.2. 89-92.
Ltr. "Y" Coy starting from CONVENT at 6-45 a.m. will proceed via JULY AVENUE and relieve "Y" Coy.GLOSTERS in J.2.93-95.
Ltr. "W" Coy. will leave the Redoubt Line at 7-30 a.m via JULY AV. and relieve "Z" Coy. GLOSTERS in SUPPORT LINE.
Ltr. "X" Coy. less one Platoon in BOSKY will leave ST NICHOLAS at 8 a.m. and take over BRITANNIA WORKS. The Platoon in BOSKY will rejoin their Coy. in BRITANNIA when relieved.
Lewis Gun Teams will relieve under orders of Lewis Gun Officer.
H.Q. Coy. will move at 8-30 a.m. and relieve H.Q. Coy. GLOSTERS.

2. **Advance Party.** O.C. Coys. will arrange to send an advance party of One Officer and One N.C.O. per Coy to take over Trench Stores etc.
The taking over must be done very carefully and must be completed before the arrival of the incoming Coy. One Copy of A.F.W,3405, will be rendered to Orderly Room not later than 6 p.m. 11th.inst.

3. **Formation.** Coys. will move by platoons in single file at three minute intervals between platoons. Troops moving through ARRAS must keep well in against the houses.
There must be no delay in the move from the CONVENT or the relief will be hindered.

4. **Breakfast.** Breakfast will be served under Coy. arrangements before the Relief.

5. **Rations.** The Quarter-Master will arrange for the meat and vegetable ration of the Battalion taken direct to the CANDLE FACTORY on the night of the 10th.inst.

6. **Kits etc.** O.C. "Y" and "Z" Coys. will arrange to keep back four dixies each for breakfast, these will be carried to trenches on relief. The remainder of dixies and cooking utensils not required for breakfast (under charge of one cook per Coy.) will be stacked at the Guard Room, at HOTEL de L' UNIVERS, by 6 p.m. on the 10th.inst.

7. **Spare Kit,** All officers surplus Kit, Blankets, of Coys etc. will be handed
Blankets etc. over to SGt. Gwinnett, at the Store Room CONVENT not later than 5-30 a.m. 11th.inst. A receipt must be obtained for all stores handed over. (Blankets will be rolled tightly in bundles of 10).

8. **Cleanliness.** All billets, cook-houses, Redoubts etc must be left scrupulously clean, latrines will be emptied and disinfected.

9. **Reports.** O.C.Coys. will report by Runner immediately the Relief is complete.

10. **Battn.H.Q.** Orderly Room will close at HOTEL de L'UNIVERS at 8 a.m. and open at Battalion H.Q. Trenches at 10 a.m.

Issued to
1 O.C."W" Coy.   6. War Diary.   11. L.G.O.
2. "   "X" "   7. "   "   12. T.O. &
3. "   "Y" "   8. Glosters.   Q.M.
4. "   "Z" "   9. File.
5. "   H.Q.   10. Brigade.

2nd. Lieut.
A/Adjutant.
15th. (S) Bn. Sherwood Foresters.

To Headquarters,

    105th. (Infantry) Brigade.

Report on Operations Morning 26th. Nov. 1916.

At 2-30 a.m. on the morning of the 26th. Nov. 1916 an attempt to raid our Trenches in the vicinity of J.11. 92 and 93 tookplace. The enemy opened fire with heavy and light T.M's. and about 2-22 a.m. exploded a Camuoflet well out in "No-Man's-Land" between CUTHBERT and CLAUDE Craters. Owing to the continuous bombardment of the preceding 48 hours our front Line Trenchesin the vicinity of J.11.93 and 92 resembled "No-Man's-Land, no bays being left and Blocks had been established on both sides of the broken in line and Sentry groups covering the part were posted as protective measures in the immediate support line. The O.C. Left Coy, Capt. Brice, on perceiving the Camuoflet go up, and suspecting an attempt at a raid with a view to the fact that a simultaneous barrage had been established between our Support and Front Line Trenches called on the Artillery for the S.O.S. Barrage.

The O.C. right Coy. Lieut. Boot, which were also being barraged did the same. Our Artillery immediately responded, and put up an effective barrage across our front within 30 seconds. In the meantime a party of the enemy entered our broken-in trenches at the top of JULY AVENUE, and attempted to seize Pte. Masnip who had just been wounded, and as he had a broken leg and was unable to move they shot him whilst on the ground. The enemy's party then turned South towards our right and ran into the block established there where a Bombing Contest took place. At this point it appears that two Parties of theenemy met as the sentry groups were engaged with the enemy on their left flank, and also with several Huns who were trying to get through from the front line.

As the Sentry group was outnumbered, and outdistanced in bombing, they retired slowly, and fell back on the next sentry group, and on being reinforced by a fresh party under 2nd. Lt. HEMSTOCK they worked their way back, and drove off the enemy. During this period a Hun apparently separated from his Party and went off to his right where he was shot at but missed crossing the Immediate Support Line, but was noticed and brought down in front of the support line and taken prisoner badly wounded, after this no further attempt was made of by the enemy. The following dispositions were made during the raid.
Immediately it was observed something unusual was happening, a platoon from the Company in Support was rushed up to the firing line with instructions to establish a Bombing block behind the broken-in part of July Avenue, whilst the remainder reinforced the front line through the immediate support.
On receipt of the news at Battn. H.Q. the Coy. in Reserve were immediately sent up to the Support Line with orders to report to Major Grellin and to replace them. All spare men i.e. Cooks, Storemen and H.Q. servants and spare signallers were collected in BRITANNIA WORKS, and STRAGGLERS POSTS placed on Avenues pending arrival Arrival of the Platoons from the Reserve Battn. All arrangements worked smoothly and Brigade H.Q. were kept fully informed of the situation. The night was particularly dark with squalls of rain, and all men in the front and Support Line were busily engaged in opening up communications and extricating buried men resulting from the previous 48 hours continuous bombardment. It was anticipated that a raid might occur and orders had been issued for all Coys.

to be in a position to move immediately if necessary.

Names of those deserving recognition will be forwarded separately.

26-11-16.   A. E. Johnson
                                              Lieut-Colonel,
              Commdg., 15th. (S) Battn. The Sherwood Foresters.

Operation
Orders, No 49
by Lieut-Col. E.H.E. Gordon,
Commdg. 15th (S) Bn. The Sherwood Foresters.

28-11-16.

1. **Relief.** The Battalion will be relieved to-morrow by the 14th. Glosters.

   Ltr. "P" Coy Sherwoods will be relieved by "P" Coy. Glosters from ARRAS at 6-30 a.m. via AUGUST AVENUE. starting
   Ltr. "P" Coy. on relief will move via AUGUST AV. to Redoubt Line.

   Ltr. "W" Coy SHERWOODS will be relieved by Ltr. "W" Coy. GLOSTERS holding ST NICHOLAS and ROSNY REDOUBT at 6-30 a.m. via JULY AVENUE.
   "W" Coy. on relief will move to ARRAS via JULY AVENUE.

   Ltr. "Z" Coy. SHERWOODS will be relieved by Ltr. "Z" Coy. GLOSTERS leaving ARRAS at 7-30 a.m. moving via JULY AVENUE.
   Ltr. "Z" Coy on relief will move to ST NICHOLAS and ROSNY REDOUBT via JULY AVENUE.

   Ltr. "X" Coy. SHERWOODS will be relieved by Ltr. "X" Coy. GLOSTERS at 7-45 a.m.
   Ltr. "X" Coy. on relief will move to ARRAS via AUGUST AVENUE.

2. **Breakfasts.** Breakfasts will be served on completion of relief.

3. **Trench Stores.** All trench and area stores will be correctly inventoried on A.F.B.3403, and handed over to the incoming unit. Great care must be taken in checking stores etc. before handing over. Signature of Officer taking over will be obtained on A.F.B.3403. One signed copy of A.F.B. 3403 will be handed in to the Orderly Room by 12 noon 27th.inst.

4. **Sanitation.etc.** All trenches, dug-outs, saps etc, will be left scrupulously clean. No articles of clothing, tins, food etc. lying about. Latrines to be emptied and well disinfected.

5. **Bombs.S.A.A.** Loose S.A.A. and bombs must not be left lying about in the
   etc.   trenches.   All bombs will be thoroughly cleaned and oiled previous to being handed over.

6. **Transport.** Orderly Room boxes, Officers Kits and Mess Boxes of H.Q."W" and "Z" Coys. will be dumped at the Candle Factory by 7 p.m. to-night 26th.inst.. The Cook Sergeant will arrange to dump all the Cooking Utensils of H.Q. "W" & "Z" Coy at the same time and place. The Stores etc. for the CONVENT and HOTEL D'UNIVERS will be stacked seperately under the supervision of the R.S.M.
   One N.C.O. or man per Coy. will be detailed to accompany these stores to ARRAS. The cooks of H.Q. "W" &"Z" Coys. will also proceed with these stores.
   The receptacles used for carrying the soup to the line to-night must be returned to the CANDLE FACTORY as soon as the soup has been issued

7. **Billets.** Company Quarter Master Sergeants of "P" and "X" Coys will be at the Convent not later than 6-30 a.m to take over Billets. Sgt. Casner will take over Billets at HOTEL D'UNIVERS for H.Q.Coy.

8. **Reports.** O.C.Coys will report by runner to the Adjutant when relief is complete.

9. **Battn.H.Q.** Orderly Room will close at 9-30 a.m. and open at HOTEL D'UNIVERS at 10-30 a.m.

Contd.

Issued at 5-30p.m.

Copies to:-

1. "W" Coy.
2. "X" "
3. "Y" "
4. "Z" "
5. H.Q.
6. War Diary.
7. "   "
8. Brigade(105th)
9. T.O.
10. Glosters.

[signature]
                2nd.Lieut. A/Adjutant.
15th.(Service) Battn. The Sherwood Foresters.

15th Bn Sherwood Foresters

Army Form C. 2118

WAR DIARY
or
INTELLIGENCE SUMMARY
(Erase heading not required.)

Vol II

Instructions regarding War Diaries and Intelligence Summaries are contained in F.S. Regs., Part II. and the Staff Manual respectively. Title Pages will be prepared in manuscript.

Place	Date	Hour	Summary of Events and Information	Remarks and references to Appendices
ARRAS	1916 Dec 1 "2 "3		Bde Reserve billets. Furnishing working parties for R.E.	
	"4		Relieved by 4th South African Infantry & moved to billets at DAINVILLE	
			Moved by march route to BEAUFORT for rest & training	
BEAU-FORT	"5 "6 "7 "8		Resting & refitting	
"	9 to 28		Training & musketry	
Dainville	28		Battn moved by march route to Dainville	
"	29 to 31		Furnishing working parties for R.E.	

11.4.

A W Farrand Lt Col
Comdg 15 Sherwood Foresters

1875 Wt. W593/826 1,000,000 4/15 J.B.C. & A. A.D.S.S./Forms/C. 2118.

WAR DIARY
or
INTELLIGENCE SUMMARY

Army Form C. 2118

Vol 12

15/SHERWOOD FORESTERS

JANUARY 1917

12.4

Place	Date	Hour	Summary of Events and Information	Remarks and references to Appendices
DAINVILLE	Jany 1st to 31st		Furnishing working parties for R.E. Training of new drafts for Battalion at Bureville	

H Morton Smith Major
Comdg 15th Bn Sherwood Foresters

9/2/17

Army Form C. 2118.

WAR DIARY
or
INTELLIGENCE SUMMARY

15th (S) Brentwood Fusiliers

FEBRUARY

Vol 13

(Erase heading not required.)

Place	Date	Hour	Summary of Events and Information	Remarks and references to Appendices
MONTS-en-TERNOIS	1917 1st to 5th		Battalion Rest & Training.	
	6th		Moved by march Route to VILLIERS L'HOPITAL	
	7th		Moved by march route to CANDAS	
	8th		Moved by march route to St VAST-en-CHAUSSE	
St VAST-en-CHAUSSE	9th to 17th		Re-organization of Coys & Platoon & beg training	
	18th		March to FLESSELLES returned to [struck] via ROELCAVE then march route to WIENCOURT. Billeted at WIENCOURT nights of 18th & 19th.	
	19th		Coy & Coy Officers & Coy Comdrs reconnoitred line at CHILLY preparatory to taking 4th from French.	
	20th		Moved by march route via CAIX to Butments at CAMP des BALLONS	
CAMP des BALLONS	21st	3pm	Bn proceeded to take over line from French in the CHILLY sector. The DEUX CIMITIERES communication trench was entered at 4.30 pm. was found almost impassable owing to mud and greatly delayed the taking over.	

Army Form C. 2118.

WAR DIARY
or
INTELLIGENCE SUMMARY
(Erase heading not required.)

Place	Date	Hour	Summary of Events and Information	Remarks and references to Appendices
	24th		of From 1 line trenches. The relief was not completed until 11.30am on 22nd inst. The line was held by X Coy on right, Y Coy on left with Z Coy in support & W Coy in reserve. Trenches were found to be in a waterlogged condition, with no trace of any description & communication between platoon & Coy Headquarters was impossible except from the top.	
	25th to 28		Troops of the large Trench into which in TRANCHEE DE PARIS the line being taken over by the flank battalions extending their front. Clearing of communication trenches to join the line system	

W. Ashe Persons
Craig's
Major
Forester

Army Form C. 2118.

WAR DIARY
or
INTELLIGENCE SUMMARY

(Erase heading not required.)

March 1917

15 Notts Derby Rgt Vol 14

Place	Date	Hour	Summary of Events and Information	Remarks and references to Appendices
HILLY	1st. 2nd. 3rd.		Battalion relieved 14th.GLOSTERS in front line trenches CHILLY sub-sector. In Trenches.	
VRELY	4th.		Relieved by 17th.LANCS. FUSILIERS and proceeded to billets at VRELY.	
CAMP des BALLONS.	5th. 6th. to 12th.		Marched to CAMP des BALLONS. In Divisional Reserve. Training and refitting.	
	13th.10a.m		Marched to ROSIERES. Battalion in Brigade Reserve and billetted in ROSIERES.	
ROSIERES	14th. to 17th.		Furnishing working parties,clearing Comm.Trenches & carrying parties for Battalions in front line.	
	17th.7p.m. to 17th.11p.m		Commencement of Enemy retirement. Battalion moved to TRANCHEE de PARIS and took over support line and Battalion Hd.Qtrs. of 14th.GLOSTER REGT. who had occupied German front line.	
	18th. 9a.m. 18th. 2p.m.		Battalion ordered to advance and occupy German front and support lines. Orders issued to continue advance and occupy enemy trench VIEUX BOCHE from BERSAUCORT to a point N.E. of HYMCOURT le PETIT.	
CHAULNES	19th.3p.m. 20th. 21st.		Battalion withdrawn and ordered to march to VERMANDOVILLERS for salvage work. In dug-outs in the vicinity of VERMANDOVILLERS resting. Marched at daybreak to ROSIERES. Battalion detailed for work on railway line ROSIERES - CHAULNES on completion of days work. W & X Coys. moved to billets at PUZEAUX. Y & Z Coys.billetted in TRANCHEE de PARIS. Battalion H.Qtrs. in ROSIERES.	
PUZEAUX	22nd. 23rd. to 27th.		Work on railway 8a.m. to 4p.m. Battalion H.Q.,Y & Z Coys. moved into billets at PUZEAUX. Work on CHAULNES - NESLE railway.	
MORLEMONT	28th. 29th. to 31st.		Work on railway. Battalion moved to billets at MORLEMONT on completion of days work. Work on CHAULNES - NESLE railway.	

Army Form C. 2118.

WAR DIARY
INTELLIGENCE SUMMARY

(Erase heading not required.)   15th. (S) Bn. Sherwood Foresters.

Instructions regarding War Diaries and Intelligence Summaries are contained in F.S. Regs., Part II. and the Staff Manual respectively. Title Pages will be prepared in manuscript.

Place	Date	Hour	Summary of Events and Information	Remarks and references to Appendices
	March			
PARADIS ROBECQ.	1st. to 7th.	—	Battalion marched from Paradis to Robecq. In Billets.	
LE TOURET	7th.		Battalion marched to LE TOURET and was attached to 10th. SOUTH WALES BORDERERS 38th. Division for instruction in the Trenches. Right Half Battalion proceeded to Trenches in the evening and were relieved on the 10th. by the Left Half Battalion, who remained in until morning of the 14th. Total Casualties - 3 Men wounded.	
MERVILLE	14th. to 18th.		Battalion marched to Merville on 14th. and remained in Billets until 18th.	
PARADIS,	19th.		Battalion marched to fresh Billets at PARADIS (Lestrem) and remained there until 25th.	
ESTAIRES.	25th. 26th.		Battalion march to ESTAIRES and billeted for the day. Battalion moved up to Trenches in the FAUQUISSART SECTION and relieved the 2nd. Bn. Scottish Rifles in the Right Sub-Section.(Operation Orders Appendix 1) Relief was carriedc out without incident by 9-40 p.m.	Operation Orders Appendix 1.
TRENCHES.	27th. 28th. 29th. 30th.		Very quiet generally . Nothing of importance occurred. Battalion was relieved by 9-30 p.m. by the 16th. (S) Bn. Cheshire Regiment and marched to LAVENTIE. Total Casualties - 2 men wounded. 2nd. Lieut. S.E. Bridgwater killed. During the occupation of the right Sub-Section the 10th. (S) Bn. Worcester Regt. were on our right, and the 15th. (S) Bn. Cheshire Regiment were on our Left.	Operation Orders Appendix 2.
LAVENTIE	31st.		In Billets.	

2449 Wt. W14957/Mgo 750,000 1/16 J.B.C. & A. Forms/C.2118/12.

April 1917 — 15th Bn Sherwood Foresters

Army Form C. 2118.

WAR DIARY
or
INTELLIGENCE SUMMARY

(Erase heading not required.)

Instructions regarding War Diaries and Intelligence Summaries are contained in F.S. Regs., Part II. and the Staff Manual respectively. Title Pages will be prepared in manuscript.

Place	Date	Hour	Summary of Events and Information	Remarks and references to Appendices
MORLEMONT	1st.		Work on NESLE – HAM Railway.	
–do–	2nd.		Work on NESLE – HAM Railway. Battalion moved to Billets at CANIZY at 3 p.m.	
CANIZY	3rd to 11th.		Work on NESLE – HAM Railway. Company and Battalion Training on 6th. and 19th. inst.	
–do–	12th.		Battalion moved by March Route to TERTRY.	
TERTRY	13th to 15th		In Divisional Reserve. Working parties furnished on Road repair.	
	16th		Brigade moved into Line in relief of 104th.Bde. Battalion relieved 17th.Lancs.Fus. in support to right Battn. in Line and occupied shelters in wood at MON de GARDE with 3 Coys. in copses and sunken Road M.32.b & d.	
	17th to 19th.		Digging a defensive line from Southern End of FRESNOY le PETIT Eastwards.	
	21st	9–30pm	Battalion moved into outpost Line in relief of 14th.GLOSTER REGT. "X" & "Y" Coy. furnishing outposts North of GRICOURT. "W" & "Z" Coys. in support in vicinity of FRESNOY le PETIT. Relief completed without unusual incident. Battalion Head Quarters established at the Quarry M.27.c.1.5.	
	22nd		No incidents by day. Reconnoitring Patrols sent out by night in the direction of MONIDEE. Quiet by day. In conjunction with 16th.CHESHIRE REGT on our left 2 small outposts were established about M.23.a.9.7. by Ltr."M" Coy.	
	23rd			
MON de GARDE	24th		Quiet. Patrolling by night. 2 small outposts established South of LES TROIS SAUVAGE about M.24.c.3.6. No opposition met with.	
	25th		No unusual incident.	
	26th		Relieved by 14th.GLOSTER REGT. and occupied bivouacs as previously held in the support Line.	
	27th to 30th		Work on defensive line. Relieved by 19th. D.L.I. at 11 p.m. 30th. and moved to billets at TERTRY.	

L.A.W. Cellin Major for Lt Col
Comdg 15 Bn Sherwood Foresters

Army Form C. 2118.

15th Sherwood

WAR DIARY
or
INTELLIGENCE SUMMARY

(Erase heading not required.)

MAY 16

Place	Date	Hour	Summary of Events and Information	Remarks and references to Appendices
TERTRY	1st to 7th. 8th.	1917	Battalion in Divisional Reserve and carrying out training.	
QUARRY	8th.		Relieved 19th. D.C.L.I. in Outpost line N of GRICOURT. Z Coy. left outpost positions. W Coy. occupying right and The relief was completed without incident. In Support X Coy. In reserve Y Coy.	
GRICOURT	9th.		An attack was carried out at 9.40 p.m. by 2 Platoons of W. Coy and 2 Platoons of X Coy. with the object of forming the enemy out of LES TROIS SAUVAGE and establish posts at the X roads M.23.d.7.8. East of Les trois Sauvage, and near the X roads at M.23.d.7.8. The posts were established with the exception of M.23.d.7.8. where strong opposition was met with but a post was consolidated about 150 yards S.W. of this point.	
—	10th.		New posts established were strengthened during the night and wiring commenced along whole front of outpost position.	
—	11th.		No unusual incidents by day or night. Wiring and strengthening posts.	
—	12th.		Battalion relieved by 14th. Glosters Regt. and moved into support position.	
MONT de GARDE	13th & 14th.		Furnishing working and covering parties for outpost battalion.	
—	15th.		At 12 M.M. W and X Coys. Carried out a raid on LES TROIS SAUVAGE with the object of destroying strong points and cellars and capturing prisoners. 2 Platoons of W. and 2 Platoons of X Coy. formed the attacking party. Forming up at the X roads at M.23.a.8.9. and moving in a South Easterly direction to the Enos side of the farm buildings. The remaining Platoons of W. and X Coys. were in Support near the X roads at M.23.a.8.9. The attacking Coys. made Good progress until our artillery fire was met with

154

WAR DIARY or INTELLIGENCE SUMMARY

Army Form C. 2118.

(Erase heading not required.)

Instructions regarding War Diaries and Intelligence Summaries are contained in F. S. Regs., Part II. and the Staff Manual respectively. Title Pages will be prepared in manuscript.

Place	Date	Hour	Summary of Events and Information	Remarks and references to Appendices
QUARRY	14th		about 50 yards east of the farm buildings. The wire was not passable and after 3 determined attempts had been made under increasing hostile rifle fire to cut saps through the wire, the attempting Coy was withdrawn having suffered 40 casualties.	
	19th		Battalion relieved 1st R. Glos. Regt. in outpost line, C Coy advancing to right, and D Coy to left outpost positions, with B Coy in support and 2 Coys. in reserve.	
	19th		Battalion relieved by the 1st Battn. 72nd Regt. 5th French Division. The relief was effected by 12 men outpost casualties double lines. Skeleton of Battalion designated as Quarry during to relief, on relief Coys moved independently to Camp at TERTRY.	
TERTRY	19th/6 22nd		} Resting and refitting.	
	23rd	3.6am	Battalion marched to PERONNE arriving at 7am.	
PERONNE	24th	—	Resting.	
	25th	6.30pm	Marched to camp at TEMPLEUX la FOSSE.	
TEMPLEUX la FOSSE	26th/6 31st		} Coy. and Battalion training. On 28th 400 of the battalion were invited by the 1st Battalion encamped at AIZECOURT le HAUT.	

W. A. W. Allin
Major Comm.
1st Bn. the Sherwood [Foresters]

2449 Wt. W14957/M90 750,000 1/16 J.B.C. & A. Forms/C.2118/12.

G.104.

To

105th. Inf. Bde.

    Forwarded herewith Report on Operations 9/10th. May.

    The Preliminary Report gave all times and orders.

    This deals with the actual occurrences, and has been compiled from Reports and statements of participators.

    Battalion Orders attached to Report.

                                    (Sd.) R.H.S.GORDON, Lt.-Col.,
                         Condg. 15th. SHERWOOD FORESTERS.

10-5-1917.

SECRET.   COPY NO.

            BATTALION   ORDERS   No. 58.

PURITY.   9-8-18

1. INFORMATION.

   Enemy is known to be in occupation of LES TROIS SAUVAGES on WEST
   side of road, and with wire on NOTH-WEST and SOUTH sides. In
   addition, he is suspected to occupy Posts in X-roads in M.23.a.9.7.
   and in the cutting in the road at M.23.b.3.5. He also holds an
   escarpement running WEST to EAST, starting from M.23.b.5.7.

2. INTENTION.

   To occupy PONTRUET - LES TROIS SAUVAGES Road from X-roads M.23.a.9.7.
   to about M.23.d.7.8., posts being established in the best possible
   positions, on, or about, the following points :-

   EAST of X-roads M.23.a.9.7.

   In the CUTTING M.23.b.3.5.

   In, or EAST of, LES TROIS SAUVAGES buildings.

   EAST of X-roads at M.23.d.7.8.

   M.29.b.2.9.

3. OPERATIONS.

   The attack will be carried out as under -

   2 Platoons of Lr. "X" Coy. each under an Officer, will furnish the
   covering and assaulting troops. The leading Platoon (Covering) will
   rendezvous in the Cutting on Road at M.23.a.7.6., and, at Zero, will
   immediately push forward, past X-roads at M.23.a.9.7., and will
   throw out a covering party running from M.23.b.2.1. to Escarpement
   at M.23.b.5.7. to EAST of LES TROIS SAUVAGES at M.23.b.8.3.
   1 Lewis Gun will accompany this party. The Assaulting Platoon
   will assemble on the Road about 50 yards behind the covering platoon,
   and will advance directly into the PONTRUET - LES TROIS SAUVAGES Road
   and assault the building at LES TROIS SAUVAGES.

   O. C., "W" Coy. will detail strong fighting patrols to occupy at
   zero hour the positions at M.23.d.7.8., and M.29.b.2.9. to act as
   flank protection to "X" Company.

4. CONSOLIDATION.

   Immediately the enemy's position is occupied the assaulting platoon
   will select the points as before detailed to be consolidated.
   O. C., "Z" Coy. will detail working party of 15 men for each point,
   accompanied by Lr. "X" Coy. to bring up tools, wire, etc. and assist
   in consolidating positions.
   O. C., "W" Coy. will detail similar parties for his two positions.
   The remainder of "W" and "X" Companies will stand-to, and be prepare
X. to give whatever support is required.

5. ARTILLERY.

   The 6" Howitzers will make a deliberate bombardment until dusk of
   the buildings and trenches round LES TROIS SAUVAGES. On their
   ceasing, 18pdrs. and Howitzers will constantly fire shrapnel on the
   buildings, also on the X-roads at M.23.a.9.7., the roads between th

5. **ARTILLERY. (CONTD.)**
X-roads and LES TROIS SAUVAGES, and the Escarpement at M.23.b.8.
until Zero.
Batteries will then be trained on enemy's trenches running
North and South through M.24.a. & C., and will be prepared to
put up a barrage on a special signal being fired.

6. **MACHINE GUNS.**
Vickers (105th. M. G. COY.) will carry out indirect fire on
enemy trench system during the whole night.

7. **AID POST.**
An Advanced Post will be established on SUNKEN ROAD about
M.23.a.7.6.

8. **ADVANCED BATTALION H. Q.**
Will be established at "Z" Coy. Headquarters.

9. **COMMUNICATION.**
O.C., "Z" Company will attach two runners to "X" Company's
Assaulting Platoon, to bring back any reports.

10. **REPORTS.**
All reports will be sent to Advanced Battalion H.Q.

11. **ZERO.**
Zero Hour will be 9.45p.m.

12. **DRESS.**
Fighting Order, less Haversacks.

13. **SPECIAL SIGNAL.**
If Artillery barrage is required, a special rockets bursting
into four red stars will be sent up by "X" Company.

14. **DETAILS.**
O. C., "Z" Company will detail a Platoon to re-occupy its
position in second line of Bombing Trenches as taken over from
D. L. I. before withdrawal.
On consolidation being completed, "Z" Company will take over
from "X" Company, and will man the Posts by day, and will
include the Post at M.23.d.8.7. before "X" Company withdraws
its Post at M.23.d.7.8.
On being recalled "X" Company's Platoons will move back through
"Z" Company. "Z" Company will detail a consolidating and
holding party to occupy X-roads at M.23.a.9.7.

(Sd.) H.MORTON, Lt. & Adjt.,
PURITY.

9-5-1917.

REPORT ON OPERATIONS ON LES TROIS SAUVAGES

On NIGHT of 9th./10th. MAY, 1917.

Map References :- Sq. M. Sheet 62B.S.W., Scale 1/10,000.

In accordance with instructions as detailed in 105th. BDE. OPERATION ORDER No. 106, dated 9-5-1917, orders were issued to the Battalion as detailed in Battalion Orders No. 55 (copy attached). The Operations resolved into two separate actions, as detailed herewith. Viz :- The assault on the FARM from the NORTH-WEST, and, second, the establishing of Posts SOUTH-WEST of the FARM. For the purpose of this narrative the two accounts are given separately.

(1). In accordance with Battalion Orders the Covering and Assaulting Platoons with their consolidation parties were in position at 9.40p.m. At zero time (9.45p.m.) the Covering Party advanced and occupied the small trench at the X-roads in M.23.a.9.7., and found it unoccupied. It then pushed forward and, leaving its L. G. Section at the forked roads at M.17.d.2.1., and the remaining three Sections at M.23.b.6.7., M.23.b.5.6., and M.23.b.7.4., which it occupied without being observed. Shortly after, the concolidation party, with its L. G. Crew having occupied the X-roads at M.23.a.9.7., the L. G. of the Covering Party was moved to a position to enfilade the bank at M.23.b.9.7., and the remaining Sections moved further South with the Right resting about M.23.b.7.4. Heavy rifle and machine gun fire was opened on the right, and, at the same time, separate parties of the enemy were seen making their way from the Bosche line at M.24.a.Central, and M.24.b.3.8. Two parties of the enemy were seen, one each approaching on either side of the bank at M.23.b.5.7. L. G. fire and Rifle fire was opened on these parties and the Rifle Grenadiers Section opened on the enemy's trench. The two parties on the bank were driven off. Casualties were inflicted, and groans were heard, the party issuing from M.24.b.3.8. disappeared down the slope and was lost to view. During this time a M. G. opened on them from approximately M.24.a.4.6. which caused two casualties to the L. G. Team. Information was sent back and more L. G. ammunition and men to replace the casualties were sent up, and arrived. During the whole of this time, heavy firing and fighting was going on in the vicinity of the FARM. The party remained out till orders were issued by the Company Commander that owing to the failure of the assaulting party to gain entrance into the FARM they were to gradually withdraw to their assembly position, and cover the retirement. This was done without loss. The night was very bright and the lightness increased very much about 12.30 a.m. on the moon rising and throwing everything into relief.

The Assaulting Party moved off in rear of the Covering Party, and on striking the road about M.23.b.1.7. changed direction and, facing the FARM, advanced with Bombers on the Right and L. G. on Left, and managed to get within 40 yards of the FARM without incident. Here they were challenged three times, but giving no reply rushed forward, but were pulled up by a strong belt of wire on iron screw pickets about 3 yards in depth, and thick. Heavy rifle fire, and bombs were thrown at them, and at the same time, a Machine Gun opened down the road towards the X-roads at M.23.a.9.7., firing approximately from M.23.b.5.0. The party opened rapid fire, threw bombs, and fired rifle grenades into the buildings, but were unable to cut their way through the wire owing to the heavy fire directed on them from the ruined buildings. During this time a heavy box barrage had been placed behind them and to the WEST by the Old German Practice Trenches, and consisted of 5.9's. from the direction of BELLENGLISE, and Trench Mortars, apparently firing from the open behind the new German trenches about M.24.a. The Platoon Commander, observing

(2).

observing/
a slackening fire on our side, ascertained that he had suffered a loss of a third of his men, and being unable to cut his way through, sent back word, and ammunition running short, gradually withdrew his men, especially as the lightness had increased, owing to the rising of the moon, notifying his Covering Party. He also brought in all wounded with the exception of one man who was very badly wounded, and personally made three separate attempts, till he, himself, was wounded in the head.

(2). The establishing of Posts SOUTH-WEST of the FARM.

The Left Party, whose orders were to establish a post as near to the X-roads as possible at M.23.d.7.8. on arrival at the X-roads were heavily fired on from rifles and machine guns. The party immediately answered the fire, and then came under a heavy fire from T.M's. from approximately EAST. After holding out for half-an-hour, the party having been reinforced, attempted again to reach its objective, but were unable to do so; the enemy at the same time attempting to turn its Right Flank, as rifle fire was suddenly opened on them from that direction. The party, thereupon withdrew back a short distance, and commenced digging in, but were unable to carry on this work, owing to heavy fire, and after remaining out till 2a.m. withdrew as ammunition had commenced to run out. In the meantime, other parties started Posts at M.29.b.2.9. and M.23.d.4.4., but work was continually interrupted by shelling. Further work will be done this night.
The Left Company occupying the trenches and Posts EAST of GRICOURT, after providing the consolidating parties, worked its remaining men into the old German trenches.
Owing to the defensive line being practically unheld I brought up the remaining two Platoons of the Support Company from the BROWN LINE and they occupied the trenches just EAST of GRICOURT. The Reserve Company at Headquarters were used for Carrying Parties; for ammunition; bombs; rations, and water, which had to be got up before daylight, and were, after arrival, placed at disposal of the O. C., RIGHT COY.
The following were noted :-
1. Enemy send up light breaking into golden rain, on which barrage was placed WEST of FARM.
2. Two green lights, each breaking into two red stars, were sent up almost instantaneously, and appeared to be taken as the special signal arranged by us for Artillery support, which was a light breaking into four red stars; at any rate our Artillery opened fire.
3. Enemy's T.M's. appeared to be in the open behind their new trench, as our Artillery, after lengthening range, the T.M's. seemed to slacken very appreciably.
4. Enemy's forces appear to have been considerable; strong working and covering, in addition to the several parties of 20 to 30 men, each seen leaving his trenches, and on whom our men fired. Observation was kept on the FARM till 9p.m., and no men were seen to enter from outside, yet, by 9.15p.m., Very Lights were going up. It is the opinion of most of the Officers that the enemy has underground rooms, and holds by day.

he result of the Operations our line now held runs from ads at M.23.a.9.7. to Old Trench M.23.b.2.0. to New Post .c.9.5. to M.29.b.2.8. Consolidation and wiring will be inued tonight, and Posts linked up.

alties, which were expected to be severe on account of the

(3).

the/
large amount of firing, resulted in being very small, and
consisted as under :-

    KILLED.............Other Ranks 4.

    WOUNDED............ "   "   18.

    Missing
    (Believed Wounded). "   "   1.

    Missing
    (Believed Killed).. "   "   1.

    Wounded, and at Duty........2/Lt. DUNS.

Names of men who performed good work will be forwarded
separately.

One point was noticed which will be borne in mind for future
occasions -   The amount of ammunition each man carried -
120 rounds - ran short.

FIELD.   (Sd.) R.H.S.GORDON, Lt.-Col.,
10-5-1917.   Comdg. 15th. SHERWOOD FORESTERS.

NARRATIVE OF OPERATIONS NIGHT OF MAY 9th./10th.

15th. SHERWOOD FORESTERS.

HOUR.	SUBJECT.
9.40p.m.	Parties in position and ready to move.
9.45p.m.	"X" Coy's. Platoons moved forward.
9.50p.m.	Message timed 9.42p.m. from O.C., "X" Coy. reports enemy firing Very Lights from practice bombing trenches.
10.35p.m.	All quiet.
10.36p.m.	Rapid enemy rifle and grenade fire heard on Right of LES TROIS SAUVAGES. Also intermittent Trench Mortar fire.
11.0p.m.	Enemy firing rockets bursting into 2 green stars.
11.10p.m.	Enemy opened strong barrage of Trench Mortars in the vicinity of LES TROIS SAUVAGES, and Artillery fire between that place and GRICOURT.
11.5p.m.	Message from O.C., "Z" Coy. timed 10.45p.m. reporting "Z" Coy. had occupied Post at X-roads and that covering platoon "X" was well forward with its left flank resting near the escarpment at M.23.b.6.7.
11.20p.m.	O.C., "W" Coy. reports his platoon at X-roads at M.23.d.7.8. had met with strong enemy resistsance and fighting was in progress since 10.25p.m.
11.25p.m.	O.C., "X" Coy. reports Consolidating Platoon held up by rifle and T.M. Fire from LES TROIS SAUVAGES buildings. Enemy M.G. firing along the road.
11.35p.m.	O.C., "X" Coy. reports verbally his covering platoon under heavy rifle fire from LES TROIS SAUVAGES and enemy reinforcing from escarpment at M.23.b.6.7. Covering party opened rapid fire on enemy and held on until ammunition was expended. The covering party then withdrew to sunken road at M.23.b.1.8.
11.40p.m.	O. C. "Z" Coy. reports verbally his consolidating parties, following up "X" Coy. were caught in barrage and had moved into the Practice Bombing Trenches, and had taken up position there.
11.50p.m.	O.C., "W" Coy. reports, verbally, his Platoon still fighting at the X-roads at M.23.d.7.8. and enemy had made two attempts to outflank the Platoon. The other Platoon of "W" Coy. had been working on consolidating at M.29.b.3.5., but had been forced to temporarily withdraw owing to accurate T.M. fire from enemy. O.C., "W" Coy. was ordered to withdraw his platoon from M.23.d.7.8. for a distance of 50 yards, and to consolidate.
12midnight.	O. C., "X" Coy. reports his consolidating party has made several attempts to rush enemy position, but owing to wire and increasing fire it could not be accomplished. "Z" Coy's. Post at the X-roads at M.23.a.9.8. assisted withdrawal.
12.10a.m.	2 Platoons of "X" Coy. arrived from BROWN LINE and put in position in support trenches.
12.30a.m.	O.C., "W" Coy. reports enemy outflanking his consolidating Platoon and was withdrawing to original trenches. The Platoon

HOUR.	SUBJECT.
12.30a.m.	(CONTD.) temporarily withdrawn from M.29.b.2.9. was being sent out to carry on consolidating.
1.0a.m.	"Y" Coy. arrived and placed in support to "W" Coy.
1.35a.m. to 2.30a.m.	DISPOSITIONS. "Z" Coy. 1 post at x-roads M.23.a.9.8. 2 platoons in Bombing Trench M.23.b.2.1. Remainder GRICOURT LINE. "W" Coy. 1 platoon M.29.c.5.4. 1 platoon M.29.b.2.5. with post at M.29.b.2.9. Establishing post at M.23.d.4.4. 1 Platoon E. of TWIN COPSES. Reserve Platoon at M.29.a.5.8.

(Sd.) H. MORTON, Lt. & Adjt.,
15th. SHERWOOD FORESTERS.

5.30a.m.

NARRATIVE OF OPERATIONS ON NIGHT OF 15th./16th. MAY, 1917.

11.50p.m. The Assaulting Company filed through X-roads and formed up about 50 yards beyond.

Midnt. Trench Mortars, Artillery and Machine Guns opened punctually at 12 midnight, and the Assaulting Company moved forward towards LES TROIS SAUVAGES, making good progress, and keeping their formation. When about 50 yards from what appeared to be a trench, several Very Lights were fired, and the position of Assaulting Company disclosed to enemy, who immediately opened a rifle fire of approximately 1 rifle per 10 yards. The O. C., Assaulting Company formed the opinion that this fire was from an enemy covering party lining a trench or bank of the Sunken Road about M.23.b.8.3. and decided to rush them. He, accordingly, gave the order to charge, and the Company rushed forward. The leading files of the platoons met with wire, but were unable to make their way through. The heads of the enemy could be seen some 20 yards away, and they were firing over the top of a bank or parapet. Our Stokes Guns were still playing on the FARM, and it was assumed the time was about 12.15a.m.

The party attempting to get through the wire suffered casualties, and as the formation of the Company at the moment was not a suitable one for over-coming the obstacle, the O. C. Assaulting Company withdrew his men for a distance of 150x and reorganised.

12.15a.m. Enemy opened T. M. barrage around the X-roads at M.23.a.8.9. and rifle fire from the direction of M.24.a.Central.

12.20a.m. The O. C. Assaulting Company, having reformed, moved forward again headed by groups of men who were to make gaps in the wire. By this time the enemy had been considerably reinforced at the point of attack, and casualties were heavier than on the first attempt. The operation of getting through the wire was proving too long. The Right Party, under 2nd. Lieut. FARMER, were almost successful in getting through and had inflicted some casualties on the enemy at that point, but unfortunately this Officer and two of his men were wounded, which delayed the attempt.

The O. C. Assaulting Company (Lt. M.M.HARVEY, M.C.) then decided to collect the men in the vicinity and make a rush. This he did together with the three Platoon Commanders, some Sergeants, and about 20 men. A cross-fire from the FARM buildings was met with, and the attempt did not succeed.

12.25a.m. Major AYLWARD, M.C., R.E., then joined up with the O. C., Assaulting Company.
All available men were collected and headed by Major AYLWARD, R.E. and the O. C. Assaulting Company, a rush was made for the trench further to the Right, but an entry could not be effected.
It was decided that further attempts would not prove successful, and the Company withdrew, bringing wounded with them.

12.25a.m. O. C. Support Company reported that a patrol sent along the track from X-roads M.23.a.8.9. towards the FARM had not returned.
Some wounded, and a few stragglers, had returned from Assaulting Company.

12.40a.m. O. C. Supporting Company reported that the Assaulting Company was coming in and were being collected in the vicinity of X-roads. The patrol sent out towards the FARM had returned and reported they were grenaded by an enemy post on the road, which post could not be exactly located.

12.50a.m. The situation was reported to the G.O.C. Brigade as follows :-
That a further attempt by the Supporting Company was not likely to prove successful. That wire existed in a continuous line towards

Secret   Copy No ___

Battalion Operation Order No 57
PURITY.

Intention.   Two companies of the Battalion
              will raid the enemy trenches at LES
              TROIS SAUVAGES tonight and will:-
              (a) Search the buildings (mopping up)
              (b) Destroy wire & tunnels in this area & from
              (c) Capture M.G. at N.W. corner of ___
              (d) A party of R.E. with explosives will
                  destroy dugouts, tunnels, &c.

Disposition. The attack will be carried out
              by an assaulting coy composed of
              2 platoons 'A' Coy & 2 platoons 'B' Coy.
              This coy will be supported, if
              necessary, by a company composed
              of 2 platoons 'A' Coy & 2 platoons 'B' Coy.

Formation of The assaulting coy will be
assaulting coy. formed as under:-
              Covering party 10 men & 1 officer NCO Jones
              1st assaulting platoon 20 men ___ Sgt ___
              2nd   do   ___ ___
              1st Mopping up platoon — do —   NCO ___
              2nd   — do —   — do —   NCO Wright

Point of   X. Rds. at M.23 a.8.9.
Assembly.

Mode of   At Zero minus 10 the assaulting coy
attack.   will move out from the two heads in
              single file in the following order:-
              Covering party, 2nd Mopping platoon,
              1st Mopping platoon, 2nd Assaulting platoon,
              1st Assaulting platoon. When clear
              of the cross roads the coy will form
              up by platoons in single file facing
              S.E. with the covering party on the
              left flank & an interval of 10 paces
              between platoons. The R.E. party will
              move with the rear file of the 1st
              mopping up platoon.
              Immediately the coy is formed up it
              will move forward as quickly as possible
              on to LES TROIS SAUVAGES the right of

Sheet 2.

directing and march straight on the track at M.23.b.3. As soon as the rear file of the 1st assaulting platoon reaches the road, the officer i/c 1st assaulting platoon will give the order right turn. The whole of [...] the covering party will [...] and rush the farm. [...] parties of the enemy [...] dealt with but the [...] must push forward to get to [...] which is the road on the [...] edge of the farm.

When the assaulting parties [...] into the farm the [...] will halt them to see if [...] any of the enemy [...]. The mopping up [...] with enemy who [...] in the cellars or [...] farm ruins, prisoners [...] direct to Ot. Suppins [...] M.23.a.8.9. who will arrange [...] removal to Ot. Suppins [...] Cheshire Regt. at M.21.a. The R.E. will be [...] destroying any items of [...] will not be exploded [...] Coy reports that the [...] withdrawn. The officer i/c [...] assaulting platoon will [...] detail his right section [...] on the road at N.W. corner [...] facing cross roads at M.23.a.9.

Withdrawal. Directly the farm [...] +prisoners +wounded for any [...] Assly. Troops will withdraw [...] farm via X Rds M.23.a.8.9. [...] GRICOURT. When the withdrawal [...] completed the O.C. Coy [...] the R.E. officer i/c Blowing up party [...] bugle call will then be sounded [...]

Sheet 3.

will be the signal for the charge to be fired. & the sapping party to withdraw. The remainder of the party will make direct for the shelter at M23a.8.9.

Dress. Drill order. Shields to be worn, and each man will carry his usual bandolier of ammunition. Bombers will carry their bomb buckets but not more than 6. The work will be carried on with all haste & if it is possible part bags will not be taken into action with them. Further the party will not go into action until all unnecessary equipment,

Supporting Coys. Will take up position at the cross roads M23a.8.9. immediately the assaulting Coy has moved forward. From this Coy will push forward a strong party to the strongpoint at M23d.5.7. to prevent any attempt by the enemy to reinforce this point. The coy will be prepared to reinforce the assaulting Coy if it is held up.

Directly the bombardment by the Stokes Mortars on LES TROIS SAUVAGES has ceased sections will be sent along the road towards the buildings to mop up any enemy on the road to protect the party in the farm & assist in removing tools at the N.W. corner. The party will be careful to discriminate between friend & foe & must use the bayonet only.

The supporting Coy will not vacate its position & cross roads until the whole of the assaulting Coy has withdrawn through them. (M.23a.8.9.)

Reports. All reports from O.C. Ass. Coy will be sent direct to O.C. Supporting Coy at X rds M23a.8.9. who will arrange to forward same direct to B.H.Q. at GRICOURT. Any message asking for assistance will be immediately acted upon by O.C. Supp. Coy. who will be i/c operations at that time. No withdrawal will take place in any case of the operation being unsuccessful until orders regarding this are received from B.H.Q.

Sheet to
which will be situated on GRICOURT at
H.Qrs of Left Brigade
Reserves. At 11.30 pm [?] Z Coy [?] ordered
to occupy Brown Line the [?]
support the two coys [?]
if required.
On completion of [?]
[?] Y Coy will stand to [?]

Medical. Stretcher bearers of [?]
be at the Ann. Rd. [?]
Y & Z at GRICOURT and [?]
to above cross roads [?]
move up & wound stretcher [?]
The aid post is [?]
GRICOURT Rd at M.29.a.87

Stragglers. O.C. Z Coy will [?]
to report at the [?]
to take names of any [?]
Any men who have [?]
not come out with [?]
will be ordered to [?]
Quarry.

Guiding A Signal lamp showing [?]
Light light will be placed [?]
All men are to be [?]
their way towards the left

Countersign. The countersign for all [?]
passing through the [?]
be "ROBINHOOD"

Zero. Zero hour will be 12 m.n.

Acknowledge.   H Morton
                       15 Sher Foresters
Copies issued to:-
No 1. W Coy
   2. X Coy
   3. Pump
   4. Z Coy
   5. Brigade.

Scale 1:10,000.   8-5-17.   Map prepared from Air Photos.
Contours from German Map.

Army Form C. 2118

WAR DIARY
or
INTELLIGENCE SUMMARY
(Erase heading not required.)

Instructions regarding War Diaries and Intelligence Summaries are contained in F.S. Regs., Part II. and the Staff Manual respectively. Title Pages will be prepared in manuscript.

15 Nott & Derby
O IV 17
16.4

W.A.W. Collins Lieut Col Comm
15th Sherwood Foresters

Place	Date	Hour	Summary of Events and Information	Remarks and references to Appendices
	June 1917			
TEMPLEUX La FOSSE	1st.		Company and Battalion Training.	
VILLERS GUISLANS	2nd.	10-30 p.m.	Relieved 17th.WEST YORKS in Support in and near VILLERS GUISLANS. H.Q., W and Z Coys. in village. "Y" Coy. in trench behind village and X Coy. in reserve in Railway Embankment. Relief carried out without unusual incident and no casualties.	
	3rd. to 9th.		Furnished Working and Carrying Parties for Front Line Battalion.	
	10th.	11-30 p.m.	Relieved 14th.GLOSTERS in front line East of Village. H.Q. in village. "Z" Coy. in front line. "W" Coy. in immediate Support, "X" & "Y" Coys. in support in Village. Relief took place without incident.	
	11th. to 13th.		Work on Trenches and patrolling, no unusual occurrences	
	14th.		Wounded prisoner was captured and identification found normal. Work commenced by Brigade on New advanced trench. "X" & "Z" Coys. finding strong covering parties.	
	15th.		Continuation of work on new Trench. W & Y covering.	
	16th.	11 p.m.	"X" Coy. occupied advanced trench.	
	17th.		Work continued, no incident of note.	
HEUDE-COURT	18th.	11-50 p.m.	Relieved by 18th.LANCS.FUSILIERS. Battalion marched by Platoons to Camp, N.W. of HEUDECOURT.	
	19th. to 25th.		Company and Battalion Training, Sports, Football Matches and Concerts.	
GAUCHE WOOD	26th.	4 p.m.	Relieved 19th.D.L.I. in Brgd.Reserve in GAUCHE WOOD SECTOR. X,Y, and Z Coys. furnished working parties for front line. "W" Coy. working under supervision of R.E.	
	27th. to 29th.			
VILLERS FAUCON	30th.	8 a.m.	Battalion left HEUDECOURT by DECAUVILLE RAILWAY and on arrival at VILLERS FAUCON pitched Camps for remainder of Brigade. The Battalion being billeted in the village.	

1875 Wt. W593/826 1,000,000 4/15 J.B.C. & A. A.D.S.S./Forms/C. 2118.

Army Form C. 2118

1/5th (S) Bn Sherwood Foresters

WAR DIARY or INTELLIGENCE SUMMARY
(Erase heading not required.)

Instructions regarding War Diaries and Intelligence Summaries are contained in F.S. Regs., Part II. and the Staff Manual respectively. Title Pages will be prepared in manuscript.

Place	Date July 1917	Hour	Summary of Events and Information	Remarks and references to Appendices
VILLERS FAUCON	1st to 5th.		Billeted in Village. Coy. and Battalion Training.	
	6th.	8-30 p.m.	"X" & "Y" Coys. moved up to "D" Sector, Right sub-sector and occupied bivouacs in SUNKEN ROAD F.4.a. and HEYTHROP POST, prior to the relief of 16th.LANCERS,3rd.CAV.BDE. in this sector.	
EPEHY	7th.	8-30 p.m.	Remainder of Battalion moved up and relieved, occupying posts as follows:- "W" Coy. CRUCIFORM POST & CATELET COPSE, 2 Platoons in each. "X" Coy. BIRD POST & THE QUARRIES. "Y" Coy. BIRD CAGE. "Z" COY. GRAFTON POST and HEYTHROP POST. H.Q. in SUNKEN ROAD running NORTH from F.4.Central to F.4.b.1.8. Relief took place quietly.	
	8th.		Battn. found covering parties for Brigade Working Parties digging Trench from OSSUS 1. to BIRD POST. Also for PIONEERS digging communication Trench from right support of BIRD CAGE to EAGLE'S NEST.	
	9th.		Covering parties again found. No unusual incident.	
	10th.	7 p.m.	"X" Coy. relieved "Y" Coy. in BIRD CAGE, the latter coming back and occupying THE QUARRIES.	
	11th.		Patrols sent out and usual Trench routine carried out.	
	12th.		Inter-Battn. Relief. "W" Coy. relieved "X" Coy. in BIRD CAGE. "Z" Coy. relieving "Y" Coy. in the QUARRIES. "X" & "Y" Coys. came back and occupied posts vacated by "W" & "Z" Coys.	
	13th.		On the 12/13th. The enemy attempted to raid BIRD CAGE, promptly at midnight he placed a heavy barrage on, in SUNKEN ROAD near THE QUARRIES and on all approaches. This lifted at 1-15a.m. and the enemy were observed in front of our wire on the right of the BIRD CAGE, rifle and Lewis Gun fire was opened and the enemy appeared to be caught in our barrage. Two green lights were then sent up from the enemy lines at rear of OSSUS WOOD and hostile Barrage recommenced, slackening at 2 a.m. and finishing at 2-30 a.m. Our casualties amounted to 23 O.R's. One of the raiding party was found dead in our wire, identification proved normal.	
	14th.		Trenches repaired after bombardment and usual trench routine carried out.	
	15th	11-30 p.m.	The Battn. was relieved by the 20th.LANCS.FUS. and moved back by platoons to VILLERS FAUCON and from there by Coys. to camp at AIZECOURT-la-BAS. No unusual occurrence.	
AIZECOURT-la-BAS.	16th 17th to 22nd.		Rest and refitting. Company and Battalion Training. Foot-ball matches, Boxing, shooting. The Battalion won the Inter-Brigade shooting Competition, gaining first and second places.	
LEMPIRE	23rd	10 p.m.	Battn. relieved 18th.H.L.I. in C.2.Sub-Sector, Left support. "W" Coy. occupied posts in LEMPIRE CENTRAL, LEMPIRE EAST AND BASSE BOULOGNE NORTH. "X" Coy. in billets in LEMPIRE. "Y" Coy. were employed with No.1.Section.180th. Tunnelling Coy. "Z" Coy.attached to 15th.CHESHIRES & were in support to them. H.Q. in billets in LEMPIRE. Relief was carried out successfully.	

Army Form C. 2118

WAR DIARY
or
INTELLIGENCE SUMMARY

(Erase heading not required.)

Instructions regarding War Diaries and Intelligence Summaries are contained in F. S. Regs., Part II. and the Staff Manual respectively. Title Pages will be prepared in manuscript.

Place	Date	Hour	Summary of Events and Information	Remarks and references to Appendices
LEMPIRE.	24th. to 28th.		Battalion in support to 15th CHESHIRES. Night and day working parties furnished. Control posts supplied. No noteworthy incidents.	
	29th.		Battalion relieved 15th.CHESHIRES in C.2. Sub-sector,northern. Relief took place quietly. "W" Coy in Left Support. "X" Coy. in GUILLEMONT FARM. "Y" Coy. in D,E,& F POSTS. "Z" Coy. in right support. H.Q. in billets near LEMPIRE CENTRAL.	
	30th.		No unusual occurrence. Patrolling and usual trench work carried out.	
	31st.		No unusual occurrence. Patrolling and usual trench work carried out.	

W. A. Cullen Lieut-Col.
W. Jt Sherwood Foresters
Cmdg 15th Cheshires

Army Form C. 2118

WAR DIARY
or
INTELLIGENCE SUMMARY
(Erase heading not required.)

Vol 19

Place	Date	Hour	Summary of Events and Information	Remarks and references to Appendices
LEMPIRE	1st.	9-20p.m.	Battalion relieved by the 17th.ROYAL SCOTS and the H.L.I. "W" Coy. relieved by the PIONEERS under H.L.I. "X" Coy. by the 17th.ROYAL SCOTS, "Y" Coy. by the H.L.I. and "Z" Coy. by 17th.ROYAL SCOTS. Battalion proceeded on relief to Camp at AIZECOURT-la-BAS.	
AIZECOURT-la-BAS.	2nd.to 16th.		In Camp at AIZECOURT. Coy and Battalion Training, Practice for the attack on the KNOLL.	
ST EMILIE	17th.	1-30p.m	Battalion moved via LONGAVESNES and VILLERS FAUCON to the neighbourhood of ST EMILIE and pitched Camp. (Map Ref. 62 c. E.23. a & b.)	
	18th.	10 p.m.	Battalion left ST EMILIE and moved to the Assembly Position for the attack on the KNOLL, via RONSSOY-LEMPIRE-TOMBOIS FARM ROAD --FLEECEALL POST --and FAG LANE to the OLD BARRIER on the SUNKEN ROAD(Op.Order.131. Bn. Order dated Aug.16th.) All Coys. were in position by 3-7 a.m. 19th.	
THE KNOLL	19th.	3.a.m.	The attack on the KNOLL was carried out successfully,(Zero time 4a.m.), in conjunction with the 15th.CHESHIRE REGT. All objectives were gained, the new defensive line in front of the Old German line was sited and dug, and a BOMBING BLOCK established on the left at a point about (F.6.c.10.6. Map 62 B.N.W. & 62C.N.E.) 50 yards or s. from the junction of BEAL LANE with TOMBOIS TRENCH. Little or no quarter was given, and few prisoners taken. The Moppers up detailed from "Y" Coy. dealt with a number of the enemy who had survived our bombardment. The German Trench was practically destroyed by our fire, the wire was well and completely cut and our men met with little or no opposition in their advance. On this right the dug-outs at A.1.d.3.0. were bombed and cleared, and two Trench Mortars captured in conjunction with a party of the 15th. CHESHIRES. Order of attack. 15th.CHESHIRES on the right.15th.SHERWOODS on the left. Our Battalion went over in three waves. "Y" & "Z" Coys. formed the first and second waves, then were the Assaulting Coys. Three platoons of "W" Coy. formed the third wave and dug the new trench in front of the Old German line. "X" Coy.were in Reserve and supplied carrying parties. Then the latter were formed up in the front trench of FLEECEALL POST, and lost two men killed there by enemy shells before the attack started about 3-30 a.m. The BOMBING BLOCK party under 2nd.Lieut.F.G.Mottershaw was detailed from Ltr."Z" Coy. The Assaulting Coy, began to withdraw about 5 a.m. and returned to billets in LEMPIRE. At one time in the morning our Artillery was firing short, also on of our Aeroplanes flew over and opened fire by mistake on our front line, wounding three men. The rest of the day was fairly quiet, but the enemy kept shelling our new position.(Ref.Op.Orders 128-132 Map.62C.N.E. & 62 D N.W.)	D.I.184
LEMPIRE	19th.	9-30p.m.	"Y" & "Z" Coys. relieved by "W" & "X" Coys. and the BOMBING BLOCK PARTY, the latter returning to the billets vacated by "Y" & "Z" Coys. During the night the work of consolidating the captured position and connecting it to our old line was carried on.	

Army Form C. 2118

SHEET 2
WAR DIARY
or
INTELLIGENCE SUMMARY
(Erase heading not required.)

Instructions regarding War Diaries and Intelligence Summaries are contained in F.S. Regs., Part II. and the Staff Manual respectively. Title Pages will be prepared in manuscript.

Place	Date	Hour	Summary of Events and Information	Remarks and references to Appendices
			A.O.T. dug from the left of our Bn. Front in the old German Line to the SUNKEN ROAD about F.6.c.3.1. The 16th.CHESHIRES supplied digging parties to work with R.E's in the new Trench began by our "W" Coy. and the 14th.GLOUCESTERS wiring parties in front of the same trench. Our "Y" Coy. acted as covering party to them 200 yards in front of the new line with "Z" Coy. in Support.(Op.Order.133).	
LEMPIRE & ST EMILIE.	20th.	9-30p.m.	Battalion relieved by the 14th. GLOUCESTERS and "Y" & "Z" Coys. moved back into Camp at ST EMILIE, "W" & "X" Coys. remaining in billets at LEMPIRE(Op.Orders.134.Bn.Order.67). Our casualties during the two days amounted to 25 Killed, 53 Wounded, 2 Died of Wounds and 5 missing.	
	21st.		New names of Trenches (Op.Orders135)	
	22nd.	9-50p.m.	"Y" & "Z" Coys. relieved "W" & "X" Coys.	
	23rd.		"W" & "X" Coys. at ST EMILIE. "Y" & "Z" Coys. at LEMPIRE.	
THE KNOLL	24th.	6p.m.	Battalion relieved the 15th. CHESHIRE on the KNOLL (Ref.Op.Orders.137. Bn.Orders75) Relief completed by 2.a.m. Aug.25th.	
	25th.	4.a.m.	At about 4.a.m. the enemy opened a heavy bombardment on the KNOLL which lasted till 5-30 a.m.	
		4-20 a.m	S.O.S. was sent up on the KNOLL. At about the same time the enemy attacked GILLEMONT FARM. No attack was made on the KNOLL. The bombardment was heaviest on our right where "X" Coy. were, then the trenches were dradly damaged and we sustained a good many casualties.	
		5-8a.m.	A message was sent to "Y" Coy to reinforce "Z" Coy. with half their number.	
		5-20a.m.	The rest of "Y" Coy. was sent for.	
		5-30a.m.	The bombardment slackened on the KNOLL.	
		6-20a.m.	The enemy shelled the TOMBOIS SUNKEN ROAD near the AID POST, there was heavy shelling round GILLEMONT.	
		6-55a.m.	A message was received that GILLEMONT FARM was lost, here the enemy took the FARM and also part of our old front line. This was regained in the evening by counter-attack by the 19th.D.L.I. REGT. leaving the situation at GILLEMONT as it had been for the a month previously. Shelling continued over the KNOLL and FLEECEALL POST at intervals during the day. Our casualties amounted to 19 Killed, and 44 wounded.	
		12noon.	A message was received from Brigade that the Battalion would be relieved by the 16th.CHESHIRES the same night. This was carried out and completed by 2-50 a.m. Aug.26.th.	
ST EMILIE	26th.	2-50a.m.	Battalion returned to Camp near ST EMILIE.	
	27th.		Battalion moved from ST EMILIE to AIZECOURT.	
AIZECOURT-La-BAS	28th.		Rest.	
	30th.		20 men from each Company to Bombing School to see new game. Battalion parade.	
	31st.		G.O.C. Corps inspected Brigade.	

L.A.W. Collin Lieut - Col
Cmdg 15th (S) Bn The Sherwood Foresters

WAR DIARY
or
INTELLIGENCE SUMMARY.
(Erase heading not required.)

15th Hampshire Regt. Army Form C. 2118.
Vol 20
1917

September 1917.

Place	Date	Hour	Summary of Events and Information	Remarks and references to Appendices
AIZECOURT-le-BAS.	1st.	4.p.m.	The Battalion relieved the 17th.ROYAL SCOTS in C.2.Sector, starting from Camp in AIZECOURT-le-BAS, at 4.p.m. "X"Coy. took over GRAFTON POST – "Y" Coy. FLEECEALL & EGO POSTS and BOMBING BLOCKS in GRELLIN and COCHRANE AVENUES. "W" Coy. was in support in SHELTERS in SART LANE, North of SART FARM, and "Z" Coy. in reserve in billets in LEMPIRE. Battalion H.Q. in LEMPIRE, at F.18.a.7.6. The work to be done was arranged as follows:- "X" Coy. to inspect the wire between "G" & "F" POSTS and to complete wiring between the two Posts. "Z" Coy. to deepen and drain FLEECEALL LANE from its commencement to the SUNKEN ROAD behind TOMBOIS FARM. "W" Coy. to clear "F" POST & FAG TRENCH where blown in by shell fire, and to furnish a patrol. "Y" Coy. to strengthen the BOMBING BLOCKS. (Battn.Order No.77.)	
LEMPIRE.	2/3rd.	10pm.	Work carried on. Covering Party supplied to the 15th.CHESHIRES. Enemy bombardment from about 11.p.m. to 12-40.a.m. Casualties - 1.O.R.	
"	3/4th.	9-30. p.m.	Inter-Company Relief. "Z" Coy. relieving "Y" Coy. in "E" & "F" POSTS. About 8-30.a.m. an enemy balloon over GILLEMONT was struck by lightening and came down in flames.	
"	6th.	9-30. p.m.	The Battalion was relieved by the 15th.CHESHIRES, and went into the SHELTERS and BILLETS previously occupied by them in LEMPIRE and SAND BAG ALLEY.(Battn.Order No.78,Bde.Order No.144.)	
"	7/11th.		Wiring Parties sent out by Coy's. alternately. 1 Coy. on duty each night with orders, in case of S.O.S., or other alarm, to occupy YAK & ZEBRA, LEMPIRE CENTRAL, and LEMPIRE EAST POSTS.	
"	11th.		The Battalion was relieved by the 20th.LANCS.FUSILIERS, and went into BILLETS, at VILLERS FAUCON. (Bde.Order No.145. – Battn.Order No.79.)	
VILLERS FAUCON.	11/18 th.		Billeted in the VILLAGE. Company Training. Musketry – Improvement of the Ranges and Revetting practice carried on. A Transport Inspection was held on Sept.13th., at 3.p.m. The Battalion Transport won First prize. Football Match & Entertainment on the 15th. There was a demonstration of Trench digging & revetting, at AIZECOURT-le-BAS.	

Army Form C. 2118.

WAR DIARY
or
INTELLIGENCE SUMMARY.
(Erase heading not required.)

Instructions regarding War Diaries and Intelligence Summaries are contained in F.S. Regs., Part II. and the Staff Manual respectively. Title pages will be prepared in manuscript.

September 1917.

Place	Date	Hour	Summary of Events and Information	Remarks and references to Appendices
VILLERS FAUCON.	18th.	7.p.m.	The Battalion relieved the 17th. WEST YORKS and 1 Coy. of the D.L.I. in the Right Sub-sector. Dispositions as follows :- "W" Coy. Right Front Line - "Y" Coy. Left Front Line. "X" Coy. in HETHROP & CRUCIFORM POSTS. - "Z" Coy. in PRIEL BANK from No. 13 Copse to CATELET COPSE. (Bin.Order No.148. Battn.Order No. 80.)	
BIRDCAGE SECTOR.	19/26th.		The Battalion had a quiet time in the line on the whole. On the night of the 22nd/23rd. the enemy shelled heavily along the line from BIRDCAGE to OSSUS POSTS, from 11 - 11-45.p.m. Inter-Company Relief. "X" Coy. relieving "W" Coy. & "Z" Coy. relieving "Y" Coy.	
	22nd.	7-30. p.m.	In the morning of the 22nd, about 8-45.a.m. 1.N.C.O. was killed near ST.EMILIE by a bomb from an Aeroplane while bringing two horses up to MALASSISE FARM. 1 horse was also killed. Work done - Revetting & improving TRENCHES & POSTS.	
EPEHY.	26/27th. to 29th.		The Battalion was relieved by the 18th. CHESHIRES, and was disposed as follows :- "W" Coy. MEATH & LIMERICK POSTS - "X" Coy. VAUGHAN BANK - "Y" Coy. 14 WILLOWS, and "Z" Coy. KILDARE POST. Battn.H.Q. in VAUGHAN BANK, near EPEHY. Lewis Gun Classes commenced. Working Parties supplied. (Battn.Order No.82.)	
"	30th.		The Battalion was relieved by "D" Battn. 168th. Bde., and marched by Coy's to AIZECOURT-le-BAS, halting on the way, at VILLERS FAUCON. (Bde.Order No. 150. Battn.Order No.83. The relief was completed without incident.	

[signature]
Major.
Commdg.15th.(S) Bn. The Sherwood Foresters.

Army Form C. 2118.

105/35 15th Bn. The Sherwood Foresters.
October 1917.

WAR DIARY
or
INTELLIGENCE SUMMARY
(Erase heading not required.)

Instructions regarding War Diaries and Intelligence Summaries are contained in F.S. Regs., Part II. and the Staff Manual respectively. Title Pages will be prepared in manuscript.

Place	Date	Hour	Summary of Events and Information	Remarks and references to Appendices
AIZECOURT le BAS	1917. Oct.1.		Battalion conveyed to PERONNE in Motor lorries. Transport moving by road.	
PERONNE	" 2nd. & 3rd.	midnight	Resting and refitting. Battalion entrained at PERONNE at 12 noon. 23rd.inst. en route for XVII Corps area and detrained at ARRAS at 4-30 a.m. 4th.inst. proceeding by march route to billets at WARLUS. Part of Battn.Transport under Command of 2nd.Lieut.R.T.Wright. proceeded by road halting on the night of 3rd. inst at BAPAUME and continuing march on 4th.inst. arrived at WARLUS at12 noon.	0.0.85
WARLUS	3rd. to 12th.		Re-organization of Coys. and Battalion Training.	
WARLUS	13th.		Battalion (less "Z" Coy.) entrained at ARRAS STATION at 12-54 p.m. and detrained at CASSEL at 8-30 p.m. marching to billets at ARNEKE. Ltr."Z" Coy. entrained at ARRAS at 8-54 p.m. and detrained at CASSEL at 3 am. 14th.inst.	0.0.86
ARNEKE	15th.		Battalion(less Transport) entrained at ARNEKE at 12 noon and detrained at PROVEN about 2-30 p.m.0.0.87 marching to D.4. Camp.	
PROVEN	16th.		Entrained at PROVEN at 12 noon and detrained at ELVERDINGHE. The Battalion relieved 1st.SCOTS GUARDS at RUGBY CAMP. Transport moved by road and occupied camp near WOESTON.	
ELVERDINGHE	17th. to 20th.		Reconnaissance of line S.of HOUTHULST FOREST preparatory to attack. Furnishing of working parties to assist in preparing forward gun positions.	
	20th.		At 5 p.m. Battalion moved to GOUVY FARM near BOESINGHE.	
	21st.		Battalion moved to assembly positions as supporting Battalion to 105th.Bde. in the general attack on morning of 22nd. inst on enemy positions S.of HOUTHULST FOREST.	0.0.8 Bde.0.0. 159.
	22nd.		Operations S.of HOUTHULST FOREST. Casualties from 21st. to 23rd. Officers O.Ranks. Killed 1 15 Wounded 1 180 Missing 1 20	Narrative "A"

2449 Wt. W14957/M90 750,000 1/16 J.B.C. & A. Forms/C.2118/12.

Army Form C. 2118.

WAR DIARY
or
INTELLIGENCE SUMMARY
(Erase heading not required.)

Instructions regarding War Diaries and Intelligence Summaries are contained in F. S. Regs., Part II. and the Staff Manual respectively. Title Pages will be prepared in manuscript.

Place	Date	Hour	Summary of Events and Information	Remarks and references to Appendices
	24th.		Relief of Battalion by 19th.D.L.I. completed at 3 a.m. Coys. moved out independently to billets at LARRI CAMP near ELVERDINGHE.	
ELVERDINGHE.	25th. to 28th.		Resting and refitting.	
"	29th.		The Battalion relieved 5th.BORDER REGT. in Right Sector Divisional Front by 7-30 p.m. Enemy very quiet whilst relief was taking place. Between 9 p.m. and 11 p.m. enemy put down a strong defensive barrage close behind our forward line, remainder of night was quiet.	O.O.89
	30th.		Casualties 1 Officer and 4 Other Ranks Killed. 1 Officer and 14 O.R. Wounded. At 4 a.m. enemy opened heavy artillery fire on the ground immediately behind our front line, developing in intensity at dawn. About 6 a.m. several of the enemy were seen running about in WOOD EAST OF MARECHAL HOUSE. Several were knocked out by snipers of Ltr. "X" Coy. Situation quietened down by 8 a.m. and remainder of day was fairly calm.	
	31st.		Quiet on the whole. Occasional heavy bursts of artillery fire on Battalion H.Q. and Support positions. From 4-30 p.m. onwards the enemy sent over constant streams of gas shells on our back areas.	

W.A.L. Collin Lieut Col.
Comdg. 1st @ 8th Sherwood Foresters

Army Form C. 2118.

105/35

1/4 (S) Bn. Sherwood Foresters.

WAR DIARY
or
INTELLIGENCE SUMMARY

(Erase heading not required.)

Instructions regarding War Diaries and Intelligence Summaries are contained in F. S. Regs., Part II. and the Staff Manual respectively. Title Pages will be prepared in manuscript.

Place	Date 1917.	Hour	Summary of Events and Information	Remarks and references to Appendices
HOULTHURST FOREST.	NOV. 1st.	2.a.m.	Relieved in RIGHT SECTOR of DIV.FRONT by H.L.I. Enemy artillery active during the period. Trenches were heavily shelled by H.E. and Gas. Casualties were suffered. The Battalion proceeded by train to DYKES CAMP.	
DYKES CAMP.	2/4th.		Rest and refitting.	
PADDINGTON CAMP.			Battalion moved by train to PROVEN, and from there marched to PADDINGTON CAMP.	
	6/8th.		Coy. and Battalion Training.	
	9th.		Coy. and Battalion Training - Visited by Army Commander. Arrival of large Draft.	
	10/13th.		Coy. and BATTALION TRAINING.	
	14th.		Working party of 500 Officers and men proceeded to KEMPTON PARK for work with C.R.A.	
BRAKE CAMP.	15th.	11.a.m.	Remainder of Battalion moved by rail and road to BRAKE CAMP in Div.Reserve.	
	16/22nd.		Coy. and Battalion Training.	
	23rd.	9-30. a.m.	Presentation of Medal Ribands by Adj.Gen.Commanding Division.	
KEMPTON PARK.	24/25th.	2-30. p.m.	Battalion relieved 18th.LANCS.FUS. in BRIGADE SUPPORT. Distribution - H.Q. & 2½ Coys. at KEMPTON PARK - ½ Coy. VARNA HOUSE - 1 Coy. CANAL BANK.	
HOULCATEM.	26th. 27th.	2.p.m.	Battalion relieved 16th.CHESHIRES in LEFT SECTOR OF DIV.FRONT. Work & Patrolling carried out. Two prisoners captured.	
	28th.	6-45. p.m.	Battalion relieved by 17th.ROYAL SCOTS. Night quiet. On completion of relief, Battalion proceeded by train to SIEGE CAMP. Total casualties whilst in the line - 13 O.R's wounded.	
SIEGE CAMP.	29/30		Rest and refitting.	

(sd.) W.A.L. Aellis Lieut Col. Commanding.
15th.(S) Bn.The Sherwood Foresters.

Army Form C. 2118.

WAR DIARY
or
INTELLIGENCE SUMMARY.
(Erase heading not required.)

Instructions regarding War Diaries and Intelligence Summaries are contained in F.S. Regs., Part II. and the Staff Manual respectively. Title pages will be prepared in manuscript.

15th. (SERVICE) BATTALION. THE SHERWOOD FORESTERS.   DECEMBER 1st. to 31st.   No.23

Place	Date	Hour	Summary of Events and Information	Remarks and references to Appendices
SIEGE CAMP.	1st to 4th.	.	Battalion in Brigade in Reserve. Company and Battalion Training.	
LANGEMARCK	5th.	1p.m.	Battalion moved forward into close Support relieving 10th. WEST YORKS, and 1 Coy. 5th.DORSETS 16th. Division. Distribution 3 Coys. EAGLE TRENCH.1 Coy CANDLE TRENCH. Relief was carried out quietly and there were no casualties.	
	7th.	Midnight	Battalion relieved 14th.GLOSTERS in Front Line.	
	8th.	11-40 p.m.	Battalion relieved by 2/11th.LONDON REGT. without incident. There were no casualties during this tour in the line.	
LE NOUVEAU MONDE	9th.	11-30 a.m.	Battalion moved by rail and road to billets in LE NOUVEAU MONDE. Transport by Road.	
	10th.		Rest.	
SCHOOLS CAMP.	11th.	10 a.m.	Battalion marched to SCHOOLS CAMP, POPERINGHE arriving at 2-30 p.m.	
	12th. to 21st.		Company and Battalion Training.	
	22nd.		Visit and Lecture by Corps Commander.	
	23rd. and 24th.		Brigade Games.	

Army Form C. 2118.

WAR DIARY
of
INTELLIGENCE SUMMARY.
(Erase heading not required.)

Instructions regarding War Diaries and Intelligence Summaries are contained in F. S. Regs., Part II. and the Staff Manual respectively. Title pages will be prepared in manuscript.

Places	Date	Hour	Summary of Events and Information	Remarks and references to Appendices
	25th.		Christmas Day.	
	26th. & 27th.		Brigade Games.	
	28th.		Company and Battalion Training. Lecture by Corps M.O. Officer.	
	29th.		Company and Battalion Training.	
	30th.		"W" Coy. moved to PIGEON Camp owing to outbreak of Diphtheria.	
	31st.		Battalion at Delousing Station.	

Graham Callos
Capt. & Adjt.

for O.C. 15th.(S) Bn. The Sherwood Foresters.

WAR DIARY
or
INTELLIGENCE SUMMARY.

Army Form C. 2118.

15th. (SERVICE) BATTALION. THE SHERWOOD FORESTERS. JANUARY 1st. to 31st. No.24.

Place	Date	Hour	Summary of Events and Information	Remarks and references to Appendices
SCHOOL CAMP.	Jan 1918 1st/2nd.		Company and Battalion Training.	
	3rd/4th.		Divisional Sports.	
	5th/7th.		Company and Battalion Training.	
	8th.		Snow. 200 men employed in clearing snow.	
WHITEMILL CAMP.	9th.		Battalion (less "W" Coy.) moved by Road and Rail to WHITEMILL CAMP, ELVERDINGHE. Road to PROVEN, rail to ELVERDINGHE. Transport and Stores by Road.	
"	10th/14th.		Company and Battalion Training. "W" Coy. rejoin, marching from PIGEON CAMP.	
	16th.		The Battalion relieved 17th.LANCS.FUS. in LEFT SUPPORT of Brigade Front, B.H.Q. at PIG AND WHISTLE.	O.O.No.2 15-1-18.
LEFT SUPPORT.	17th/20th.		Improvement of shelters and Trenches, wiring Corps and Main lines of defence. Special wiring party 1 Officer and 25 O.R under 2nd.Lieut.J.Keeling.	
	18th.		Casualties. Killed Major.W.A.McClelland & 2nd.Lieut.G.S.Hopkinson. Captain.K.W.Morell took Command of Battn. 2nd.Lieut.C.W.Pamplin Adjutant.	
	20th/21st.		The Battalion relieved the 14th. GLOSTER REGT. in LEFT FRONT SUB-SECTOR of Brigade Front. Relief complete without incident by 8-45 p.m. B.H.Q. SOUVENIR HOUSE.	O.O.NO.3. 19-1-18.
LEFT FRONT SUB SECTOR.	21st/24th.		2nd.Lieut.C.W.Pamplin proceeded on leave on the 21st. and Capt.M.M.Harvey became Acting Adjutant. Improvement of Posts and wiring was carried out. A new Post was completed at WATER HOUSE. A new belt of wire was constructed in front of REQUETE FARM in advance of the existing belt.	

WAR DIARY
or
INTELLIGENCE SUMMARY.
(Erase heading not required.)

Army Form C. 2118.

Instructions regarding War Diaries and Intelligence Summaries are contained in F. S. Regs., Part II. and the Staff Manual respectively. Title pages will be prepared in manuscript.

Place	Date	Hour	Summary of Events and Information	Remarks and references to Appendices
	22nd.		Enemy M.G's were definitely located at V.7.b.0.7. and V.7.b.55 .55 pill boxes were also located at the same spots. A patrol reconnoitered a mound 330 yards M.W. OF REQUETE FARM which was found to be unoccupied A patrol of 1 Officer and 1 N.C.O. reconnoitered MENLING FARM getting within 20 yards of it. Another patrol reconnoitered GRAVEL FARM but could not get further than about 70 yards owing to meeting a strong patrol of the enemy. They reported a strong belt of wire from GRAVEL FARM to the WATERVLIETBEEK and entrenching in front of the Farm; also that the enemy had a post between the FARM and the WATERVLIETBEEK.	Ref. Map Sheet. BROEMBEEK
	23rd.		Contact was obtained between our Left Coy and the Right Coy of the Battalion on our left by means of patrol.	
	23rd.		Casualties. Wounded 4 O.R.	
	24th.		Killed. 2nd.Lieut.S.H.Price.M.C. & 2nd.Lieut.A.A.Hogan. and 2 O.R. were killed.at FERDAN HOUSE by an incendiary shell which entered the pill-box. Wounded. Lieut.G.H.Boot and 2 O.Rs were wounded on the same occasion. The Battalion was relieved by the 17th.LANCS.FUS and moved to IRISH FARM. The relief was completed without incident.	O.O.NO.4: 22-1-18.
IRISH FARM.	24th./28th.		Rest. Baths and Foot Treatment.	
	29th./31st.		Working parties supplied as follows:— 2 Officers 72 O.R. to EAGLE HOUSE. Map Ref. U.20.d.4.5. 1 Officer 72 O.R. to BEER TRENCH Map.Ref. U.17.d.2.2. 3 Officers 150 O.R. working on drainage of PHEASANT TRENCH and its dug-outs to improve the accommodation for Infantry stationed therein. 1 Off.30 O.R.Improvement of accommodation in EAGLE TRENCH. 20 O.R. Improvement of accommodation between MINTY FARM and PHEASANT TRENCH in PHEASANT TRENCH.20 O.R. work on Light Railway between MINTY FARM and PHEASANT TRENCH	

Wwmorel Captain, Commdg.

15th. (S) Bn. The Sherwood Foresters.

105TH INF. BDE.

15TH BATTN. THE SHERWOOD FORESTERS (NOTTINGHAMSHIRE AND DERBYSHIRE REGIMENT)

FEB 1918

MISSING.

105th Inf.Bde.
35th Div.

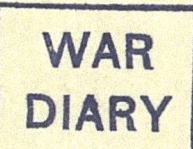

15th BATTN. THE SHERWOOD FORESTERS (NOTTINGHAMSHIRE AND DERBYSHIRE REGIMENT).

M A R C H

1 9 1 8

Army Form C. 2118.

35
75/105

WAR DIARY
INTELLIGENCE SUMMARY.
(Erase heading not required.)

15th.(S) Bn.The Sherwood Foresters. 1/4/18.

Place	Date	Hour	Summary of Events and Information	Remarks and references to Appendices
	MARCH 1918.			
LANGEMARCK.	1st.		Battalion relieved in support by 18th.LANCS.FUS. and on relief proceeded to HUDDLESTONE CAMP.	
HUDDLESTONE CAMP.	2nd.		Rest and refitting.	
	3/8th.		Working Parties on Army Battle Line.	
CHAUNY FARM CAMP.	9th.		Battalion moved by Rail & Road to CHAUNY FARM CAMP. The Division being in G.H.Q.Reserve and ready to move to any part of the Line at 12 hours notice.	
	10/22nd.		Training.	
	23rd.		Battalion moved by Train from ROUSEBRUGGE at 9 am. to MERICOURT arriving there at 9.30 pm.and then marching throughout the night reaching MARICOURT at 6 am. A halt was made then till	
CURLU WOOD	24th.	12 noon.	8.30 am. when we pushed on to CURLU WOOD. At 12 noon orders were received to counter-attack "Y" & "Z" Coys.at once moved forward and held the advancing enemy, with the 15th.CHESHIRES on the RIGHT. No touch could be got with any troops on the LEFT, and towards 4.30 pm. the enemy was outflanking the two front Coys.who had very few survivors.	
CURLU MAUREPAS RD.		5 pm.	At 5 pm.Orders were received to withdraw which was successfully carried out and a fresh position occupied on CURLU-MAUREPAS ROAD. The Battalion had the 15th.CHESHIRE REGT.on the RIGHT and the 104th.Brigade on the LEFT.	
	25th.	10.30 am.	At 10.30 am.Owing to heavy enemy shelling from the rear the troops on either flank retired and to avoid being isolated the Battalion withdrew to a defensive Line in front of MARICOURT	
MARICOURT.		12 noon 11 pm	where it witheld the enemy, who again were round our left flank, until 8.30 pm.when we were relieved by the 18th.LANCS.FUS. On relief the Battalion marched by parties to a position EAST of the BRAY-ALBERT ROAD and put forward Outposts.	

Army Form C. 2118.

WAR DIARY
or
INTELLIGENCE SUMMARY.
(Erase heading not required.)

Instructions regarding War Diaries and Intelligence Summaries are contained in F. S. Regs., Part II. and the Staff Manual respectively. Title pages will be prepared in manuscript.

Place	Date	Hour	Summary of Events and Information	Remarks and references to Appendices
E OF BRAY. ALBERT RD.	26th.	10 am.	At 10 am. On receipt of warning that the enemy were approaching, the Outpost Line was manned and touch was quickly gained with the 15th.CHESHIRE REGT. On the RIGHT, but no British Troops could be seen on the LEFT. The enemy were heavily engaged during the day particularly on the left flank which was exposed, except for some valuable assistance rendered by Tanks.	
		5.30pm.	At 5.30 pm. Orders were received, to retire and a withdrawal having been effected a position was occupied West of the RIVER ANCRE in front of BUIRE VILLAGE.	
		7 pm.		
BUIRE.	27th.	4 pm.	The day passed without incident and at 4 pm. the Battalion was relieved by the 12th.H.L.I. and on relief removed to SUPPORT POSITION in QUARRY behind BUIRE.	
	28th.	10 pm.	The Battalion relieved the 10th.D.L.I. in RIGHT SECTOR of Div Front. All quiet.	
	29/30th.		No incident worthy of record.	
	31st.	7 am.	Battalion relieved by AUSTRALIANS and proceeded to billets at LA HOUSSOYE. Total casualties since the 24th. Officers 12 -- O R's 458.	

W.A.B. Collin
.... Lieut.Col. Commanding
16th.(S)Bn.The Sherwood Foresters.

SECRET. Wareham Copy No. 6

15th.(S)Bn.The Sherwood Foresters
Operation Order NO16.   1-3-18.   2.

1. The Battalion will be relieved in SUPPORT to-night by the 18th.LANCS.FUS.

2. "W"Coy. relieved by "X"Coy. 18th.LANCS FUS.
   "X" "   "   "Y" "   "   "   "
   "Y" "   "   "Z" "   "   "   "
   "Z" "   "   "W" "   "   "   "
   H.Q. "   "   H.Q. "   "   "   "

3. On relief Coys. will proceed independently to HUDDLESTONE CAMP.

4. All Trench Stores, A.A.Positions etc. must be carefully handed over & receipts forwarded to Adjutant by 9 am.March 2nd.

5. 1 Guide per platoon & Coy.H.Q. will report to the Adjutant at 5 pm to-night at Bn.H.Q.

6. The Q.M. will arrange a hot meal to be ready from 7 pm.

7. Lewis Gun Limbers will report at following places as soon as possible after dusk. "W"Coy. EAGLE DUMP - "X"Coy.JUNCTION OF HUNTER ST & KOEKUIT RD "Y" & "Z"COY.LANGEMARCK STR.
Mess Cart will report at Bn.H.Q. at dusk.

8. Accommodation at HUDDLESTONE CAMP will be arranged by the 2nd.in Command.

9. The T.O. will arrange to convey all packs, blankets etc to HUDDLESTONE CAMP & the Q.M. will see these issued out to Coys. this evening.

10. O.C."W"Coy. will detail a Lewis Gun team to man A.A.Position at C.7.d.1.2. NO 19 & O.C."X"Coy. will detail a Lewis Gun Team to man A.A.Position at C.1.c.7.3. NO 20. These positions must be occupied 12 noon March 2nd.

11. Baths are being arranged for to-morrow, details will follow.

12. Completion of relief to be notified to Bn.H.Q. by phone. Code Word "BUCKED"

ACKNOWLEDGE.
Copies to NO1.C.O.
        2.2nd.in Command.
        3."W"Coy.
        4."X" "
        5."Y" "
        6."Z" "
        7.T.O.
        8.Q.M.
        9.Bde.
       10.18th.LANCS FUS.
       11.File.
       12.War Diary.

(Sd.)Graham Callow.Capt.A/Adjt
15th.(S)Bn.The Sherwood Foresters.

SECRET.   COPY NO.

15th.(S)Bn.The Sherwood Foresters,
Operation Order No.17.   March 9/1918.

1. **INTENTION.** The Battalion will move tomorrow the 10th.inst. by Road & Rail to GRANDE PARE CAMP - Sheet 19X 18.b & c.

2. **MOVE.** The Battalion will proceed by Road to BOESINGHE STATION BROAD GAUGE, arriving there by 9.30 a.m. & entraining at 10 a.m. for INTERNATIONAL CORNER.

3. **ORDER.** Order & Time of Move :-
   "W"Coy. & B.Q. 8.15 a.m.   "X"Coy. & Drums 8.20 a.m.
   "Y"Coy. .... 8.25 a.m.   "Z" " . ... 8.30 a.m.

4. **ENTRAINING OFFICER.** 2nd.Lieut.H.German will act as Entraining Officer, he will report to the R.T.O. BOESINGHE, at a.m. 10th.inst.

5. **DETRAINING OFFICER.** Lieut.J.V.Potter will act as Detraining Officer at INTERNATIONAL CORNER.

6. **STORES.** All Blankets, Officers Valises, Mess Kits etc. must be stacked by Coys. at HUDDLESTONE X ROADS ready for loading on to Lorries, by 8 a.m.   Blankets to be rolled in bundles of ten & clearly labelled. The Mess & Maltese Carts will report at Battn.H.Q. at 8 a.m.

7. **LOADING PARTY.** Loading Parties of 2 men per Coy. & 1 N.C.O. from Battn.H.Q. will report to the Quarter Master, at 8 a.m. at Battalion Orderly Room.

8. **TRANSPORT.** Transport will march brigaded under Brigade Transport Officer.

9. **MEALS.** Reveille 6 a.m. Breakfasts 7 a.m. Dinners on arrival in new Camp.

10. **DRESS.** Full marching Order.

11. **SANITATION.** All Billets, Ablution Places, Latrines & Cookhouses must be left clean & sanitary. Each Company must obtain Certificate from the Camp Warden to that effect.

    ACKNOWLEDGE.
                            Issued at 5 p.m.
Copies to:- No.1.C.O.
            2."W"Coy.
            3."X" " .
            4."Y" " .
            5."Z" " .
            6.H.Q. .
            7.Bde.
            8.T.O.
             .Q.M.
            10.R.S.M.
            11.File.
            12.War Diary.

                                (Sd.)Graham Callow. Capt. A/Adjt.,
                                15th.(S)Bn.The Sherwood Foresters.

Army Form C., 2118.

WAR DIARY
or
INTELLIGENCE SUMMARY.
(Erase heading not required.)

16th.(S)Bn.The Sherwood Foresters. 30/4/18.

Place	Date	Hour	Summary of Events and Information	Remarks and references to Appendices
	1918. APRIL.			
LAHOUSSOYE.	1/3rd.		Rest & reorganization. Small Working Parties supplied for work on Corps Line.	
LA NEUVILLE.	4th.	5 pm.	Battalion marched to Billets in LA NEUVILLE.	
	5th.		In LA NEUVILLE.	
HERISSART.	6th.	4 pm.	Battalion moved to Billets in HERISSART arriving there at 10.30 pm.	
HEDAUVILLE.	7th.	8 pm.	Battalion marched to Billets in HEDAUVILLE in relief of a Battalion of 115th.Inf.Brigade in Reserve.	
BOUZINCOURT.	8th.	9.15 pm.	Battalion relieved 2 Coys. of the London Regiment in Support in Right Sector of Div.Front. Occupying Bivouacs in Sunken Road N. of BOUZINCOURT. Large Draft arrived amounting to approximately 350 O.R's	Sheet 57D.Ed2. V.7.bad
FRONT LINE.	11th.	10 pm.	Battalion relieved 15th.Cheshire Regt. in Left Sub-Sector of Brigade Front without incident. Active patrolling was maintained throughout the night. Work was continued on improvement of Trenches.	
FRONT LINE.	12/13 14th.		Constant patrolling each night. Improvement of Trenches & Shelters worked on. Casualties slight.	
	15th.	1 am.	Battalion relieved by 18th.H.L.I. & proceeded to HEDAUVILLE. Remainder of day devoted to Baths, & absorption of Draft.	
HEDAUVILLE.		6.30 pm.	Village of HEDAUVILLE shelled, troops temporarily moved out of the village, no casualties in the Battalion.	

Army Form C. 2118.

WAR DIARY
or
INTELLIGENCE SUMMARY.
(Erase heading not required.)

Instructions regarding War Diaries and Intelligence Summaries are contained in F. S. Regs., Part II. and the Staff Manual respectively. Title pages will be prepared in manuscript.

Place	Date	Hour	Summary of Events and Information	Remarks and references to Appendices
HEDAUVILLE.	16th.		Battalion moved to Bank E of HEDAUVILLE, the village being evacuated owing to enemy shell fire.	Sheet 57D Ed.2.P.35.
AVELUY WOOD.	17/18th.	7.15 pm	Battalion moved forward in relief of 17th.Lancs.Fus. in Left Sub.Sector of Brigade Front. Dispositions - "W" & "X" Coys. in Front Line. "Y" Coy. in Support, "Z" Coy. in Reserve. Fighting Patrols went out during the night & succeeded in making a little ground.	
	19/20th.		Our fighting patrols several times came into contact with the enemy, finding him in strength. Casualties - 1 Officer, 8 O.R's.	
	21/22nd.	10 pm.	Inter Coy. relief. "Y" & "Z" Coys. relieving "W" & "X" Coys.	
	22nd.	7.30 pm.	Battalion attacked in conjunction with 15th.Cheshire Regt., 19 th.D.L.I. & 59th.Div.all on right. Objective Ride from W.4.c.4.7 to Ride Junction W.4.c.85.40 inclusive. The attack at first progressed favourably, but in a short time we were held up on the right by M.G.Fire. After 2 hours fighting a defensive flank was formed running from W.4.c.25.40. through W.4.a.8.4.of Operations. W.4.a.6.4 to Original Line W.4.a.4.2. where connection was established with 15th.Cheshire Regt. Casualties - Officers 5, O.R's 112.	O.O. NO.28 Account of Operations.
	23/24th.		Battalion relieved by 12th.H.L.I. & proceeded to Camp, near HEDAUVILLE.	P.28, c & d
HEDAUVILLE.	25th.		Rest & reorganization.	
BOUZINCOURT.	26/27th.		Battalion relieved 19 th.D.L.I. in Reserve in Right Sector of Div Front Occupying Shelters in Sunken Road N. of BOUZINCOURT.	V.7.; & d.
	28/30th.		Working parties supplied for work on Support, & Reserve Lines.	

N Morris Mantle Lieut-Col. Comdg., 15th.(S)Bn.The Sherwood Foresters.

Army Form C. 2118.

WAR DIARY
or
INTELLIGENCE SUMMARY.

(Erase heading not required.)

15TH SHERWOOD FORESTERS
MAY 1918

Place	Date	Hour	Summary of Events and Information	Remarks and references to Appendices
BOUZINCOURT	1/2		Battalion relieved in Reserve by the 10th S.W.B. & proceeded to Billets in HERRISART.	
HERRISART	3/4		Training	
	5		Inspection by Corps Commander.	
	9/10		Training	
FORWARD AREA	11		Battalion moved to FORWARD AREA for work with R.E's.	V.S.L.
	12/14		Working Parties supplied. 3 casualties.	
HERRISART	15	2pm	Battalion relieved by 1st d. Staffs & returned to Billets in HERRISSART.	
	16		Training	
	17		Divisional Anxiety Competition	
	18		Training	
	19		Platoon Rifle Competition	

Army Form C. 2118.

WAR DIARY
or
INTELLIGENCE SUMMARY.
(Erase heading not required.)

Instructions regarding War Diaries and Intelligence Summaries are contained in F. S. Regs., Part II. and the Staff Manual respectively. Title pages will be prepared in manuscript.

Place	Date	Hour	Summary of Events and Information	Remarks and references to Appendices
RESERVE POSITION	20/21	1.40 a.m.	Battalion moved to FORWARD AREA & relieved 10th S.W.B. in Bgde. Reserve. Two Coys. W & Y forward in PURPLE LINE. Two Coys. X & Z in Reserve.	V.16.c.4.2.
BOUZINCOURT	22/23		Battalion moved to new positions as follows:— H.Q. in BOUZINCOURT. X & Z Coys in Sunken Rd. N.W. of Village. W Coy in PURPLE LINE & Y Coy in OLD FRENCH LINE S. of Village. Working Party of 1 Coy supplied.	
FRONT LINE	23/24	12.35 a.m.	Battalion relieved 11th J. Staffs in left sub. sect. of Bgde Front. W & Y Coys in front line, W Coy on right Y Coy in Reserve.	
	25/26		Patrolling, wiring & work on Trenches.	
	26/27	12.30 a.m.	Inter Battalion relief. W Coy relieving X Coy in left front line, Y Coy relieving Z Coy in right front line.	
BOUZINCOURT	29/30	12.30 a.m.	Battalion relieved by 15th Cheshire Regt. & moved into Bgde Reserve. Bn. H.Q. in BOUZINCOURT. X & Z Coys in Sunken Rd. N.W. of Village. W & Y Coys in PURPLE and FRENCH LINES S. of Village.	
			Casualties during tour in front line :— 1st O.R. killed 1 " 15 O.R.s wounded	

(A7092). Wt. W12839/M1293. 750,000. 1/17. D. D. & L., Ltd. Forms/C.2118/14.

Army Form C. 2118.

WAR DIARY
or
INTELLIGENCE SUMMARY.
(Erase heading not required.)

Place	Date	Hour	Summary of Events and Information	Remarks and references to Appendices
BOUZINCOURT	30/31	7 am 4 am	Area bombarded with gas shells	Graham Callers Capt & Adjt for Lt Col Comdg 15th Sherwood Foresters

Army Form C. 2118.

WAR DIARY
or
INTELLIGENCE SUMMARY. 15th.(S)Bn.The Sherwood Foresters.
JUNE 1918.
(Erase heading not required.)

Place	Date	Hour	Summary of Events and Information	Remarks and references to Appendices
RIGHT FRONT LINE.	JUNE 1918. 1/2nd.	1.am.	Relieved 4th.NORTH STAFFS in RIGHT FRONT LINE. "Z", "Y" & "X" Coys. in Front Line, "W" Coy. in Reserve.	
	3/4th.		Patrolling & Wiring.	
FORCEVILLE.	5/6th.	1.30 am	Relieved by 17th.D.L.I. and proceeded to Camp near FORCEVILLE. Few casualties during the Tour.	P.27.1.8.0.
	7/8th.		Resting & Training.	
LINE IN FRONT OF BOUZINCOURT.	9/10th.		Relieved Four Coys. of 104th Brigade in Line. Dispositions, "X" Coy. Front Line, "W" Coy. Support, "Y" & "Z" Coys. Reserve.	
	11th.		Patrolling & work on Trenches.	
FORCEVILLE.	12/13/14th.		Relieved by 17th D.L.I. & proceeded to Camp, near FORCEVILLE.	P.27.1.8.0.
			Rest & Refitting.	
	15th.		Training.	
	16th.		Relieved by 7th NORFOLK'S & proceeded by Road to Rest Billets in PUCHEVILLERS. Re-Organization. Battle Surplus rejoined.	
PUCHEVILLERS.	17th.			
	18/27th.		Training.	
	28th.		Brigade Field Day.	

Army Form C. 2118.

(Sheet 2)

WAR DIARY
or
INTELLIGENCE SUMMARY. 15th.(S)Bn.The Sherwood Foresters.
JUNE 1918.

(Erase heading not required.)

Instructions regarding War Diaries and Intelligence Summaries are contained in F.S. Regs., Part II. and the Staff Manual respectively. Title pages will be prepared in manuscript.

Place	Date	Hour	Summary of Events and Information	Remarks and references to Appendices
	JUNE 1918.			
	29th		Divisional Rifle Meeting. Battalion won the Rapid Fire Competition.	
	30th.		Orders received to move.	
			Preparing to move by Train from CANDAS.	

..........................Lieut-Col., Commanding.

15th.(S)Bn.The Sherwood Foresters.

=*=*=*=*=*=*=*=*=*=*=*=*=*=

Army Form C. 2118.

WAR DIARY
or
INTELLIGENCE SUMMARY.

15th(S)Bn.The Sherwood Foresters.

JULY 1/18.

(Erase heading not required.)

Instructions regarding War Diaries and Intelligence Summaries are contained in F. S. Regs., Part II. and the Staff Manual respectively. Title pages will be prepared in manuscript.

Place	Date	Hour	Summary of Events and Information	Remarks and references to Appendices
CANDAS.	JULY 1/18. 1st.	5.50 am	Battalion moved by train to WIZERNES and was billetted there for night of 1st/2nd.	30/15
WIZERNES.	2nd.	4 pm.	"W" & "X" Coy. marched to ARQUES and were billetted there for the night. H.Q., "Y" & "Z" Coys. remained in WIZERNES.	I 27.6.
ZERMEZEELE.	3rd.	4.30 am	"W" & "X" Coys. marched to ZERMEZEELE.	
		5.30 pm.	H.Q., "Y" & "Z" Coys. embussed for ZERMEZEELE, where the Battalion was billetted.	K 33~34
BEAUVOORDE WOOD.	4th.	2 pm.	Battalion marched to BEAUVOORDE WOOD and bivouaced for the night	
RESERVE.	5th.	11 pm	Battalion relieved the 358th French Inf.Regt. in Reserve Position of KEMMEL CENTRE SUB SECTOR	
	6/8th		In Reserve.	
SUPPORT.	9/10th	12 M/N.	Battalion relieved the 4th N.STAFFS REGT. in SUPPORT. 4 casualties.	
	11/12th	12.30am	Night Working Parties.	
FRONT LINE.	13/14th.	1 am.	Battalion relieved the 4th N.STAFFS REGT. in Front Line. "W" & "Z" Coys. in Front Line, "X" & "Y" Coys. in Support. Patrols sent out.	
	15/16th		Patrolling & work on Front Line.	
	17/18th 18th	12 m/n	Battalion relieved by 15th CHESHIRE REGT. & proceeded to RESERVE BILLETS. 38 casualties during tour in Front Line & Support.	
RESERVE.	9/20th.		Resting & refitting.	

25Y

J Webb

Army Form C. 2118.

WAR DIARY
or
INTELLIGENCE SUMMARY.

(Erase heading not required.)

15th.(S)Bn.The Sherwood Foresters.

JULY 1918.

Instructions regarding War Diaries and Intelligence Summaries are contained in F. S. Regs., Part II. and the Staff Manual respectively. Title pages will be prepared in manuscript.

Place	Date	Hour	Summary of Events and Information	Remarks and references to Appendices
	JULY 1918.			
SUPPORT.	21/ 22nd. 23/ 24th.		Battalion relieved 4th. N.STAFFS.REGT. in SUPPORT. Night working parties & patrols furnished.	
FRONT LINE.	25/ 26th.		Battalion relieved 4th.N.STAFFS.REGT in Front Line. "X" & "Y"Coys. in Front Line, "W" & "Z"Coys. in Support.	
	27/28th.		Patrolling & work on Front Line.	
	29/30th.		Battalion relieved by 15th.CHESHIRE REGT. & proceeded to RESERVE POSITION, West of BOESCHEPE.	R.C.S.
RESERVE.	31st.		Rest & refitting.	

................................Major,

Commanding 15th.(S)Bn.The Sherwood Foresters.

=

105TH INF. BDE.
35TH DIV.

15TH BATTN. THE SHERWOOD
FORESTERS (NOTTINGHAMSHIRE AND
DERBYSHIRE REGIMENT)
AUGUST 1918
MISSING.

Army Form C. 2118.

"WAR DIARY" or INTELLIGENCE SUMMARY.

15th (S)Bn.The Sherwood Foresters

(Erase heading not required.)

SEPTEMBER 1/18.

Place	Date	Hour	Summary of Events and Information	Remarks and references to Appendices
ST SYLVESTRE CAPPEL	SEPT 1st		At St SYLVESTRE CAPPEL resting.	Attached Notes
	1/2nd		Marched to WHINFIELD CAMP (27/L.4.a.9.5.) on Poperinghe Watou Road. Started 6.25am arrived 11am	O/H.%.51
POPERINGHE	3/4th		At WHINFIELD CAMP resting. Usual Inspections, Refitting &c.	
YPRES. (Support)	4/5th	10 pm	Relieved part of 120th American Regt. in L.Sub.Sector of Canal Sector (S.E. Of Ypres) Marched from WHINFIELD CAMP (27/L.4.a.95.) to BLUE GRASS SIDING (27/F.28.a.2.0.) on POPERINGHE PROVEN ROAD & entrained on Metre Gauge Railway to YALE SIDING (28/H.15.d.0.4.) Marched from thence to SUPPORT AREA. Relief complete about 10 pm	O.O.No.62/63
	5/8th		In Support Area L.Sub.Sector CANAL SECTOR. Usual routine	
(Reserve)	8/9th	6 pm	Relieved in above sector by 19th D.L.I. (104th Inf.Bde) & marched to LAWRENCE CAMP (Reserve Brigade Area) (28/G.11.c.6.3.) Relief complete 6 pm. Arrived new area at 8 pm.	O.O.No.64
	9/12th		At LAWRENCE CAMP in Div. Reserve. Light training in addition to usual routine.	O.O.No.65
FRONT LINE	12/13th		Relieved 17th ROYAL SCOTS in L.Sub.Sector CANAL SECTOR. LAWRENCE CAMP vacated at 7 pm. Relief complete	O.O.No.66
	13/15th		Front Line. Intense patrolling.	
	15th		105th Inf.Bde carried out a minor operation in conjunction with 104th Inf.Bde on the Left with complete success. The Outpost Line being advanced 1000 yards. Operation included the capture & consolidation of SPOIL BANK & ROAD JUNCTION (28/I.32.d./0.55.) which was carried out by this battalion. "Y"Coy. attacked SPOIL BANK & raided dugouts beyond. ZERO hour 11.30pm Prisoners taken by battalion numbered 7.	O.O.No.67
	16/17th		Dispositions altered in conjunction with 4th N.STAFFS.	
	18th		Front Line. Usual routine.	

Army Form C. 2118.

WAR DIARY
or
INTELLIGENCE SUMMARY.   15th(S)Bn.The Sherwood Foresters

SEPTEMBER 18

(Erase heading not required.)

Place	Date	Hour	Summary of Events and Information	Remarks and references to Appendices
SCHOOL CAMP. (resting)	19/20th	10 pm	Relieved by 6th Wilts.Regt. Relief complete by 10 pm. Proceeded to SCHOOL CAMP by march & rail. Entrained at YALE SIDING & detrained at BLUE GRASS SIDING on Metre Gauge Railway. Last Coy. arrived in billets at about 3 am 20th.	O.O. No 68
	20/21st		Resting & refitting. Inspection by G.O.C. 35th Div. on 20th.	
FRONT LINE	22/23rd		Moved by Lorry & march route to line & took over part of the Front occupied by 18th H.L.I. Left School Camp at 7 pm & moved by lorry to WHITE MILL near VLAMERTINGHE & marched from there to line. Boundaries of Line occupied as follows :- 28/I.27.d.7.1. to 27/I.28.c.1.9. Relief complete midnight.	O.O. No 69
	23/24th	2.30 am	Battalion relieved by 15th CHESHIRE REGT. in the line, & proceeded to SCHOOL CAMP. Arrived billets at 2.30am.	O.O. No 70
SCHOOL CAMP	25th		At School Camp. Resting.	
FRONT LINE.	26/27th		Battalion moved forward leaving School Camp at 7 pm under same arrangements as on night 22/23rd & reoccupied same section of Front Line relieving 15th CHESHIRE REGT. Relief complete midnight.	O.O. No 72
	27/28th		Operations on a large scale were commenced. Assembly for attack was completed by the Battalion about midnight,At ZERO (5.30am) the attack commenced supported by a very good artillery barrage. Everything went according to arrangement, the enemy shewing little or no resistance & surrendering freely. All objectives were reached & consolidated by 8.30 am. Shortly after commencement of assault rain started to fall & continued heavily until dusk. During the afternoon the 41st Divn. continued the attack through our objectives. The night 28/29th was quiet.	
	29th		At 4.30 am Orders were received to continue the attack. The battalion assembled at 5.30 am in BATTLE WOOD and moved off at 8.30 am. The battalion was now in Brigade Reserve.The Battalion moved forward to position in rear of the attack & remained during the afternoon. At 4.50 pm 2-45 pm Orders were received to attack the village of ZANDVOORDE in conjunction with 4th N.STAFFS, the 15th CHESHIRE REGT having failed to advance during the morning. "W" & "Y" Coys. moved forward 2.55 pm to the attack about 2.50 pm & encountered heavy M.G.Fire from long range. The village was taken & the attack progressed & positions finally taken up on the Northern Side	O.O. No 71

Army Form C. 2118.

WAR DIARY
or
INTELLIGENCE SUMMARY.   15th(S)Bn.The Sherwood Foresters

(Erase heading not required.)

Instructions regarding War Diaries and Intelligence Summaries are contained in F. S. Regs., Part II. and the Staff Manual respectively. Title pages will be prepared in manuscript.

Place	Date	Hour	Summary of Events and Information SEPTEMBER '18	Remarks and references to Appendices
OF TENBRIELEN.	SEPT.'18 30th		"Y" & "X" Coys. in Front Line, "Z" & "W" Coys. in Reserve. Weather good until evening when rain commenced & continued throughout the night. The 106th Inf.Bde continued the attack at dawn occupying our frontage at 6.30am. "Z" & "W" Coys. moved forward & the battalion assembled at DEVOORSTRAAT CABARET & from there moved forward to reserve position on Northern outskirts of TENBRIELEN.	

..................Lieut-Col.

Commdg 15th(S)Bn.The Sherwood Foresters.

Army Form C. 2118.

WAR DIARY
or
INTELLIGENCE SUMMARY.

(Erase heading not required.)

15th(S)Bn The Sherwood Foresters
OCTOBER 1918

Place	Date	Hour	Summary of Events and Information	Remarks and references to Appendices
RESERVE	OCT.'18 1st		Battalion relieved from position on NORTHERN outskirts of TEMBRIELEN by 6th CHESHIRE REGT. of 34th Division, and marched to Camp at 28.J.30.C.5.5.	
	2nd		Resting at Camp in 28.J.30.C.5.5.	
	3rd		At 04.10 hours the Battalion marched to area around DOLL'S HOUSE (28-H.19.b.25.	
	4th		Resting and refitting.	
	5th		Battalion moved into line and relieved K.R.R's 34th Division.	
FRONT LINE	6th		Front Line	
"	7th		Front Line. Lieut-COL.W.A.W.Crellin,D.S.O. Wounded. Battalion relieved by 18th H.L.I. 106th Bde and on relief Coys marched to billets vacated by them on the 5th inst. at DOLL'S HOUSE.	
DOLL'S HO.	8th/10th		At DOLL'S HOUSE. Resting and refitting. Lieut-COL.W.A.W.Crellin,D.S.O. Died of wounds in 10th C.C.S.	
HALDEN HO	11th		The Battalion moved to Forward Area arrived HALDEN Ho.K.27.B.7.6.	
SUPPORT	12/13th		In support at HALDEN HOUSE.	
	14th		Operations on a large scale were continued. The Battalion assembled E. and W. OF the VIETWEGEN RD at 03 hours in rear of the 15th CHESHIRE REGT. At ZERO (05.35 hours) the CHESHIRE'S advanced with good artillery support. Little opposition was met with and the Battalion passed through the CHESHIRE'S at the line of the first objective and continued the advance. Owing to the dense mist directions was extremely difficult to keep. Nearing CABIN COPSE the resistance was stronger and at dusk we had established ourselves on the line running N.E.through 28.L.35.b.5.2	
	15th		At dawn the 4th N.STAFFS went through our positions, and continued the advance. The Battalion remained in the positions already gained by them	

Army Form C. 2118.

WAR DIARY
or
INTELLIGENCE SUMMARY.
(Erase heading not required.)

Instructions regarding War Diaries and Intelligence Summaries are contained in F. S. Regs., Part II. and the Staff Manual respectively. Title pages will be prepared in manuscript.

Place	Date	Hour	Summary of Events and Information	Remarks and references to Appendices
	OCT'18 16th		The Battalion were withdrawn to billets about TAMIL FARM 28.L.28.D.2.3.	
	17th		Resting and refitting at TAMIL FARM.	
SUPPORT	18th		The Battalion marched to forward area in support to the 104th Bde, who were attacking MARCKE the following morning.	
	19th		At 03 hours the Battalion were assembled in position, in 29.M.10.E. of the Railway, when the 104th Bde. advanced the battalion followed up behind and at 8 hours were in support about 29M.6 and N.1. A patrol was sent into COUTRAI and reported enemy evacuation of the town.	
	20th		The advance was continued and the Battalion assembled E. of the Road in 29.H.34 central with the 15th CHESHIRE'S on the Right Flank and 4th N.STAFFS on the Left. At ZERO(5.45) the advance began and the leading Coys. were greatly troubled by M.Gun resistance. On nearing the outskirts of SWEVEGHEM the attack was held up by M.G.Fire and the 15th CHESHIRE'S who had encountered a stout resistance had not come up - thus exposing our right flank. After a heavy enemy barrage the Bosche evacuated the village and at 15 hours the Battalion marched through, eventually taking up the line of the Road running N.E. through 29.O.7. central.	
	21st		The 31st. Divn. continued the advance and at 11 hours the battalion was withdrawn and marched to billets about 29.H.34.c. At 16 hours new areas were allotted and the Battalion moved to billets in COUTRAI about 29.A.27.c.0.0.	
	22nd		At 14 hours the Battalion moved to another area S of COUTRAI about 29N.1.B.3.	
	23rd		Resting and refitting.	
	24th		The Battalion moved back to COUTRAI and took over billets from 106th Bde (29.H.32.d.29)	
	25th		Resting at COUTRAI.	
	26th		The Bde moved into Reserve and the Battn. occupied billets in ESSCHER and at LOCK NO.6.E. OF SWEVEGHEM.	

Army Form C. 2118.

WAR DIARY
or
INTELLIGENCE SUMMARY.
(Erase heading not required.)

Instructions regarding War Diaries and Intelligence Summaries are contained in F. S. Regs., Part II. and the Staff Manual respectively. Title pages will be prepared in manuscript.

Place	Date	Hour	Summary of Events and Information	Remarks and references to Appendices
	Oct. '18			
In Reserve Billets.	27/31		Usual Inspections and Routine carried out.	
	28			
			.... Lieut.-COL.,	
			Commdg. 15th (3) Bn The Sherwood Foresters.	
			=*=*=*=*=*=*=*=*=*=*=*=	

15th Glamorgans

Army Form C. 2118.

WAR DIARY
INTELLIGENCE SUMMARY

NOVEMBER 1918.

Place	Date	Hour	Summary of Events and Information	Remarks and references to Appendices
	1st.		The Battalion was relieved by the Lancs. Fus. and marched from Lock No 5. (Map Ref) 29.0.2.b.5.4. to billets S.E. of Marcke. Bn. H.Q. was established at the Mill M.19.d.40.85.	
	2nd. 3rd.		Resting and usual routine. Training Commenced. A Bde. Thanksgiving Service was held in Marcke. After the service the Bn. marched past the Divisional Commander.	
	4th.		Bathing commenced. At 12 noon orders were received for the Bn. to move forward and take over part of the front line from the 10th Queens Regt. The Bn, started to march at 2-30 p.m. and went via Courtrai, Sweveghem, Kappart, Ooteghem, Ingayhem to p.18.c.33. which was Bn.H.Q. The Bn. acted under the orders of the 103 Bde. Y. Coy in Front Line occupying 105th.Bde Frontage for the proposed attack from P.30.D.00. Meerschstraat (inclusive) Z and W Coys were in support and Sterenbek and X Coy in reserve about p.10.d Central.	
FRONT LINE.	5th. 6th. 7th. 8th.		Intense patrolling of western bank of river Lyseaut. Lt. Col. H.Morton D.S.O. M.C. went to Hospital and Command was taken over by Major Johnson M.C. Intense Patrolling. At 11.45.p.m. message was received to say troops had crossed the river at Meersche and we had orders to cross opposite our front. From that time no sound was heard on opposite side of river but crossing owing to having no material ready crossing was not started until the morning of the ninth.	
	9th.		At 07.00 hrs. the Bn Commenced to cross by ferry and bridges with orders to assemble along the railway track running N.E. through Q.25.b.1.9. Z Coy crossed by a bridge at Tenhove. W.Y and H.Q. Crossed by ferry at Q.25.b.1.5. X Coy crossed by a bridge at Q.25.c.0.0. at 11 hrs the Bn, was assembled behind Railway Embankment as follows. Y on the left and W on the right. Z in support to Y and X in support to W. At 12 noon orders for a General advance were received. No opposition was met and progress was rapid. At 14.15 hrs. the Objective(which was a line running N and S 800 yds west of Wrasal) was reached Outposts were pushed forward to the Renaix; Sukerke Road and remained during the night.	
	10th.		The 104 Bde. passed through us at about 09.00 hrs. proceeding in an easterly direction on orders being received to move into billets the Bn. marched into Zandstraat and Mont-Ma..rs. Cruche. Batt N.H.Q. was at Xa.B.95.95. Z,W, and X Coys were in billets at Mont de la Cruche. Z.n. and Y Coy about Mill in X.7.b.2.6. At 17.00 hrs. news was received that Germany had signed the Armistice and that hostilities would cease at 11.00hrs the following day.	

Army Form C. 2118.

WAR DIARY
or
INTELLIGENCE SUMMARY.
(Erase heading not required.)

Instructions regarding War Diaries and Intelligence Summaries are contained in F. S. Regs., Part II. and the Staff Manual respectively. Title pages will be prepared in manuscript.

Place	Date	Hour	Summary of Events and Information	Remarks and references to Appendices
	11th.		Resting and reorganizing.	
	12th.		The Bn. moved to billets at Marie Louise in the morning and Bn. H.Q. was established at the Convent in the village. All Coy were in Billets in the village.	
	13th.		The Bn. moved to Nukerke Area starting at 09.45 hrs. On arrival no billets were to be had there still being occupied by the 41st. Div. B.H.Q. was finally established at the Chateau in X.3.C. and the Coys were distributed on the outskirts of Nukerke.	
	14th.		Billets were rearranged and B.H.Q. and all Coys moved to the billets previously arranged to them allotted in Nukerke. A Bn. Officers and Sgts. mess were formed.	
	15th. 16th. 17th. 18th. 19th.		In Nukerke. Training carried out during the morning and sports in the afternoon.	
	20th. 21st. 22nd. 23rd.		The Bn. marched to billets in Vichte W.24.a. and I.30.b. starting at 9.15 hrs The route followed was via Berchem Ivgeayhem to Vichte. Billets in the Heule district were reached by midday. The march was resumed at 09.00 hrs. and	
	24th.		Training carried out by Coys during mornings.	
	25th.		A Church service was held in Heule for the Bn. A Bde. Route March was held The Bn. paraded to square at Heule and moved off at 09.35 hrs. The route was from Heule via Cappelle Road Junction G.2.c.30, G.2.d.7-7. to Heule M and Z Coys proceeded to 30 yds range at G.24.b central and G.4.c.9.5. respectively. The remainder of the Bn continued training.	
	26th.		Training for Bn. except W. Coy who used Range at G.24.b. central.	
	28th.		The Bn. started marching by stages to Monschove. Menin being the first stage. The Bn. started from Heule at 09.50 hrs. and marched to billets in Rue de Lille in Menin. Route taken was Gulleghem-Wevelghem to Menin.	
	29th.		At 08.50. hrs the Bn Marched frm Menin to Vlamertinghe. Billets in the village were reached at 15 hrs.	
	30th.		At 09.00 hrs the Bn Marched from Vlamertinge to Tergeghem via Poperinghe, Abeele and Steenvoorde. The new billets were reached at 15.00 hrs,	

................Major Commdg.,
15th. (S). Bn. Sherwood Foresters.

Army Form C. 2118.

Vol 35

WAR DIARY
or
INTELLIGENCE SUMMARY.
(Erase heading not required.)

15th(S)Bn The Sherwood Foresters

DECEMBER 1918.

Ref:ST.OMER MAP 1/40,000.

304

Place	Date	Hour	Summary of Events and Information	Remarks and references to Appendices
	DEC/1918 1st		The battalion marched from Camp at LEDEGHEM to billets in BROXEELE, starting at 10.00 hrs, and following the route via Switch Road N of CASSEL & LEDERZEELE. A halt was observed for dinners, and the Battalion arrived in BROXEELE at 15.30 hrs.	
	2nd		The final stage of the move was completed by marching from BROXEELE to original VIII Corps School Camp at MONSCOVE. The Battalion moved off at 08.30 hrs and marched via CROMB STRAERT and WATTEN, arriving at MONSCOVE at 15.00 hrs.	
	3rd/ 31st		Education, Musketry & Training carried on between 09.00 & 12.30 hrs. Recreation & Sports organised to occupy afternoons.	

A. M. Colson.......Lieut.Col. Commdg.,

15th(S) Bn The Sherwood Foresters.

###################

Army Form C. 2118.

WAR DIARY
or
INTELLIGENCE SUMMARY.
(Erase heading not required.)

Instructions regarding War Diaries and Intelligence Summaries are contained in F. S. Regs., Part II. and the Staff Manual respectively. Title pages will be prepared in manuscript.

JANUARY 1919.

Place	Date	Hour	Summary of Events and Information	Remarks and references to Appendices
	Jan. 1st. to 27th.		Demobilization of 8 Officers and 229 other ranks. Educational training. Company Drills.	3 6
	28th.	1a.m.	Received orders to proceed to CALAIS to quell a riot. 16 Officers and 300 other ranks moved by Lorry and arrived BEAUMARAIS camp 21.00 hours.	
	29th.		Relieved 4th. North Staffordshire Regt. on picquet duty on bridges over Canal, facing No. 6 Leave Camp East. Held bridgeheads to prevent rioters leaving their camp.	
	30th.		Disturbance quelled at 11.00 hours. Battalion remained on picquet duty until 19.00 hours when it returned to Camp No. 6 West.	
	31st.		Resting.	

A.M Colson Lieut-Col., Commanding,

15th. (S). Bn. The Sherwood Foresters.

Army Form C. 2118.

15TH (S) BN. THE SHERWOOD FORESTERS
WAR DIARY
or
INTELLIGENCE SUMMARY.
(Erase heading not required.)

WO 3/4

324.

Place	Date	Hour	Summary of Events and Information	Remarks and references to Appendices
BEAUMARAIS	Feb 28 1919.		BATTALION AT BEAUMARAIS CAMP. NR. CALAIS. DEMOBILIZING AND BASE DUTIES. STRENGTH FEB. 28TH 24. OFFICERS 208. O.RS.	

R.W.Marsh. MAJOR. COMMDG.
15TH (S) BN. THE SHERWOOD FORESTERS.

Army Form C. 2118.

15th (S) BN THE SHERWOOD FORESTERS.

WAR DIARY
or
INTELLIGENCE SUMMARY.

(Erase heading not required.)   MARCH, 1919.

Instructions regarding War Diaries and Intelligence Summaries are contained in F. S. Regs., Part II. and the Staff Manual respectively. Title pages will be prepared in manuscript.

Vol 38

Place	Date	Hour	Summary of Events and Information	Remarks and references to Appendices
BEAUMARAIS CAMP CALAIS	1.3.19		MOBILIZATION AND BASE DUTIES. 10.OFFICERS AND 40. OTHER RANKS DEMOBILIZED.	
—do—	14.3.19		THE BATTALION PARADED ON THE 14TH INST., TO HAVE IT'S REGIMENTAL COLOURS PRESENTED. LIEUT. R.A.C. BEATES RECEIVED THEM FROM DIVISIONAL COMMANDER, MAJOR-GENERAL HARTHOIN.	
—do—	25.3.19		THE BATTALION MOVED BY RAIL TO ST OMER AND MARCHED TO MONNECOVE.	
MONNECOVE CAMP	26.3.19		O.C. ARRIVED ABOUT 1800 & 15.00 HRS. TRAINING AND DEMOBILIZATION. STRENGTH. 31ST.MARCH. 16.OFFICERS. 109. OTHER RANKS.	

M Robin Hood
o/c.
15th (S) BN THE SHERWOOD FORESTERS.

1st (S) Bn. The Sherwood Foresters

Army Form C. 2118.

WAR DIARY
or
INTELLIGENCE SUMMARY.
(Erase heading not required.)

Place	Date	Hour	Summary of Events and Information	Remarks and references to Appendices
MONNECOVE	April 1919 1/17		Camp Duties & Demobilization	
	18		3 Officers & 80 O.Rs proceeded to 73 POW Coy HAVRE. Batn Transport moved to St. OMER, prior to entrainment for DUNKIRK.	
ST. OMER	19	10.00	Bn Cadre entrained from ST. OMER, arriving DUNKIRK at 02.00 hrs. to 20th	
DUNKIRK	20/21	16.00	On loading stores on boat, Stores on the CLUTHIA, personnel embarked on a Russian boat at 16.00 hrs.	
	22	05.00	Left DUNKIRK and sailed for SOUTHAMPTON at 05.00 hrs.	

N M Corton
Lt. & Adjt.
1st Sherwood Foresters

www.ingramcontent.com/pod-product-compliance
Lightning Source LLC
Chambersburg PA
CBHW080437240426
43662CB00049B/2081